Sept 4 (1,16,18)
Sept 11 (5,6)
Oct 2 (2,34)
Oct 16 (9,17)
Oct 23 takehm
Oct 30 (12,13,15)
Nov 13 (19)
Nov 20 (10,11,14)

EMERGING OFFICE SYSTEMS

COMMUNICATION AND INFORMATION SCIENCE

A series of monographs, treatises, and texts

Edited by
MELVIN J. VOIGT
University of California, San Diego

WILLIAM C. ADAMS • Television Coverage of the Middle East
HEWITT D. CRANE • The New Social Marketplace: Notes on Effecting Social Change in America's Third Century
RHONDA J. CRANE • The Politics of International Standards: France and the Color TV War
HERBERT S. DORDICK, HELEN G. BRADLEY, and BURT NANUS • The Emerging Network Marketplace
GLENN FISHER • American Communication in a Global Society
EDMUND GLEN • Man and Mankind: Conflict and Communication Between Cultures
BRADLEY S. GREENBERG • Life on Television: Content Analyses of U.S. TV Drama
JOHN S. LAWRENCE and BERNARD M. TIMBERG • Fair Use and Free Inquiry: Copyright Law and the New Media
ROBERT G. MEADOW • Politics as Communication
WILLIAM H. MELODY, LIORA R. SALTER, and PAUL HEYER • Culture, Communication, and Dependency: The Tradition of H. A. Innis
VINCENT MOSCO • Broadcasting in the United States: Innovative Challenge and Organizational Control
KAARLE NORDENSTRENG and HERBERT I. SCHILLER • National Sovereignty and International Communication: A Reader
DALLAS W. SMYTHE • Dependency Road: Communications, Capitalism, Consciousness and Canada
HERBERT I. SCHILLER • Who Knows: Information in the Age of the Fortune 500

In Preparation:

WILLIAM C. ADAMS • Media Coverage of the 1980 Campaign
WILLIAM C. ADAMS • Television Coverage of International Affairs
MARY B. CASSATA and THOMAS SKILL • Life on Daytime Television
ITHIEL DE SOLA POOL • A Retrospective Technology Assessment of the Telephone
OSCAR H. GANDY, JR. • Beyond Agenda Setting: Informtion Subsidies and Public Policy
BRADLEY S. GREENBERG • Mexican Americans and the Mass Media
CEES J. HAMELINK • Finance and Information: A Study of Converging Interests
VINCENT MOSCO • Pushbutton Fantasies
KAARLE NORDENSTRENG • The Mass Media Declaration of UNESCO
JORGE A. SCHNITMAN • Dependency and Development in the Latin American Film Industries
INDU B. SINGH • Telecommunications in the Year 2000: National and International Perspectives
JENNIFER D. SLACK • Communication Technologies and Society: Conceptions of Causality and the Politics of Technological Intervention
JANET WASKO • Movies and Money: Financing the American Film Industry
OSMO WIIO • Information and Communication Systems

EMERGING OFFICE SYSTEMS

based on Proceedings of the
Stanford University
International Symposium
on Office Automation

Robert M. Landau,
Science Information Association
James H. Bair, *BNR, Inc.*
Jean H. Siegman, *Stanford University*

 Ablex Publishing Corporation
Norwood, New Jersey 07648

Copyright © 1982 by Ablex Publishing Corporation.
Second Printing 1984.

Printed in the United States of America.

Library of Congress Cataloging in Publication Data

Stanford University International Symposium on Office
    Automation (1980)
    Emerging office systems.

    Includes index.
    1. Office practice--Automation--Congresses.
2. Business--Data processing--Congresses. I. Landau,
Robert M. II. Bair, James H., 1943-   . III. Siegman,
Jean H. IV. Stanford University. V. Title.
HF5548.2.S7733 1980   651.8'4   82-4086
ISBN 0-89391-075-9   AACR2

ABLEX Publishing Corporation
355 Chestnut Street
Norwood, New Jersey 07648

TABLE OF CONTENTS

v

PREFACE

This book is a result of the Stanford University International Symposium on office automation held at Stanford in March, 1980. It includes three kinds of contributions: papers by several of the invited speakers, reprints contributed by the speakers, and invited papers. The last category includes papers from invited respondents to the speakers, and from the editors of these proceedings.

The papers differ widely in form, from fairly "chatty" pieces to major papers that are a significant contribution to the field. All the contributions have a similar thread in that they address a problem area that has received too little attention at previous forums on office automation in the United States: the human and organizational factors.

Over a year and a half ago, a group of key people at Stanford recognized this problem area as critical to the widespread, direct use of information technology by the university's faculty and staff. Even though most had no prior experience with direct usage, they would ultimately be thinking, writing, and communicating on a daily basis using computer and communication technology. In fact, some already were, such as Joshua Lederberg, the Stanford Nobel Laureate in genetics.

Several ways to approach the problem were pursued including a rather novel idea. The idea was not to sponsor another conference, workshop, or tutorial, but to combine all three to address a question: Why have some organizations failed in their attempt to use the technology and how could such failures be prevented at Stanford? Perhaps insight is just a daily practice at Stanford. To my surprise the basic answer was immediately recognized: the human and organizational factors have not been given adequate attention. Certainly the technology for office automation has been the focus of effort to date. In fact, the technology is going to be tried no matter what.

Having decided to address the human and organizational factors, what better way to begin than to hear from the leading experts who have actually dealt with these factors? It was not difficult to identify the experts: our criteria included having direct experience with electronic office systems (EOS), having gathered empirical data (hopefully in some scientific way) on EOS implementations, having struggled with implementation in real organizations, and having questioned the whole notion of using EOS to automate offices. Perhaps more importantly, the speakers were not selling equipment or services. We even attempted to avoid speakers who are known as consultants, but it has become difficult to find an expert who is not offering his expertise in some profitable manner.

Of course there are more experts than could possibly tell their story in three days. The notion of a "respondent," frequently used in academic conferences, was employed to expand the exposure of people and ideas. There is nothing like the vitality of two experts with divergent views, especially when one is playing the role of devil's advocate.

The symposium raised a plethora of issues because of the tremendous diversity of backgrounds and disciplines represented. Some of the disciplines are so diverse that we could well use a language translator. But this very diversity is essential because the innovation being conceived for the office exists in an "interdisciplinary twilight zone."

The symposium and these proceedings represent a departure from the comfortable intellectual zones we all have created for ourselves in our respective disciplines. Understanding each other's perception may be as challenging as the subject matter itself. But then this challenge may be the very catalyst that unfreezes conventional ways of thinking and allows us the unfettered view from which new solutions spring. Perhaps we can divest ourselves of the preconceived positions of businessman, computer scientist, human scientist, manufacturer, user, or philosopher. Perhaps we can focus our efforts toward creating a working life in the office that is more humanly satisfying as well as more efficient.

James H. Bair
Program Chairman

ACKNOWLEDGEMENTS

The Symposium was the result of the energy and commitment of dozens of persons who directly contributed or indirectly supported those who did. At Stanford, Jon Sandelin was the Symposium Chairman. His leadership and liaison with Stanford management made it not only possible, but a great success. Jeannie Siegman's coordination and contribution to program content as well as logistics were crucial, and Pentti Kanerva's insights and crisp statements of purpose and goals were of immense value. We also gratefully acknowledge those responsible for hosting the symposium: the Committee on Office Systems and Technology, with special thanks to Sanford Rockowitz (audio/visual), Allison Bishop (Symposium administration), and Val Akana (assisting in Symposium administration.)

Indirect support from Bell Northern Research enabled the Program Chairman to be supported with time, secretarial help and patience for over a year prior to the Symposium. Jimmy Bates, the Director of Design Interpretive, Jim Gale, a senior manager at Bell Northern Research in Ottowa, and John Buchan, President of BNR INC. in Palo Alto, were the key supporters. Without their commitment, the Program Chairman would not have been able to devote the time and energy needed to make the Symposium a success.

EMERGING OFFICE SYSTEMS

CHAPTER 1

INTRODUCTION

James H. Bair

PURPOSE OF THE SYMPOSIUM

The purpose of the Stanford symposium was to examine emerging office systems to better understand why some work and others fail. Emerging office systems were defined to include both the technological and the behavioral innovations in the office. The technological innovations were viewed as being primarily based on computers and digital communications. We concluded very early in the planning of the symposium (the spring of 1979), that it was no longer a question of whether or not the technology was going to be used in new ways in the office. It was clear that *new office systems based on computer and communication technology are coming no matter what.*

This view assumes that new office systems will be justified— one way or another. Selection of the most technically advanced equipment, projection of productivity improvement, calculation of

return on investment, and the like are but short-term issues—
important for gaining corporate commitment. The question
becomes, once corporate commitment is achieved, whether the
new office systems will be successful and not just another
"gimmick" or corporate "new deal."

More specifically, the question becomes, what are the key
issues concerning the "office-of-the-future"? The symposium team
concluded that they are the human and organizational factors. The
success of emerging office systems was viewed to be determined
by how well these factors are taken into account during design
and implementation. Implementors must be aware of the specific
factors and understand the consequences for individuals,
organizations, and, ultimately, society. For example, what in the
design of a terminal contributes to user efficiency? What office
procedures must change to ensure sensible use of the new
technology? For every consequence there is a large and complex
set of factors, some of which have been studied in actual
implementations.

The goal of the symposium was to identify critical success
factors and their consequences. The invited symposium leaders
were Americans and Europeans who have researched, developed,
used, and managed the most advanced office technology avialable.
They have been recognized in the trade and research communities
for their contributions to the understanding of the human and
organizational factors. The achievement of the symposium's goal
would have resulted in the identification of ways to recognize
pitfalls in design and implementation. This proceedings suggests
that some proximity to the goal was achieved.

THE PURPOSE OF THIS PROCEEDINGS

The purpose of this book is to make generally available a
collection of papers stimulated by the theme of the symposium, as
well as ones actually prepared for the meeting at Stanford. Those
who attended the symposium had the opportunity to hear many
different ideas about practical ways to avoid pitfalls. They also had
the opportunity to assess the state of knowledge about the human
and organizational factors, and office systems in general.

Synthesizing these ideas is a formidible task, far beyond the
scope of this publication. However, it is a task worth mentioning as
a goal that might only be achieved or even adequately addressed
by an organization of sages, supported by resources that
transcended special interests.

The state of knowledge about office systems was shown to be in its infancy. As many of the contributors state, we are only beginning to understand what we must understand to make this change in the behavior of humans in offices as constructive as possible. We are at a stage analogous to the introduction of the automobile into American society, an innovation that restructured the fabric of our existence beyond what could have been imagined—let alone managed. Introducing office technology differently from the automobile so that we choose the consequences rather than just live with them is a philosophical question. What this symposium proceedings hopefully can do is to encourage us to proceed *experimentally* rather than *exploitatively* recognizing the limited state of knowledge.

These papers illustrate some general characteristics of the early stage of knowledge: (a) There is a difference of opinion about most issues; (b) The driving forces for the advancement of the knowledge are mostly special interests, ranging from vendors to those climbing the corporate ladder of using institutions; (c) There is a great diversity of approaches to office systems, ranging from scientific research to practical business administration; (d) Some of what has been reported is difficult to understand due to special research techniques and cliques of "insiders." In actuality, probably only a few persons have more than a superficial understanding of office systems, while many claim to (a basis for caution on the part of those just entering this field). These characteristics apply to any innovation less than 10 years old.

Awareness of the current state of office automation has guided the preparation of this proceedings and maximizes its valadity. This awareness does not dispute its value, but rather establishes a context for its use.

ORGANIZATION OF THESE PROCEEDINGS

The proceedings have been divided into four parts based on the similarities among issues and approaches. The first part has a management perspective and business orientation, and the second has a more technical consideration of design. The third is a research-oriented discussion of evaluation, and the fourth is a review of long range concerns of the the implications of user evolution for organization management and society. The papers vary considerably in detail within each part, but tend to be consistent in difficulty of comprehension for the practitioner.

Part I is most oriented toward the business practitioner; Part II is oriented the most toward the designer/implementor at a technical level; Part III is best understood by the social scientist/evaluator; and Part IV is best for planners and those concerned with the broader issues. Of course, the parts are not mutually exclusive, nor can the organization into parts withstand serious tests of consistency or intellectual rigor. But the organization can be useful to guide the reader and illuminate some of the ways in which perspectives differ.

Part I, "User Experience and Strategies," begins with a summary of the context at Stanford which spawned the conference. It becomes apparent when reviewing the events at Stanford, that they are representative of the situations that arise in any corporation. The next two papers describe strategies at two kinds of corporations planning for the large scale use of office technology: a large, multi-national petroleum company and a large, high-technology manufacturer. The Exxon project has required consideration of the issue of centralized planning in a decentralized organization. At DEC, concern is more directed toward the rationalization of a new use of the technology which has been its livelihood.

Part II, "Designing the Social and Technical Components of the Office System," starts with the clarification of the differences between traditional uses of technology, particularly computers, and the novelty of the unstructured office which processes mostly text and requires an interactive, custom system design. Office system design requires that the behavioral questions about meeting user needs be studied, particularly to determine what conventional office behaviors can be successfully changed—a tough question considered in the next paper. Departing from the social-psychological view, a computer scientist lists practical pointers and needs for users of computers, based on wisdom from pioneering experiences at Stanford. Similar wisdom is applied in the next paper to the design of a computer conferencing system, acknowledging the vital importance of the human-computer interface. Lastly, the impact of the vastly differing views of vendors, designers, users, and researchers is identified as most often resulting in "working non-solutions" to office problems. A reconciliation of these views requires a humanistic, multi-disciplinary approach to system design.

Part III, "Evaluating Office Information Systems," begins with questions similar to those in Part II about what actually happens in offices, but quickly moves toward methods for evaluating office changes. The first two papers offer similar frameworks and methods for evaluation and argue for the need to apply the tools of scientific method to answering such questions as, what is the impact on productivity? The third and fourth papers report findings from scientific, field research into a precursor of office automation systems, computer conferencing, which include generalizable methods as well as conclusions. In a quick return to "bottom-line" issues, the last paper takes a businessman's look at cost-benefit determination, arguing for more of the research discussed in the preceding four papers.

Part IV, "The Management and Evolution of Office Systems," starts with a review of the interdisciplinary twilight zone surrounding the close coupling of computers and humans in offices, offering some of the applied wisdom so desperately needed by managers. Lest the enthusiasm of a perspective born of technology remain unchallenged, the next paper counterpoints with an argument for a humanistic path toward technological innovation based on humanistic management science. Then, a description of socio-technical innovations in general is considered briefly in light of early office technology. Innovation in offices is most likely an evolutionary rather than revolutionary process, a notion that has been argued for years. The next two papers are by the father of office "augmentation" systems, Douglas Engelbart. Dr. Engelbart was invited to provide this proceedings with some of his wisdom that has guided much of the evolution, a point of view acknowledged by the resounding response of the symposium attendees. These companion papers describe both the technological prototype of office systems to date ("Augment") and the human system solutions that have been amply demonstrated in the twenty years of his work. Concluding the proceedings is an invited paper by our principal co-editor that combines the practical and technological into an application-oriented approach for the management of information resources.

CONCLUSION

Many readers of this proceedings will be looking for answers to their needs as practitioners, designer-manufacturers, and students. I have suggested that the symposium represents the relatively immature state of knowledge about office systems. This does not imply that there are no answers, merely that they require some digging to uncover. This is particularly true of these proceedings because of the divergent disciplines and perspectives, ranging from academic research to business pragmatism. As a whole, this heterogeneous collection will not stand the tests of either extreme. However, the conclusions and insights presented represent the best available in the field and are here for the digging.

This examination of why some office systems work and others fail does not reveal what might be considered an answer. It is embedded in the concept of "human and organizational factors." It is the essence of the message from the most senior of social scientists, such as Lodahl and Conrath, and the senior computer scientists, such as Engelbart and Turoff. And it is in danger of being lost in a plethora of platitudes.

The concept of human and organizational factors basically serves to focus on the users of technology rather than the technology. It is represented by many office automation programs today that begin with an examination of current office activities, methods, and procedures to determine human needs rather than uses for current technology. The program at DEC reported in Part I is representative of this approach. However, it is a giant leap from office needs to a socio-technical system that will increase organizational productivity and effectiveness. An examination of the systems at any office automation equipment show reveals a diversity that is difficult to comprehend, let alone relate to any consistent behavioral criteria. Similarly, a comparison of the implementation strategies for these systems does not reveal any consistency. The apparent lack of concern for the human and organizational factors stems partly from the difficulty of applying behavioral knowledge to system design. To wit, during the closing session of the symposium, a senior designer for Xerox Corporation, one of the most active in this field, raised a question at issue: How is all this behavioral knowledge supposed to help me when I'm programming software code for our office system product?

Posing that the answer to the design question lies in more research is not very realistic or comforting. The answer that *design is an art* and never will be determined by research results is more likely the case. Do we need then to have a new community of "office system design artists"? Perhaps yes, and if so, how do we establish a new generation of artists? I think the answer is that we must continue to experiment with the diversity of technology in the variety of human and organizational settings, combining our research rigor and business pragmatism. Only if this experimentation is done with great sensitivity to humans and their social setting can we expect to advance the art of design and innovation in office systems.

PART I

USER EXPERIENCES AND STRATEGIES

CHAPTER 2

PLANNING ELECTRONIC OFFICE SYSTEMS IN A UNIVERSITY SETTING: EXPERIENCES AT STANFORD

Jon Sandelin and Jean Howard Siegman
Center for Information Technology
Stanford University

INTRODUCTION

More than an academic interest lay behind Stanford University's sponsorship of the symposium on which this book is based. Human and organizational factors were, we felt, the least understood of the issues surrounding planning and implementation of electronic office systems, but among the most important. What better way to educate ourselves, as planners for the university, than to bring together some of the most innovative and respected people in the field—and then listen, question, and stimulate debate?

A community of about 20,000 people, Stanford University had a consolidated budget approaching $500 million in 1980. The purpose of the University is to provide instruction to a student body of nearly 12,000 and to conduct research in a wide variety of disciplines. The primary product is knowledge—recorded in its scholarly publications and carried into society by its graduates.

Exchange of information is fundamental to both the creation and dissemination of knowledge, and to the infrastructure (budgeting and funds accounting, admissions processing, people and space administration, etc.) required to support instruction and research. The impact of computer and communications technology on the creation and dissemination of knowledge will be comparable in magnitude to the introduction of the printing press—when our current transitional systems mature, perhaps before the end of this century.

This odyssey began about 15-20 years ago in computer science laboratories of major universities when work began on computer programs to help people write, to send messages, to collaborate by sharing access to electronic files, and to store and retrieve information conveniently. The continuing decline in the cost of computer function, and the continuing rise in the cost of labor to perform functions that computers can do better, make the widespread use of this technology inevitable.

In terms of the "three R's"—reading, writing, and arithmetic— a shift is taking place. In the 1960's, numerical computation was by far the dominant use of computers. By the mid -1970's, some university computers were used as heavily for writing as for computation. In the 1980's we are entering an era in which, thanks to the evolution of network communications technology, we can expect to *read* much information through computers as well. By the 1990's, assuming unfettered growth of communications networks, we can expect reading to be the dominant use.

In a university setting, the use of computers as a medium for all aspects of written communications—for reading, writing, revising, filing, retrieval, printing, and distribution—is by far the most broadly valuable of the multitude of "office system" applications now beginning to appear.

PIONEERS WITH NO FOLLOWERS

Stanford, paradoxically, is both rich and poor in the availability of computer tools to help people write and communicate. The University is fortunate in that very powerful tools were developed by some groups for their own use several years ago, and many of the people who developed these tools are still in residence. Extensions to their programs are under development, and advanced work on computer-assisted document preparation techniques is in progress under the leadership of Professor Donald Knuth in the Computer Science Department.

These tools, however, have been available to only a small segment of the Stanford population (a few hundred people). This is because the funding for these organizations (e.g., the Institute for Mathematical Studies in the Social Sciences, the Artificial Intelligence Laboratory, and the Stanford University Medical Experimental Facility) typically comes from government agencies and is restricted to supporting specific research projects. Access is thus limited to people directly working on those projects. The relatively high productivity of people within these environments and the noticeable lack of clerical personnel (typically 25-40 professionals per clerical worker vs. the university-wide average of about 2 to 1) provided a tempting model for the university as a whole.

In 1978 a small ad hoc group called COST (Committee on Office Systems and Technology) began to consider whether such tools might be extended more broadly at Stanford. COST was unique in that its members came together because of common interest, not executive directive, and they reported to no university unit. Members came from a variety of departments. The process COST followed to develop a comprehensive, institution-wide plan, and obtain support for its implementation, is described in detail in the following section.

A FRAMEWORK FOR ACTION

From the beginning, some basic premises provided us with a framework for action. These premises were strongly influenced by our observations of common characteristics at those places where computer tools for writing and communicating were in effective use:

1. The availability of a good context (or "full screen") editor.

2. The convenient availability of workstations—similar in accessibility to the telephone, i.e. at the place of work, within easy reach, and available also at home if desired.

3. Integration of a range of related software modules (e.g., message systems, spelling checkers, filing systems) and hardware components such as printers, phototypesetters, etc.—even if in some cases some "kludging" was needed to create the links.

4. A critical mass for effective communications, i.e., almost everyone with whom frequent contact was important was on the system.

Based on these observations, our own experiences, and discussions with many people at Stanford and elsewhere, COST adopted the following premises:

1. Quantity is more important than quality. *Given a minimal standard,* we felt that widespread use of a basic tool-set for writing and communication would do more to further the University's goals than limited availability of very powerful workstations.

2. To achieve widespread use, a system must have a relatively low entry price to encourage experimentation by potential users.

3. The expected useful life of systems should be no greater than 5-6 years. For all practical purposes, communications bandwidth is currently restricted to 9600 bits per second between on-campus locations and 1200 bits per second to homes. Beginning in the mid-eighties, we expect multi-megabit transmission capabilities. Declining costs in processor and storage technology, together with better software for graphics and video applications, will then permit a transition to much more sophisticated systems. But first the transmission capability to make them effective must be in place.

4. Writing and communicating by messages are the broadest applications of computers in the university and are therefore the logical foundation for building an integrated system. By contrast, if many kinds of separately designed, special-purpose terminals were installed, it would be very expensive to make the different systems compatible.

EARLY PREMISES ABANDONED

Two other early premises were subsequently abandoned or modified as additional information was gathered and results analyzed:

1. We thought a single approach would suffice for the Stanford community. Expectation of achieving 100% homogeneity in the university seemed both very unlikely and not even desirable, but we did believe a single system could become the de facto standard among most users. However, as we learned more about the characteristics and organizational dynamics of major communities (e.g., faculty vs.

administration) and more about the limitations of what the market had to offer, it became clear that none of the available "solutions" would work well for all. Planning thus had to be adjusted to provide for linking different kinds of systems together so that interorganization information mobility was not lost. To contain the expense of the work on links, only a small variety of systems could be supported.

2. We felt that system(s) on which much of the university would soon become dependent must be commercially supported. This position was subsequently modified. Although we were well acquainted with the perils and pitfalls associated with locally developed software, we could find no commercial alternative that provided the functions needed by the academic community at a cost that would encourage widespread experimentation. Commercial, turn-key systems were judged adequate for many of the administrative applications. For the faculty and the student communities, we adopted a plan that calls for standard off-the-shelf hardware and operating-system software, but that uses locally developed application programs for the text preparation, dissemination, storage, and retrieval functions. These programs had been developed within, and optimized for, the academic environment.

THE ACTION TAKEN

Given these premises, a group of COST members with complementary skills and a common vision set out in early 1978 to see what could be done. In retrospect, what transpired can be partitioned into the following phases:

1. The Survey (Where are we now? Who is interested? What systems are in use?)

2. The Needs Assessment (What capabilities should be provided both in the near term and several years in the future?)

3. The Evaluation of Alternatives (What is available today and what is likely to appear in the foreseeable future?)

4. The Development of a Strategy (Where to start, what to do, and how to get it done?)

5. Implementation (Turning plans into action, evaluation and adaptation.)

It is important to understand that these phases do not occur in discrete, serial steps. The process is dynamic—new products that must be evaluated enter the market, needs are not static (and indeed perception of needs changes as consumers become more knowledgeable and begin to experiment with new technologies), people enter and leave the organizations bringing with them (or taking away) notions of what ought to be done, and explaining the concepts seems to be a never-ending process.

What follows is a description of these phases as they have evolved at Stanford. They reflect the environment of a major research university—with organizational structure and operating characteristics differing from many other types of organizations.

THE SURVEY PHASE consisted of a telephone canvassing of the many departments of the university to determine who (if anyone) within each department was actively using or evaluating computer-assisted tools (e.g. commercial word-processing equipment or time shared services from central computer resources) for text preparation or communication purposes. The survey was conducted by two people from the Computer Center and one person from a large department who—at this stage—were interested in the area and concerned that no organized planning was being done nor was there any apparent concern that it should be done.

The information they gathered served two useful purposes. First, a data base of existing equipment was compiled. This data base has been continually updated to track the growth in acquisition of text preparation systems. Second, many people who were interested and/or involved in this area were thereby identified. A meeting was held where these people could discuss areas of mutual interest and concern. From that group, a few were seriously interested in better understanding the technology and influencing where it might lead the university. It was these people who formed COST. COST continues to exist today, and its work in teaching others about computer-assisted writing and communication tools and also its contributions to university planning have positioned the university to more readily accept the organizational changes required to exploit this technology.

THE NEEDS ASSESSMENT PHASE was an important period for us. We were beginning to develop some specific ideas on what we felt was needed. More and more, it seemed to us that the University needed an official coordinator in this area. Word processing salespeople were becoming very active on campus, spreading their own "vision" of what was good for us. In what in hindsight seems a somewhat naive move, we wrote a memo to the University's provost and vice presidents, recommending that a coordinator be appointed. We received a courteous reply that led essentially nowhere. The magnitude of what was at issue had not yet been made clear.

After this slight pause, we regained our momentum by preparing a formal document that permitted widespread review of our emerging ideas within the institution. The reactions and responses thereby generated led to important refinements in our thinking, and also led (eventually) to a general consensus as to what ought to happen among the many people who needed to be involved in implementing new technologies. The end result was a clear written statement of what was needed and a series of questions for potential suppliers, the answers to which allowed us to judge how suitable their system were for our needs.

One fortuitous event that occurred during this phase was Stanford's creation of a task force to study future use of computer technology by the institution. COST volunteered to provide a planning document on the potential for network-based text systems, thus acquiring the endorsement of a high-level Task Force in its efforts to acquire information and solicit support.

THE EVALUATION OF ALTERNATIVES PHASE involved distributing the needs assessment document to potential suppliers and evaluating the responses. This process not only provided valuable information on what products were available at that time, but also established channels of communication with some vendors so that new product developments could be previewed.

In judging alternatives and developing plans, it became clear that three areas of equal importance needed to be addressed:

1. Technical analysis. What are the components of this new technology, who are the potential suppliers, and what are the implications of design differences?

2. Financial and economic analysis. What are the economic issues and financial implications of introducing this new technology broadly within Stanford?

3. Human and organizational issues. How does, or more importantly how should, this new technology appear to the end user, and what organizational changes must occur for it to support institutional goals effectively? What factors distinguish successful installations from those that fail?

R.O.I. IN THE IVORY TOWER

The next phase, THE DEVELOPMENT OF A STRATEGY, began with the issuance of COST's report to the Task Force. The COST report discussed in some depth a range of technical, economic, and human and organization issues, described various alternatives, and provided recommendations on things to be done. At the time the report was issued, there was no enabling group with assigned resources and accountability to carry recommendations into action. COST was an ad hoc, volunteer group held together by common interest but with no accountability to manage a University program. The newly formed Center for Information Technology with its broad charter to guide the University in application of all manner of information systems, was a natural home. Thus the Text Network Program was formed as an arm of C.I.T.—to develop an overall strategy, to present specific action plans (with time-lines and resource requirements) to senior management for review and, if approved to implement them.

In formulating strategy, some elements we had to consider included:

1. Territorial and definitional boundaries. The distinctions between telecommunications, reprographics, and computing services functions are blurring. The campus is awakening to the potential impact of direct computer assistance to professionals wherever they choose to work. A "bandwagon" effect is developing that complicates efforts to provide a single focal point for coordinating organization-wide planning. In the broadest context, text preparation and communication "systems" encompass most of the traditional telecommunication, reprographics, and computational activities, and thus careful definition of scope is necessary to avoid perceived threat to other parts of the organization. Where organizational entities remain independent of the initiating group, they must be approached as contributors and partners in the planning process, otherwise they are likely to undertake independent planning efforts.

2. Managing expectations, both present and future. There is a need to avoid overselling, of committing to what can be accomplished only if everything goes perfectly. Small sure steps are generally more successful, as seen by the end user, than giant leaps that fall short. Our general philosophy has been to partition major projects into two components—a production service which uses only off-the-shelf, proven

components, and a research effort—to test, and introduce on an experimental basis if warranted—components "in development."

3. Avoiding technology-induced paralysis. A very real danger is the lure of the "better" product just over the horizon. There will always be improved products under development, and although careful judgments on timing must always be made, the "better" is the enemy of the "good." A good strategy takes advantage of what is available today, yet provides flexibility to evolve to future product generations—not an easy order to fill.

4. Recognizing group differences. Our own experience is that a single approach would not work because of differing needs of the major communities within the University. Faculty members tend to write a good deal, frequently choose to work at home, typically require special character sets for technical equations or foreign languages, and, as a group, tend to have infrequent turnover and are good self-teachers of new ideas. Administrators tend to communicate a good deal via short messages, work mostly in their office, generally require only standard symbols, and, especially among the clerical support work force, experience high turnover rates and are thus more dependent on good training aids (e.g., extensive use of menus). Different approaches were clearly needed, but there is sufficient overlap that links will be supported to permit information flow between the groups.

THE IMPLEMENTATION PHASE is about six months old at this writing. Three major projects are underway under the sponsorship of the Center for Information Technology: commercial word processor support, a project known as "Terminals for Managers," and a project intended to provide writing and communications tools to scholars. The first, commercial word processor support, sprang from a recognition that stand-alone word processors have inherent limits we hope to grow beyond, and that the piecemeal acquisitions taking place in numerous departments were amounting in the aggregate to significant expenditures. Any hope of using this equipment in other than stand-alone fashion depended on limiting the proliferation of brands. Such a policy was established, and special efforts have been made to assist the users of the approved brands.

The second project, Terminals for Managers (TFM), is a one-year experiment in which senior officers and their staffs are using a message system. The president of the University himself often turns to his terminal in preference to the telephone. Judged on user acceptance, the project is a huge success.

The TFM project, unlike the scholarly writing project, was conceived amd initiated—as an experiment—in only a matter of weeks. That could not have happened without a dedicated staff and access to existing computer capacity. But further, it would not have happened without the enthusiasm of the Director of the Center for Information Technology, who as a new user of an earlier message system recognized its potential and was a vigorous lobbyist to enlist his colleagues in the experiment.

Unlike the TFM system, the third project, the scholarly writing system, requires a commitment by the university to make a significant investment in new hardware, and thus has moved less rapidly. We believe the recommendation of enthusiastic colleagues will be just as important with it as with TFM, however, and have accordingly encouraged some long-standing users of similar systems to participate in a faculty advisory committee.

We are at this writing just at the point of selecting initial installation sites for this service. Our hope is to be able to achieve a concentration of users in a few departments rather than have scattered users in separated locations. This is important not only because of the "critical mass" phenomenon in message systems, but because users close to each other are able to help each other during the learning phase. New users are thus less dependent on instant access to system consultants and less vulnerable to the frustration and discouragement of not having help when it is needed. We expect this will promote faster incorporation of the new methods into people's work routines..

In other ways, too, the success of the project hangs in the balance as the initial users are selected. In *Decision Support Systems; An Organizational Perspective,* Peter Keen and Michael Scott Morton have this to say on what they call the "entry" stage:

> Entry involves ensuring legitimacy for action: defining the problem situation, the nature of a solution, the critera for evaluation, and the allocation of responsibilities and resources, even if only at a general level. . . Entry requires subtle skills and, in many instances, far more time and effort than any other aspect of implementation. Far too often, analysts respond to the pressure of visible results, and focus on formalizing the system, leaving "people" issues to be sorted out later. However,

most of the critical decisions are made at entry. . .
Moreover, it is at entry that the client's expectations
are set. . . Many failures occur not because a
"good" system was not delivered, but because the
right one was not or because the user had
excessively high expectations that led him or her to
enthusiastically support the effort but that could
never be met in practice.

The word processing industry in the past few years has inundated
us with stereotyped images of sophisticated secretaries operating
feature-laden super typewriters. Sometimes it is quite a job just to
erase that image and get people to think beyond it.

The papers in this collection have served us as a source of
inspiration in this work. We hope they will be equally valuable to
our readers.

CHAPTER 3

CAN CENTRALIZED PLANNING FOR OFFICE AUTOMATION EVER WORK IN A LARGE CORPORATION?

Robert M. Dickinson
Exxon Corporation

The answer to the question raised in the title of this paper is, from our perspective, both yes and no. I prefer to speak from our experience, rather than attempting an answer on the basis of a speculative theoretical analysis. One proof of successful planning is whether or not it has helped to bring about desired results. Exxon's offices today are far from fully "automated," in the sense of having work stations in every manager's, professional's, and secretary's office, tied together into a network via appropriate communications. Therefore, planning at the Exxon corporate level has not yet finished working. The votes are not all in yet.

Also, we have a plan, in fact, a series of plans and planning documents. However, these plans are not yet integrated in the corporate business plans and, therefore, do not enjoy the full understanding and support of top management. Our *program*, of course, is endorsed by management. That is, the office systems technology activity that I head up has achieved organizational legitimacy and is replicated throughout many parts of Exxon.

Finally, answering yes or no in this case is affected by one's definition of centralized planning. Exxon is composed of many distinct organizations, highly autonomous and frequently large. Many are planning for office automation, so there are, to a certain extent, many Exxon answers, not one.

Thus, in detailing my answers to the question, "Can centralized planning for office automation ever work in a large corporation?" I'm going first to describe our corporate effort in Exxon; how we got started, where we are today, and where I think we are going, which will lend credibility to our planning efforts. Second, I'm going to illustrate the variety of Exxon answers by describing briefly two specific examples at different levels in the organization. Finally, I'm going to describe our corporate planning efforts and hopefully, set the stage for further discussion by presenting a series of office automation planning issues that we've developed.

ORGANIZING A LARGE CORPORATION'S EFFORT IN OFFICE AUTOMATION

Exxon has been using computers to support its business operations for many years. It has been using modern office equipment even longer, and began acquiring sophisticated word processing equipment in the early 70s; however, the first real interest in office automation and "the office of the future" came in 1975, stimulated by an S.R.I. report by Alan Purchase and a cover story in *Business Week* on the subject. That interest was centered in two corporate headquarters' departments, the Administrative Services Department and the Mathematics, Computers, and Systems (MCS) Department.†

As a result, the Administrative Services Department carried out a scoping survey in mid-1976, with the goal of recommending an appropriate corporate response. The survey identified the two major thrusts that were bringing about the demand for office automation: (1) User pull, i.e., stable productivity, increasing office costs, and a growing awareness of the need for increased efficiency and effectiveness to handle the information explosion in the office; and (2) Technology push, i.e., the rapidly changing technology, dramatic reductions in cost brought about by the "computer on a chip," and the opportunities for synergism resulting from integrated electronic office solutions. The survey

---

†MCS is the Exxon term equivalent to such terms as EDP, MIS, Systems Development, etc., used by other organizations.

report recommended that a small project team be established at the corporate level to further study and recommend plans and actions regarding office technology.

In the fall of 1976, Exxon's Advanced Office Technology Project (AOTP) team was formed. It was jointly sponsored by the Administrative Services and Mathematics, Computers, and Systems departments, and initially staffed by me as manager and three analysts. One of the analysts came from Administrative Services and had been involved in implementing word processing in the corporate headquarters. One analyst was a relatively senior person from the MCS Department with a strong computer sciences background. The third analyst came from another part of the corporation, but had five years of prior service in systems development work in the MCS Department. My own background was largely in finance, accounting, and personnel, but I had had previous assignments as an advisor in Exxon's Office of Management Information Coordination and as Information Services Manager for Exxon Chemical. Thus, I think we avoided, at the beginning, some of the political problems relating to which organization will be responsible for office automation. Also, we had a good mix of skills and experience for our small team.

The announcement forming the AOTP team, which went to all Exxon directors and chief executives of Exxon's Regional and Operating Organizations, stated that the team's responsibilities would be world wide in nature and broad in scope, covering all aspects of the technologies and methodologies involved in the creation, production, transmission, storage, and retrieval of text and data. These responsibilities were limited, however, to coordination, communication, and developing recommendations, with a heavy emphasis on planning recommendations.

One of the first things the team did was to develop an action plan for itself, which is shown as Figure 1. The letters "BCS" in the plan stand for Business Communication System, which is the term adopted by the team to describe the scope of its activities. The BCS turned out to be quite useful in explaining concepts in management presentations, in categorizing office work in order to generate meaningful costs and statistics, and in providing a framework for planning.

The action plan indicates an end to the team's activities by the 4th quarter of 1978. In fact, the team was dissolved at the end of 1978, and was replaced by a new permanent organization, the Office Systems Technology Division, as described below. Also, most of the activities shown on the action plan were completed, at least on a first pass basis. Sometimes, they were carried out

Figure 1

AOTP NEW YORK
2 YEAR ACTION PLAN

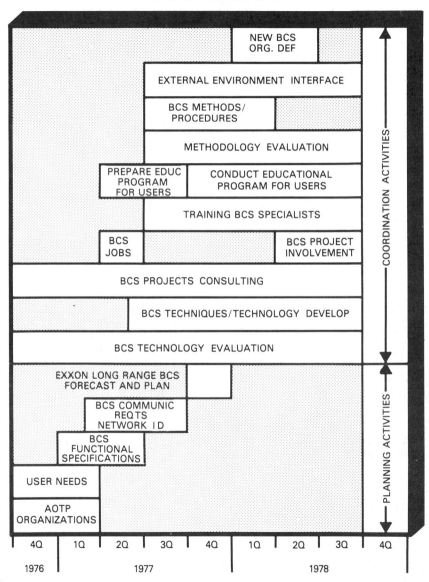

differently than originally anticipated. For example, we had expected to produce an audio-visual "dog and pony show" to help educate Exxon users. Instead, most of that is done via presentations that I, and various members of my staff, give on frequent occasions. We concluded that a canned A-V presentation would risk becoming out of date, and would not be suited for tailoring to meet the different needs and levels of understanding of our various audiences.

However, I can begin to say that centralized planning, as it applied to my group's activities, worked in helping to bring about desired results. During 1977 and 1978, we did indeed help to stimulate the formation of counterpart groups in other parts of Exxon (sometimes consisting of just part of the time of one person!). We quantified user needs, and we maintained state-of-the-art awareness of technology. We developed techniques for office systems studies and provided consulting services. We established an information exchange program, consisting of such things as a periodic newsletter, annual conferences, visits to affiliates, reports, seminars, etc. We also increased the AOTP staff to 6 by the end of 1978. In addition, the MCS Department was providing three man years of technical support to the AOTP. We carried out prototype evaluations and helped implement some advanced minicomputer-based systems to support office work, particularly in the areas of correspondence control and information retrieval.

In the meantime, as Exxon personnel were becoming more aware of the potential impact of office automation, major developments were also occurring in classical data processing and telecommunications. The trend toward distributed computing was bringing computing power closer to the end user, and was beginning to enhance office automation capabilities. The need to link these capabilities together via telecommunications became apparent just as technology was becoming available to make it possible. Thus, an Exxon headquarters organization study, in 1978, concluded that improved coordination was required in all these areas. The study recommended that: (1) MCS, Telecommunications (which had been part of the Administrative Services Department), and AOTP should be merged into a single department; and (2) AOTP should be expanded (to give it the capability to design and implement computer-based office systems software) and given permanent status. On January 1, 1979, the Communications and Computer Sciences (C&CS) Department of Exxon was formed. AOTP became the Office Systems Technology (OST) Division of C&CS. At the end of 1980, my staff consisted of 23 people, 8 of them in Exxon's New York office building and the rest in the C&CS Department's main offices in Florham Park, New Jersey. I divide my time between the two locations. An organization chart of the C&CS Department is shown in Figure 2.

In addition to carrying on the work of the AOTP, OST put considerable effort into developing and maintaining office systems software packages, participating in long range office systems planning studies for Exxon clients, conducting "R & D" into integrated electronic office systems, and increasing the tempo of our communications activities within Exxon. Our long range planning activities will be covered later.

Examples of office systems software we develop and/or support include a sophisticated information management and indexing system for large information centers, a correspondence control system, a calendar management system, a tickler (follow-up) file system, and a project status system. The planning studies we participate in for Exxon clients represent an encouraging trend. Originally, most of the studies we were asked to do were short term projects designed to reduce secretarial and clerical costs and improve support services. We justified doing them, even though it took effort away from our R & D and planning programs, because they improved our understanding of office work and user needs, and because they provided entries with users for increasing awareness of other aspects of office technology. Starting in 1979, our studies tended increasingly to involve developing long term plans oriented toward the integrated electronic offices of the future. More and more parts of Exxon recognized that the real target for office automation was the managerial and professional worker. This is where the biggest costs are, and where the greatest needs and opportunities lie. While the truly integrated, cost effective, user oriented, flexible, friendly electronic office system for managers and professionals isn't here yet, Exxon organizations are more and more convinced that it is definitely coming, and plans must be made to implement the new systems properly. Thus, the demand for our services in conducting planning studies has displaced most of the short term consulting we used to do and has reached a level difficult to accomodate within our available resources.

LEVELS OF PLANNING WITHIN EXXON

This leads to my second approach to answering the question, "Can centralized planning for office automation ever work in a large corporation?" Exxon is not only large, it is decentralized, with a great deal of autonomy delegated to its major subgroupings. We call these subgroupings Regional and Operating Organizations, or

FIGURE 2

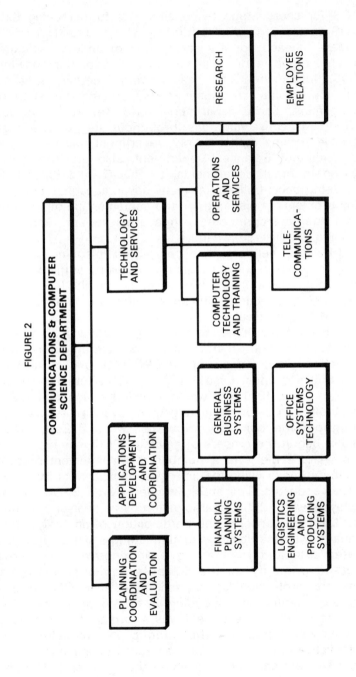

COMMUNICATIONS & COMPUTER SCIENCE DEPARTMENT

PLANNING COORDINATION AND EVALUATION

APPLICATIONS DEVELOPMENT AND COORDINATION

TECHNOLOGY AND SERVICES

RESEARCH

EMPLOYEE RELATIONS

GENERAL BUSINESS SYSTEMS

OFFICE SYSTEMS TECHNOLOGY

FINANCIAL PLANNING SYSTEMS

LOGISTICS ENGINEERING AND PRODUCING SYSTEMS

OPERATIONS AND SERVICES

COMPUTER TECHNOLOGY AND TRAINING

TELE-COMMUNICA-TIONS

ROOS for short. Much responsibility is further delegated by the ROOS to the individual affiliates, which actually carry out the business in each country and/or line of endeavor. Figure 3 is a summary organization chart for Exxon Corporation showing all the ROOS. Not shown are the headquarters departments, each headed by a vice president or manager, that provide staff support to top management. These departments have stewardship responsibility for their respective functions throughout the ROOS and affiliates, but have no line authority. My department, the Communications and Computer Sciences Department, also provides a variety of services to other departments, to ROOS, and to affiliates.

Being decentralized has many advantages, but it also presents many problems in planning for and implementing office automation within the interconnected office environment. Some of these problems are listed in Figure 4.

I believe, therefore, that "centralized" planning can be carried out by the parts of a large organization. Many of the parts of Exxon are huge entities in themselves. Also, each major level should carry out planning activities, with appropriate coordination effected by the next higher level.

Thus, my first illustrative example starts with an affiliate, Esso Petroleum (England) and its 5-year strategic plan for office automation. Esso Petroleum, or EPCO, is one of several billion dollar affiliates under Esso Europe. EPCO's formal planning study began in June, 1979 and was completed in January, 1980. It was kicked off with a formal management overview to insure support throughout the company. However, we and Esso Europe had actually begun the process of gaining EPCO management support three years earlier, via a number of management presentations. The study began when the time was deemed right by the project's internal sponsors. The study was led by an EPCO management employee, with full time participation by an analyst from my group. Esso Europe sponsored the participation of an analyst from Esso Germany, with the objective of stimulating a similar project there at a later date and transferring experience gained. The project focussed primarily on the business communications needs of managers, professionals, and secretaries in EPCO's head offices, with the intention of extending it to the field later.

The result of the project was a formal, documented strategy plan which highlighed the conceptual way ahead, but was conservative in terms of implementation recommendations to help insure success and minimize acceptance problems. The plan looks out ten years and contains specific phases and developments for five years. It concentrates on hard (cash) benefits and estimates a

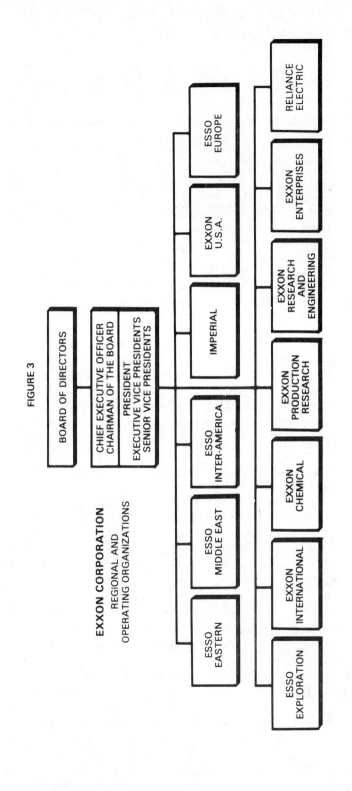

FIGURE 3

EXXON CORPORATION
REGIONAL AND
OPERATING ORGANIZATIONS

BOARD OF DIRECTORS

CHIEF EXECUTIVE OFFICER
CHAIRMAN OF THE BOARD

PRESIDENT
EXECUTIVE VICE PRESIDENTS
SENIOR VICE PRESIDENTS

ESSO EASTERN

ESSO MIDDLE EAST

ESSO INTER-AMERICA

IMPERIAL

EXXON U.S.A.

ESSO EUROPE

ESSO EXPLORATION

EXXON INTERNATIONAL

EXXON CHEMICAL

EXXON PRODUCTION RESEARCH

EXXON RESEARCH AND ENGINEERING

EXXON ENTERPRISES

RELIANCE ELECTRIC

Figure 4
Problems of a Decentralized Organization

- Geographic, functional, business line decentralization
- Variation in capabilities/understanding/management and employee attitudes
- Variation in opportunities and availability of solutions
- Variation in government regulations and requirements
- Different rates of progress
- Different approaches
- Incompatibilities; sub-optimum solutions
- Penalty for delay vs. moving too fast

---

very high, discounted cash flow (DCF) rate of return for the project's investment costs. Basic recommendations include extensive decentralized word processing, electronic filing, electronic mail, some professional work stations, enhanced graphics, emphasis on dictation, and interfaces to data processing.

Because of solid work done by the study team, employing effective communications and methodology, user acceptance and support throughout and after the study was high. Management endorsement was obtained at the completion of the study; and implementation was begun.

I think we can readily conclude, in this case, that centralized planning has worked. At this writing, implementation is ahead of schedule and benefits are greater than anticipated. Perhaps more importantly, the success of the project has provided stimulus and guidance for similar studies in other affilitates, and has helped convince Esso Europe to concentrate more effort in this area, and to begin looking at region-wide considerations.

The next level in my answer is the Regional (ROOS) answer. My example here is Esso Eastern's Integrated Electronic Office Concept. Esso Eastern is Exxon's regional management company for the Far East, and is located in Houston, Texas. Unlike Esso Europe, where office automation activities started really bubbling at the affiliate level, Esso Eastern has taken the lead for all of its region. Being located in the U.S., Esso Eastern had access to advanced office technology earlier than its affiliates. The region it manages is characterized by great communications distances, voluminous communications needs, significant time differences, long delays with conventional mail, and rapidly and constantly shifting situations requiring fast responses.

Esso Eastern recognized the potential of office automation shortly after the formation of Exxon's AOTP team, and formed their own combined office automation and telecommunications group. They adopted the concept of the Business Communications System (BCS) and developed an extensive communications program. This program, which included participation by Exxon's AOTP team, was aimed at employees at all levels. It identified hard benefits, but focussed more on medium (professional time savings) and soft (quality of work output, quality of work life) benefits. The heart of their program *and* their planning efforts has been a series of scenarios for a staged approach to the Integrated Electronic Office. Figures 5, 6, 7, and 8 are selected examples of the simple visuals they used to communicate these scenarios within Esso Eastern headquarters, to their affiliates, to other parts of Exxon, and externally where appropriate.

All implementation, in accordance with their staged plan, has been cost justified. Their plan stresses compatibility at all appropriate levels between headquarters and the affiliates. Esso Eastern has been the most aggressive part of Exxon in pursuing teleconferencing (in their case, slow-scan video). Interest in this technology is now spreading to other Exxon groups. They have also been the most successful in encouraging the widespread, extensive use of dictation, based primarily on the micro-cassette, hand held recorder. Many Esso Eastern affiliates are following headquarters' lead and are rapidly implementing various aspects of office technology, with significant successes and a high degree of acceptance.

Thus, we can again conclude that centralized planning can work in a large organization, this time at the regional level. Conditions, of course, were right. Management was enthusiastic, needs were great, and opportunities were becoming available. Effective communications and dedicated efforts were key to the success of their planning efforts.

THE CORPORATE CHALLENGE

Back now to the corporate level. Can centralized planning work at this level? As I said at the beginning, the answer is both yes and no. I don't believe we can develop a grand master plan and impose it throughout Exxon. First, this would be contradictory to

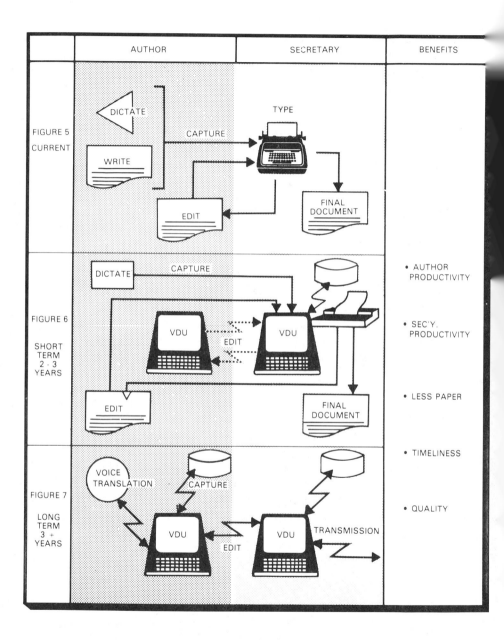

	AUTHOR	SECRETARY	BENEFITS
FIGURE 5 CURRENT	DICTATE / WRITE / CAPTURE	TYPE / EDIT / FINAL DOCUMENT	
FIGURE 6 SHORT TERM 2 - 3 YEARS	DICTATE / CAPTURE / VDU / EDIT	VDU / FINAL DOCUMENT	• AUTHOR PRODUCTIVITY • SEC'Y. PRODUCTIVITY • LESS PAPER
FIGURE 7 LONG TERM 3 + YEARS	VOICE TRANSLATION / CAPTURE / VDU / EDIT	VDU / TRANSMISSION	• TIMELINESS • QUALITY

Figure 8

A LONG TERM CONCEPTUAL VIEW OF A LOCAL AFFILIATE INTERNAL
COMMUNICATIONS SWITCH SERVING THE FUTURE ELECTRONIC OFFICE

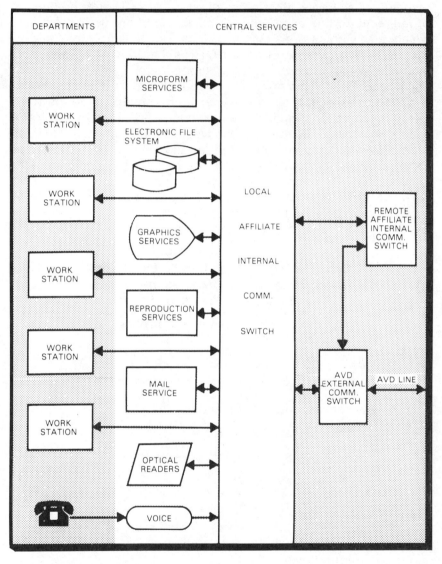

our decentralized organization and management philosophy. Second, we don't have the time or capability to develop such a plan in the detail necessary to reflect all the variations in needs and opportunities that exist throughout Exxon.

However, I believe we *can* contribute to more effective planning at all levels. Most of my division's work is devoted directly or indirectly to this end. Figure 9 is a listing of our work programs, which are planning-related.

Annually, we publish an Office Technology *Forecast,* internally within Exxon, indicating what developments we think will occur, and when. This material is also included as a component of a broader forecast by my department covering computing, telecommunications, and office technology, in order to reach the widest possible audience. We also issue, periodically, a brief status report to managements throughout Exxon on our outlook for Exxon's offices of the future (note the plural). It is comparable to Esso Eastern's scenarios, except that the stages are described in narrative form and only the grand design is depicted graphically.

Concept development, such as the Business Communications System (BCS), supports planning by providing a framework for

Figure 9
Centralized Planning: Can it Ever Work
IN a Large Corporation—
The Exxon Headquarters Answer

Exxon OST Planning Activities

- Forecasting

- Concept development

- Awareness and understanding

    —Management presentations

    —Information dissemination/exchange

- Tools and techniques

- Technology evaluation

- Integrated office systems: Office systems studies
    —Functions and considerations
    —Prototypes

- OST planning projects

thinking, analyzing, and exchanging information. Figure 10 is a description of the BCS and its seven components. We have also used the BCS to categorize costs and volumes and estimate benefits. For example, when we tell management that the expansion ratio throughout Exxon is 19:1 (i.e., for every original piece of text, 19 copies are made), it really catches their attention.

Our presentations to managements help gain support for planning projects. Our information dissemination and exchange activities help transfer experiences and minimize the likelihood of duplication of effort. At several different types of Exxon conferences, presentations about affiliate and regional planning projects have stimulated interest in conducting similar projects by other Exxon groups.

We have developed tools and techniques for data collection and data analysis which provide assurance that implementation of

Figure 10
Office Systems Technology
Scope

● Business communications system

— Includes all business communications which are documented or recorded

— Includes internal business communications and business communications from/to the outside

● Consists of seven components

— Creation - Act of thinking and formulating a communication

— Capture - Placing the communication onto a medium

— "Keyboarding" - Entry to/processing by/output from a keyboard

— Distribution - Message carrying, mail handling, electronic transmission

— Expansion - Copying, printing, microfilming, duplication of magnetic records

— Storage and Retrieval - Indexing, storing, searching for and finding information

— Disposal

---

plans will truly respond to user needs and yield meaningful benefits. We have been packaging these tools and techniques to increase their transportability within Exxon.

Maintaining state-of-the-art awareness through our technology evaluation program, of course, supports our forecasting and information dissemination activities. Detailed evaluations of specific products, often carried out jointly with the Computer Technology and Training Division of the C&CS Department, are frequently the basis for specific system selection decisions.

Our Integrated Office Systems program consists of the Office Systems Planning studies for Exxon clients already discussed, the ongoing development and refinement of a document called "Functions and Considerations of the Integrated Electronic Office," office systems software development, and prototype evaluations. The office systems planning studies we participate in represent the most direct influence we have at the affiliate and regional level. Our problem is that these are on request only, are time and resource consuming, and represent a relatively small percentage of all the entities within Exxon.

The Functions and Considerations report is a "living" (i.e., constantly being refined and improved) document describing the details of the ideal office system, as we see them. It is used for systems comparisons and evaluations, for specific systems selections, as a stimulus for new development work, and as a basis for communicating with Exxon user groups and with vendors. Our prototypes have been installed to gauge demand, determine needs and benefits, and develop proprietary office systems software. Initially, our prototypes were relatively small scale, but we expect that a number of large production prototypes will be installed over the next two or three years.

OST projects, which specifically fall under our planning program, and not otherwise described, include a variety of activities. Early in the life of the AOTP, the team prepared a lengthy exploration report on office automation opportunities, investment costs, and benefits. It was global in nature and projected huge savings, as extrapolated from a variety of internal and external sources. It received very limited distribution, even within Exxon, because of the sensitivity of the numbers; but it remains useful for reference purposes.

Annually, we receive limited data on office technology from the ROOS, as part of their C&CS plans, submitted to my department. In order to minimize reporting burdens, the submissions on office technology are limited to narrative descriptions of activities, and plans and data on OST manpower and communicating word processors. The information we receive has limited usefulness, since the overall planning horizon is only one year forward. We are concentrating on communicating word processor data because of the growing interest, throughout Exxon, in linking these devices together in a store-and-forward network.

Our most recent work has been to focus on the strategic planning process involving premises, issues, objectives, and strategies. With participation by ROOS and affiliates, we have reached the stage of having developed a list of office technology issues. The final list of 10 issues that was circulated within Exxon is shown in Figure 11. These were derived from earlier lists developed at an Exxon OST conference, in the fall of 1979, and a European OST conference, in February, 1980.

Figure 11
Issues

The Challenge: Office systems change must be managed!

1. How do we prepare Exxon?

2. How should Exxon determine guidelines for design of office systems?

3. How do we deal with human factors?

4. How do we insure an effective working relationship with (remote) groups?

5. How do we improve ability to deal with user needs?

6. How do we determine commonality of solutions?

7. What skills are required to plan, implement, and maintain TOOTF?*

8. How do we implement TOOTF* with the varying degrees of existing systems?

9. How do we measure the success of office systems change?

10. How do we determine and implement interconnect-ability among Exxon offices?

*The Office of the Future!

This list has been made available within Exxon as a basis for discussion; for the identification of R & D projects; and, for each of the levels within Exxon as appropriate, for the development of objectives, strategies, and action plans. While it still may not be possible to develop an overall grand strategy for Exxon, for the reasons cited above, we think the issues list will be useful at various levels. It will encourage some consistency, while permitting tailored approaches. We think, also, that we may be able to single out one or more specific issues, set up task group(s) composed of Exxon OST and ROOS/affiliate personnel, and recommend broad objectives and strategies for the issues so selected.

CONCLUSION

Centralized planning for office automation can work in a large organization such as Exxon, at the affiliate level, at the regional level, and even at the corporate level. Effective planning and effective planning support are not necessarily the same as having a single adopted corporate plan. I believe we have the former even if we don't have the latter. The offices of the future will become a reality throughout Exxon because of the combined and coordinated efforts of affiliates, ROOS, and corporate level groups, such as my own, other divisions of C&CS—in particular Telecommunications and Computer Technology and Training, and other corporate departments. The kind of planning I have talked about, carried out at all levels, *will* bring about our desired goals.

NOTE

Certain reports and material referred to herein, such as the Office Technology Forecast, Status Report on Exxon's Offices of the Future, Functions and Considerations of the Integrated Electronic Office, Data Collection and Analysis Tools and Techniques, etc., are considered proprietary and are not released outside Exxon.

CHAPTER 4

OFFICE AUTOMATION AT DIGITAL EQUIPMENT CORPORATION

Robert Erickson
Manager
Office Information Systems
and
Richard Hill
Manager
CSI Investment Strategy
Digital Equipment Corporation†

INTRODUCTION

Office automation. . . just another computer "buzzword?" Or, is the carefully planned and implemented application of computer technology to the office, a wave of the future? At Digital Equipment Corporation, a leading manufacturer of computers, professionals and non-professionals have found that technology at their fingertips changes the way they accomplish their day-to-day activities—and even the way they think.

At the present time, it seems clear that there are as many definitions of "office automation" as there are people who would define the term. At Digital, there are four valid elements which can

---

†The ideas and opinions expressed herein are those of the authors and are the sole responsibility of the authors; they do not express or imply Digital Equipment Corporation products, plans for products, or direction in product offerings.

be implemented, and examination of the current progress provides insight into the overall role of technology in the office, as well as clearly defining the problems that need to be solved to provide a useful technology.

First, *interpersonal communication* is a key component which is required and contributes to the effectiveness of all levels of activity. Digital is a decentralized, highly-matrixed organization in which communication—at all levels, between levels and between different organization entities—is key to success. Because of these communication needs, interpersonal communication support systems must be flexible, reliable and easy to use. This would include any system or service that assists people to communicate with each other. The list includes electronic mail systems (EMS), facsimile (FAX) systems, telephone, teleconferencing, message switching, etc.

Second, *office processing* has been used with success. While "word processing" is moving forward in various formats and using a wide range of computer equipment, the concept of total processing—data processing *and* word processing—is an important one in the overall scheme of office automation. Computer hardware technology and its price are moving steadily toward the point where it can be assumed that processing power can be inexpensively provided in every office. The question is raised, however, about how that power can be effectively implemented. Dedicated, stand-alone word processing is finding its way into many offices—for the express purpose of automating "clerical" functions. While extremely useful, even in its current state of development, we have found that the real leverage comes from automating professional resources, through the use of integrated systems which provide more than simple clerical automation.

Third, *information retrieval* has become an extremely important component of the overall office need. A recent study by a large manufacturing company indicates that the cost of a single file cabinet, maintained for one year, is about $5,600. Retrieval of a memorandum or other piece of hard-copy information, if not where it should be (misfiled or missing) costs about $80. Even more interesting is their determination that it costs about $23,000 just to create the file cabinet and that only 30% of the information within the file cabinet is accessed, even once, during a year. With this pricing information, applied to a specific office environment, goals for information storage and retrieval are provided for the automation of the file cabinet function. Key to success of the information retrieval activity is easy access to large banks of information. A successfully implemented system can increase the effectiveness of both clerical and professional resources.

Fourth, *information mobility* is a key consideration. Information is useful only if it can be moved to where it is needed and can be used. Much of our useful information, stored in various forms on various computer systems, is in computer-readable form, but extremely difficult to access and move. Capabilities that the casual user can directly utilize to move information easily to and from the office must be implemented.

The "office automation" project at Digital, then, faced the challenge of providing these four capabilities, in various forms: interpersonal communication, office processing, information retrieval, and information mobility.

After an understanding of the various technology components that could be used to enhance office efficiency and effectiveness had been gathered, we considered it useful to determine the individuals, within the office, who would derive benefits from application of this technology. It became clear, at Digital, that the key target audience consisted of managers and the professional staff. In planning and implementing the various elements of our office automation project, we adopted the classification of *knowledge worker,* and focused our efforts at increasing the effectiveness of this class of individual.

Nearly all organizations have become dependent on this knowledge worker. Many of the skill groups represented are in short supply and are expensive to obtain and retain. As a rapidly-growing, high-technology company, Digital has found this to be especially true. The opportunity to extend the effectiveness of the knowledge worker became both an exciting challenge and a real opportunity to contribute to corporate success.

As we looked at this group of individuals (the knowledge workers), it became clear that information is their raw commodity. They deal with information constantly, and the ease of information manipulation is a key factor in their effectiveness. The product of the activity of these knowledge workers is *value added* to information. How a manager processes information and the measure of his or her effectiveness remains a "black art;" however, when attempting to relate a manager's work flow to a process where automation can be applied, interesting opportunities are uncovered.

The number of knowledge workers is increasing. The major cost in industrialized countries is in their white collar labor force. If productivity is going to increase, it must be reflected through increased effectiveness in this segment of the work force. In addition, the demand for information is increasing. Government regulations, need for control in large corporations and organizations within corporations, and changing economic conditions all contribute to this demand.

Even more critical, in our industry, is the demand for computer and business professionals. This demand is increasing at a dramatic rate. And, the supply of qualified individuals is not satisfying the demand. Conventional wisdom acknowledges that Office Automation will indeed happen; however, the belief seems to be that it will be a long time coming. The need at Digital, and our experience in pilot programs, indicates that it may occur earlier than expected.

With this challenge in mind, and its significant opportunity, we focused our EMS and other office capabilities directly toward achieving benefits to the knowledge worker segment of the work force. We felt that the secretaries are an important key to successful implementation, and in the future will become part of the professional staff. This should be especially true as they are provided with more effective tools. However, the initial thrust was to increase the effectiveness of our managers and professional staff.

The benefits of office automation are becoming clear to us, even with our current state of evolution in supplying technology to the office. Office automation allows organizations to manage the use of information as a valuable resource. A primary goal of the office automation project is increasing the effectiveness (productivity) of knowledge workers—the managers and professional staff. While this has long been the foundation of office automation, there is a real challenge to develop methodologies to quantify this benefit. Because office automation brings new capabilities to our office workers, the potential benefits are subject to be questioned until experience and metrics can be obtained and analyzed.

With this basic background, some of which has been developed in retrospect, we will now explore the various elements of office automation that have been implemented at Digital.

INTERPERSONAL COMMUNICATIONS

There are several specific projects which have evolved into an interpersonal communications capability. This collection of capabilities has grown to high usage. The specific components within this area of office automation are as follows:

1. *EMS (Electronic Mail Systems):* currently have 2,500 subscribers. An internal production system operating on three different nodes. The acceptance and use have been very high, and the demand has not yet been satisfied.

2. *Store and Forward (S&F) Message Switch (MS):* currently processing 12,000 messages per day. It is a worldwide system of 500 terminals operating on a forced delivery basis.

3. *Word Processing (WP) Connectivity to EMS and MS:* currently we have 1,200 word processing units with communications capability. Although word processing as a communication terminal has been underutilized, efforts are now being made to increase its connectivity to other systems.

4. *Facsimile (FAX) Units:* currently we have 200 units. These are point-to-point analog and digital facsimile units.

Electronic Mail Systems (EMS)

The evolution of electronic mail at Digital is interesting, and perhaps unique. As an engineering, manufacturing and marketing company, and because of the interactive nature of our computer systems, many managers and professionals "grew up" with a terminal in his or her office. Several years ago, the concept of using the terminal as a message station evolved with departmental "electronic mail" systems. Various technical departments within Digital wrote primitive mail systems, which allowed them to exchange "notes" with their colleagues. There was no control over this evolution; however, many basic technical principles, such as concurrency, lock-out, disk/data accessing privileges, and others, were explored during this time period.

A major drawback of the various systems that evolved was their "unfriendliness" to the inexperienced or casual user. A great deal of knowledge and information about how the system was set up was required for use. This, of course, proved no inconvenience to the highly technical user of one of the various systems; however, the casual user had no chance for success. In addition, it was often necessary to gain access to a mail system through the use of monitor-level (operating system) commands, rather than user-oriented interfaces.

In 1978, Digital initiated a Corporate-level EMS pilot project. The EMS facility was introduced as a pilot, for many reasons. First, introducing EMS as a pilot assisted EMS to be accepted within Digital. Second, users accepted changes because they understood it was a pilot operation. Thus flexibility in development was preserved. Third, the pilot helped greatly to set user expectations. The level of availability and the extent of functionality did not have to attain the level the users may have demanded from an internal production service. Fourth, the pilot report was the end result of the project, rather than the service or the system. The focus of the pilot was to learn and document the results. Fifth, the pilot provided the basis for a production-level service plan. The experience gained during the pilot served as basis for proceeding to an integral production service, which is now in operation.

EMS pilots were in operation from January, 1978, until August, 1979. This seems to be a long time for a pilot, but this time period allowed changes to be made to improve the system and allowed three complete sets of questionnaires to be circulated and analyzed for the pilot report. The total number of users to participate in the pilot was 1,200.

Although complete details of the pilot report are beyond the scope of this document, it is interesting to analyze several aspects of the pilot program which may be of use to those intending to implement EMS systems.

Terminal Use.   Terminals are still the most expensive element of this type of system. Therefore, we had to know the demand for new terminals if additional users were added. It was determined that for each three EMS users, one additional terminal would be required. This ratio is perhaps unique to Digital, because of the already heavy terminal usage throughout the company. Figure 1 illustrates the terminal usage profile at the end of the EMS pilot.

Another interesting piece of data came out of the terminal-usage portion of the questionnaires. Since existing terminals were used, it was determined that 64% of the terminals were video terminals (clearly the preference of those who use terminals for data processing or other interactive usage) as opposed to only 36% hard copy (which may be thought of as more practical for word processing activities). It became apparent, however, that video terminals are preferred by most EMS users, but access to a hard copy terminal is required to allow printing of EMS messages in special situations.

EMS Costs.   (See Figure 2.) EMS costs consist of three major elements: terminal cost, communications costs, and cost to operate

Figure 1

EMS PILOT – TERMINAL USE

	USERS HAVE THEIR OWN TERMINALS	USERS SHARE A TERMINAL
TERMINAL USE DEDICATED TO EMS	19%	30%
TERMINAL HAS MULTIPLE USES	34%	17%

VIDEO TERMINALS   64%

HARDCOPY TERMINALS   36%

A video terminal is preferred by most EMS users.

Figure 2

Costs of EMS

Terminal Cost   Communications Cost ➤   Service Cost

Service Cost is $25/User/Month

This Includes

— Equipment at Node

— Operating Expenses for Node

— Personnel Costs (System Manager, User Support, Operators)

     Internal costs to Digital average about $600 per year for each user. This may be higher if the user has a private terminal or is remote from the EMS node.

on an EMS node (referred to as service cost). It was determined that internal costs to Digital during the pilot phase and succeeding service phases averaged to about $600 per year for each user. This cost may be higher if the user has a dedicated, private terminal for EMS, or if the user is remote from the EMS node (must use common-carrier communications). Approximately half ($300/year) was determined to be the service cost, which includes the equipment at the node(s), operating expenses for the node(s) and personnel costs (system manager, user support, operators, etc.)

Types of Communications Sent on EMS. Although the system was not designed to monitor and determine the type of communication sent via EMS, questionnaires sent to all users resulted in the following communication types:

1. *Broadcast Information:* the ability to reach a group of individuals quickly by one group.

2. *Information Inquiry/Response:* the answer command in EMS facilitates this ability. By a simple keystroke command, the user creates a complete memorandum header and has only to enter a short answer to complete an interpersonal transaction.

3. *Task Assignments:* managers often provide task assignments to others via EMS.

4. *Followup on Task Assignments:* the "forward" command, within EMS, permits a manager to assign a request that he or she has received to one of his or her subordinates, add comments to the forwarded message, and copy the original requestor. The message can also be posted to a tickler file for follow-up at a later date.

5. *Status Reports:* in essence, a variety of "memoranda."

6. *Requests for Action:* again, previously described under task assignments and prior to EMS, accomplished by hard-copy note, memorandum or personal discussion.

7. *Meeting Agenda and/or Minutes:* in analyzing the way executives spend their time, it becomes apparent that a mechanism through which meetings could be eliminated or made more effective would be a key area for improvement. While EMS utilization at Digital has not resulted in replacement of meetings by use of EMS, the users felt that information flow before and after a meeting can assist materially in making the meeting more effective.

8. *Follow-up Conversations:* at Digital, as in most organizations, business issues are discussed in halls, the cafeteria, etc. After these short discussions, it is extremely useful to confirm an issue or an agreement from the conversation. EMS provides an excellent medium to accomplish this task.

9. *Informal Discussion of Issues:* this capability comes close to a meeting substitute in the use of EMS in Digital. For EMS to make a major impact on meetings, however, it will have to have special features that promote its use in that way. Also, training may be needed to get people to think of working solutions with a different approach, such as EMS or teleconferencing, rather than meetings. As Digital continues to distribute geographically, however, the impact on efficiency and effectiveness would be significant.

Primary User Services Requested.   Although it is beyond the scope of this paper to explore the specific capability of the Digital EMS system, it might be useful to those planning EMS implementation to explore the issues raised from the three sets of questionnaires and the user feedback mechanism (called "feedback") on the EMS system. First, editing capabilities were cited as a key requirement. This requirement may be somewhat unique within Digital, however. Most of our technical users were accustomed to having access to powerful and sophisticated editing systems—much beyond those on the EMS pilot. Second, interconnectivity is a must. The users at Digital felt that once a terminal is available in an office, it must have access not only to EMS, but other systems as well. Third, anything that makes an office system more approachable is a plus. Most felt that an on-line "help" facility is a must. User manuals may not be available at all times; therefore, on-line help is needed and must be extremely easy to use (a user could forget almost anything, and be led through a tutorial to refresh his/her memory on system usage). Fourth, a "return receipt" capability would be helpful. EMS is like physical mail in many ways. The need for a return receipt capability raises an important question, however: Should the system observe what the user is doing, such as reading his/her mail? Fifth, a calendar capability is desired. There is considerable overhead in maintaining on-line calendars. Also, everyone needs to do it if it is to be effective. So far, in our implementation, the calendar capability appears to have only limited success. Sixth, a tickler file automation would be useful. The tickler is really a message to the user from the user (to himself/herself). This appears to be a natural feature of the system and it is expected that future research will show increased usage.

Effects of EMS. Although the real goal of EMS metrics is to determine how the effectiveness of managers and professionals is impacted, the questionnaires contained a series of questions on the effect of EMS on the way the user performed his/her job. The questions centered on four areas, and the results were as follows:

1. Number of telephone calls *decreased.* A majority indicates this was true with between 5 and 25% decrease in the actual number of telephone calls.

2. Number of interoffice memoranda *decreased.* Again, a majority responded with a 5-20% decrease in interoffice memoranda. This figure in part is based upon the fact that the pilot project and subsequent production operation cannot serve the number of users that are requesting EMS; therefore, continued use of interoffice memoranda to reach non-EMS users was strong.

3. Number of meetings *remained the same.* Potential possibilities here but more capability and training appear to be needed.

4. User productivity *increased.* A majority indicated that, in their opinion they are more productive with EMS as a tool. The users' opinion of their increase in productivity ran between 5 and 15%, but clearly was extremely subjective. A 5% user productivity increase was used as a cost justification for providing the EMS production service to the Corporation.

What Did Digital Learn From EMS?

User's Viewpoint. Both the EMS pilot and the three-node production systems now in operation have provided some interesting insights on office information systems. First, user assistance is a must. A user support and assistance group has been available during the pilot and production phases of the EMS service. We believe this is a key factor in its success within Digital. Second, managers *will* type! The majority of managers and professional staff personnel use the terminal directly, and they range from good touch typists to those who use the "two-finger" approach. Third, EMS activity is a productive use of managers' time. Managers with several hundred people reporting to them have indicated that the time spent at the terminal is the most productive time they spend each day! Fourth, there is a constant demand for more features and more functions. Any widely-used office system must be very approachable and easy to use; however, the users quickly start to demand more features. The constant balance between simplicity and ease of use and the demand pull for more complexity, flexibility, sophistication, is a continuing challenge.

Management's View of EMS. An important aspect of the evolution of EMS at Digital was a series of one-on-one interviews with key managers. They feel that the benefits of EMS fall into four categories:

   1.   Distribution of information is easier and more timely. Ease and speed of getting information from the system appear to be the key factors in its success.

   2.   Potentially explosive situations are defused. The ability to keep informed with minimal overhead and then being able to react quickly is important. Also, more acceptance of vertical communication is apparent with EMS.

   3.   Geographical boundaries become transparent. Many managers at Digital have direct reports in different buildings and sometimes in other time zones and countries.

   4.   Time spent at the terminal is highly productive. Again, the view that the time spent at the EMS terminal is useful and productive in accomplishing the work of a manager was held by those interviewed.

Interpersonal Communications Future

With the experience of the pilot program and over a year in production operation, plans are being made for future enhancements and additional capabilities in the system. Although time schedules and implementation plans are not appropriate for this paper, these are some of the new capabilities and pilot systems in Digital's plans at the present time.

Store and Forward Facsimile. Image information, as well as character data, is required in the office. A pilot S&F (store and forward) FAX is being explored to use underutilized data capacity between major mailroom locations during off hours.

On-Line Corporate Locator. A locator system, supporting a centralized telephone answering service and connected to the distributed EMS network to identify proper mail and message switch codes for individuals not on EMS is planned.

Store and Forward Voice. This capability, along with EMS, may remove the need to have an individual answering his or her telephone. There should be training offered to assist in proper use of this tool.

Common Editor for WP and EMS. Office systems should converge to common ways of doing similar functions. This will assist in training and ease of continuing use of the system.

Before leaving the discussion of EMS, it may be worthwhile to include a major system block diagram of the hardware used to implement the production system. Figure 3 illustrates the equipment configuration established in August of 1979. This configuration was expanded (also shown in Figure 3) to include an additional node in September of 1980. Maynard, Massachusetts and Marlboro, Massachusetts are geographic locations of two of Digital's office buildings.

OFFICE PROCESSING

Office processing makes available powerful and flexible processing capability in the office. With the cost of computer hardware decreasing dramatically over time, this is now starting to be economically feasible in many more areas than previously possible. Such capability allows knowledge workers to directly manipulate information. If knowledge workers are able to write simple routines, using an approachable office language, they can then process information at any time in the manner most useful to them. This capability permits the processing of data that has a fast rate of diminishing value. It also facilitates the processing of constantly changing information in a rapidly changing environment.

The delay in getting a change made to any production Data Processing system cannot always keep up with our changes in the economic system (interest rates, gold prices, tax rates, etc.), government policies, technique and technology changes, etc. The dependence upon the formal Data Processing development process is getting to be a major issue in corporations today. Through the use of office processing systems, Data Processing can still maintain control over corporate standards, data bases, and company-critical information; however, the knowledge worker can deal with data and processing power commensurate with his or her individual needs. The office processing system has the added

Figure 3

EMS PHASE I PRODUCTION SYSTEM

This is the equipment configuration established in August, 1979. This configuration will be expanded in August, 1980 with a VAX node.

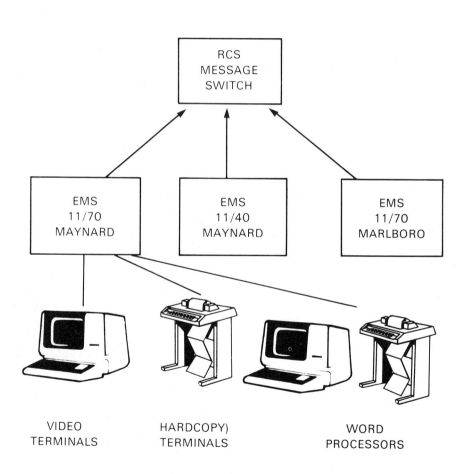

| VIDEO TERMINALS | HARDCOPY) TERMINALS | WORD PROCESSORS |

advantage of allowing the information worker to process data independent of information specialists or secondary workers.

The casual user in the office cannot stand the pain of going through a difficult learning curve and maintaining a high level of technical expertise. Knowledge workers are becoming more specialized in today's rapidly changing business environment. We must remember that this professional or manager has a primary job to accomplish. Therefore, good application development tools are a must. Innovative research is needed here to evolve better ways of programming a system to solve routine office processing problems, which will be acceptable to the casual user.

Information must also be easily available. The extent of information and the ease of access both require significant improvement. A friendly voice available on the telephone at any time to get over what may appear to the casual user as a stone wall, is a necessity. Good training must also be available to those who wish to be formally trained.

Although Digital has many years' experience in the implementation of systems to leverage professionals, integration of many diverse Department systems into a unified Corporate Office Information and Process System is underway. Issues are going to become evident as we gain experience with this capability. Some that have already surfaced are:

1. Who owns and maintains the information?

2. To what extent is the casual user able to be trained (and willing to be trained) to use technology?

3. Type of network needed for the office. How do office systems relate and integrate with the voice and data networks?

4. Can a complex system be approachable? This is a big open question that could slow the implementation of office processing systems.

INFORMATION RETRIEVAL

The concepts of information warehousing, data structuring, production data access, inquiry data access, plus the privacy and security aspects of information retrieval contain a discipline that may be provided to each office or individual within an office by a local electronic library. The capability will be significantly enhanced by local area networks. If an electronic library is available, then a local area network will make the information retrieval transparent to the user. The information retrieval system must operate on unstructured as well as structured data. In today's economy, external information is part of some managers' information and data.

Information retrieval systems may be the key to MIS success in the 80s. Easy access, in presentable form, to large quantities of information could result in management information systems finally achieving a wide acceptance by management.

INFORMATION MOBILITY

If information is to be available, it must be moved easily and then it must be understandable in its new environment. A typeset system, for example, should be able to deal with the format structure of a word processing document. At the present time, the Digital implementation of word processing, EMS and typeset is as appears in Figure 4.

As new mobility opportunities are explored, information may be transformed into many different media (EMS to FAX, EMS to voice, etc.) A diagammatical illustration of such a concept is also shown in Figure 4.

WHERE DIGITAL IS

In analyzing where the Digital office automation implementation is at the current time, it is most descriptive to consider our development to be in the middle of an expansion stage of using many different capabilities. After experience is obtained in the various capabilities areas, integration of the successful technologies into a true automation stage will be possible.

In line with this expansion and experience phase, the following projects/capabilities are being explored at the present time:

1. Personal Work Station: with the size and cost of computers decreasing to a point where they are reasonable for office use, this possibility is opening up new areas of opportunity.

2. Effective Use of Word Processing: with about 1,200 word processing systems, Digital has an extensive base of WP

Figure 4

INFORMATION MOBILITY – FUTURE

As new mobility opportunities are explored, information may be transformed into a different media (EMS to FAX or voice).

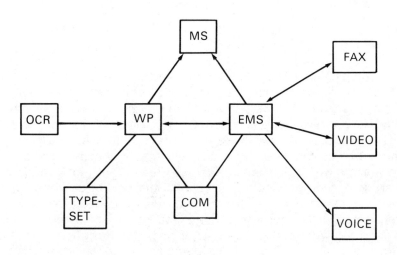

capability. Initial studies indicate opportunities to increase the effectiveness of their use.

3. Encouraging Decentralization: Digital will continue to decentralize; therefore, the information system needs to change with the organization.

4. Testing a Distributed EMS Architecture: the multimode EMS system is providing excellent data from which we can continue to learn as we proceed.

5. Studying How to Quantify Office Activities: even though little has been done successfully in this area, efforts must continue to answer the questions on cost versus benefits and provide real and measurable data.

6. Developing and Analyzing Pilot Office Automation Test Groups: Digital will continue to test new applications and approaches and use that experience to proceed to the next step.

SUMMARY

The Digital Office Automation activity has progressed well over the two years since the initial pilot EMS project was begun. Digital has taken a "tools" approach in that no turnkey applications software was available, at that time, to provide the functions that initial studies showed were required. The future of office automation is clear to us: productivity and effectiveness of the knowledge worker is an area in which significant corporate leverage can be obtained. In fact, with the growth of white-collar worker numbers and the growing shortage of trained professionals, such productivity improvements may be key to continued success. At Digital, we have proceeded slowly (although faster than originally expected), and have gained experience through pilot projects and limited production systems. In every case, user demand has outdistanced capability at every turn. In the future, we expect this trend to continue.

PART II

DESIGNING BOTH THE SOCIAL AND TECHNICAL COMPONENTS OF ELECTRONIC OFFICE SYSTEMS

CHAPTER 5

DESIGNING THE AUTOMATED OFFICE: ORGANIZATIONAL FUNCTIONS OF DATA AND TEXT

Thomas M. Lodahl
The Diebold Group, Inc.

The basic metaphor for early office automation is borrowed from the factory: the term "word processing," for example, conjures up images of words passing through various mechanical processes, to emerge as shiny, perfect products. One of the major selling points for word processing equipment was, "You've been using these methods in your factory—now, finally, you can also get your office under control." Strongly implied in this message is not mere technology as such, but also production-style organization: centralization, tight control, rationalization and standardization of work, extensive rules and procedures, replacement of people by machines, and hardnosed cost-benefit calculations (see Table 1.) As appropriate and effective as this style is for processing large volumes of routine work, it does wreak havoc with the custom office, which is by definition unpredictable, chaotic, and improvisational. Applying this organizational philosophy to the custom office predictably led to an assembly-line psychology

Table 1
Traditional WP Office System Designs:
The Factory Model

- Cost-justified on secretarial and clerical costs

- Designed around analysis of paperwork flows

- Emphasis on capture of repetitive work and large volumes

- Telephone input system ("TANK")

- Large, centralized centers, centrally managed

- Author proofing

- Rigid priorities, long turnaround, FIFO and GIGO

- Low skill operators

- Emphasis on line-count, high production

Typical Results of Traditional
WP System Design

- Off-loads clerical work on managers or professionals

- Low user satisfaction

- Increased conflict over work priorities

- Low satisfaction of administrative secretaries, medium-high satisfaction of typists

- Increased work loads which cannot be performed adequately—"Freeway Effect"

- Dictation decreases, longhand goes *up*

---

among its workers: complaints of boredom and routine, low job satisfaction, high turnover, dissatisfied managers, and high conflict. For the custom office, there can be no "one best way," because things are constantly changing and because different subgroups have widely different needs.

There is another reason why different standard designs didn't solve the problem. All office environments, we have seen, are mixed with some custom and some production elements. The design task then becomes one of identifying where and how much of each exists in an office, and providing each subgroup with a subsystem with appropriate performance characteristics. Under this scheme, there are as many "best ways" as there are different subgroups in the office, and the attempt to identify standard designs begins to falter. But we have found that the "standard design" concept dies hard in the minds of many. People still want some overall model or organizing concept that is simple, clear, and elegant. That's why the prototypical word processing system is centralized, first-in, first-out, has tight rules, keeps line counts, rejects poor input, etc., etc. People tend to view system designs as some kind of standard product, such as a sedan, station wagon, sports coupe, or whatever. We view design as a *process,* rather than a *product;* a process whose aim is to discover differences among subgroup needs, rather than to force similarities by imposing a common system for all.

This leads us to the third reason why the "standard-design" approach hasn't worked well. To apply it effectively requires a fair amount of organizational sophistication. To identify different subgroup needs accurately requires far more than a paperwork study. The separate missions and goals of each department must be understood, and the specific workstyles and methods must be appreciated. The overall organizational structure must be taken into account, along with the uniquenesses of each subgroup. Work flows must be described accurately, and intergroup dependencies must be teased out. Given that organizational analysis is still a young science, it is not surprising that these skills were not available to system vendors.

A fourth (and final) reason why standard designs haven't solved the problem is that most of them make no provision for the human problems of managing the change itself. Office automation deeply affects every aspect of office life: ways of doing work, work flows, the distribution of work, and the quality of relationships among managers and between managers and secretaries, to name but a few. Small wonder that the prospect of adopting it gives rise to fear, anxiety, resistance, rumors, and resignations. Until recently, the most common tool for managing these things was power; for example, in one organization, in which we did research, all of the typewriters were removed from the floors between a Friday and a Monday, to make sure everyone would have to use the new processing center. Usually, the use of power tactics like this simply leads to more resistance, then to more severe power tactics, and so on, until a nobody-wins vicious circle is established.

ORGANIZATION OF THE CUSTOM OFFICE

In our minds, the custom office is best exemplified by a corporate headquarters operation. How is one to describe the typical headquarters organization? First of all, its basic function is to coordinate the actions of organizational elements, and the type of coordination depends on what kind of interdependence exists among the elements. According to James Thompson (*Organizations in Action,* McGraw-Hill, 1976), there are three basic types of interdependence: pooled, sequential, and reciprocal. Pooled interdependence is when the elements depend on the whole, but not much on each other, as among the different branch offices of an insurance company; sequential interdependence is when A must act before B, as in an assembly process, and reciprocal interdependence is when A's outputs become inputs for B, and vice-versa, as in the drafting of a complex memo by several authors.

With the relatively simple pooled interdependence, *coordination by standardization* is appropriate; rules and routines are established to treat everyone the same, which requires a high degree of stability and repetition of situations or work. The typical word processing production shop (as in a consumer correspondence office), for example, operates just this way. With sequential interdependence, *coordination by plan* is appropriate: this involves the establishment of schedules for the actions of the different organizational elements. Scheduling work and establishing priorities for turnaround in a WP center would be such coordination. With reciprocal interdependence, coordination is by mutual adjustment, which requires extensive attention and quick, accurate feedback. A multi-authored document undergoing revision would be an example of this.

Where does this take us? For one thing, it means that you can afford to centralize and standardize where there is low or pooled interdependence. Where there is high reciprocal interdependence, it is desirable to put such elements close together into locally autonomous groups, because doing so facilitates mutual adjustment. For these reasons, big WP centers usually don't work well in the complex, headquarters organization; we find that small centers, placed close to the originators, do the job much better, although they don't maximize line count.

Using this terminology, we can analyze the headquarters office environment as one in which the departments or divisions have high *reciprocal* interdependence (that's why they have so many meetings), and there is high *sequential* interdependence between the automated office system (such as a WP center) and the organizational subunits. To serve the subunits effectively, there has to be a good deal of collaborative *planning* between the system and its users, and a lot of *mutual adjustment,* because of constant changes, crises, and because that's the typical user style. The most effective WP coordinators I know make it a point to see every user weekly, to discuss problems, and opportunities, etc. Some of them also hold weekly problem analysis and planning sessions with support system people, to facilitate mutual adjustment. By now it should be clear why the centralized, standardized, large WP center is inappropriate for the custom office: it is not able to deal with the complexity and valid differences among its user subgroups.

ANOTHER VIEW OF THE CUSTOM OFFICE: THE FUNCTION OF TEXT

A headquarters office is the brains and nerve center for an entire organization. It processes large amounts of information, and the structure and process of the office form the information flow and determine its effectiveness. The organization chart is a map of the organization's current theories about how it must function in relation to its environment. Learning and experience are captured in the form of structural alterations; the organization's competence is determined by how well its theories match environmental reality. As Cohen, March, and Olsen point out, however, that reality is always ambiguous. "An organization is a set of procedures for argumentation and interpretation as well as for solving problems and making decisions. A choice situation is a meeting place for issues and feelings looking for decision situations in which they may be aired, solutions looking for issues to which they may be an answer, and participants looking for problems or pleasure."

Given this tenuous grasp on reality, organizations have to be careful in adapting new technology to their present structure and process. However badly it might work now, the organization got where it is by learning, and must be respected for its unconscious adaptiveness as well as being laughed at for irrationality and clumsiness. In most offices, the computer has already digested much of what is programmable and routine, and reduced it to numbers and models; poorly structured problems still arrive and depart in the form of text. For example, Keen (1978), contrasts typical MIS functions with the nine customized "Decision Support Systems" (see Table 2). It is precisely because text is the medium for poorly structured problems that we must not act as if all text and text-processing needs are the same. Although we are tempted to adopt factory-like organization for text processing, to do so is to ignore the basic nature of the messages it is carrying. Rather than forcing text-processing (and other office automation) into a long-

Table 2

Management Support System Designs:
The Custom Approach

- Cost-justified on professional, managerial time savings
- Designed around differentiated departmental and user needs
- Emphasis on user work facilitation: dictation, revision, retrieval and storage, communications
- Telephone input systems, plus many portable dictation units
- Small centers close to authors
- Center proofing
- Flexible turnaround, "soft" dedication
- High-skill, highly selected operators
- Emphasis on service to users

Typical Results of Management
Support System Designs

- Off-loads some manager and professional work to administrative secretaries (Delegation)
- New work appears—25-100% more from same number of users ("Uncaptured" work)
- High user satisfaction and involvement
- Low conflict over work priorities
- High satisfaction, involvement of all support personnel
- Dictation increases, longhand decreases, much new repetitive work appears

© 1978 Office Systems Research Group

linked (e.g., assembly-line) technical organization just because words all look the same, we have to pay attention to the messages it is carrying and the needs it is trying to serve. In fact, the headquarters office more nearly resembles an *intensive* technology (again, Thompson's term), which is characterized as the application of a variety of knowledge and techniques being brought to bear on a given situation or problem or object, the application being determined by feedback from the object itself. As Thompson puts it,

> "The intensive technology is a custom technology. Its successful employment rests in part on the availability of all the capacities potentially needed, but equally on the appropriate custom combination of selected capacities as required by the individual case or project." (*Ibid*, p. 18).

We would go on to say that the custom office similarly requires "the appropriate custom combination of selected capacities as required by the individual department or subgroup." In the next section, we will describe interactive design methods for doing this.

To summarize, the factory metaphor worked in those offices which resembled factories; it failed, spectacularly, in the custom office, where intensive technologies abound. What is required, then, is a design methodology which is sensitive to variation in office functions and processes, over time and across organizational subunits. Because of the high rate of change in the custom office, members of user groups must participate in the design process, in order to be able to modify designs as the office changes. The objective of the design process is to arrive at appropriate technology *and* appropriate organizational support structures, and to facilitate user acceptance through their participation in the design process. There is a built-in dilemma in this process: in assessing user needs, the designer would like to be able to ask the client, "What do you need?" But since the client normally does not know what is possible, available, or practical, s/he can't answer the question. And since there are so many different ways an office automation (OA) system can support office work, tight definition of problems to be solved does not make sense. Therefore, we have adopted a "Sociotechnical Systems" approach to OA design, which begins with a generalized diagnosis of office organization, functions, and processes; from this, designer and client together decide what problems to address in the design process.

This differs importantly from the typical DP/MIS Project lifecycle process, which normally begins with a careful definition of the problem(s) to be solved; often, responsibility for that definition rests with the client. Perhaps users are more familiar by now with the capabilities of DP/MIS systems, and, therefore, can arrive at practical and sophisticated problem definitions. Because OA equipment and systems are so multi-functional, general diagnosis must precede problem definition.

There are three major elements in office system design: technical design, organization design and an implementation design. Typically, we spend most of our attention on the first one. We visit exhibits and look at the technology, asking what can it do. Usually, we give less attention to the second, and even less attention to the third element. The importance of the design process to the success of the resulting system is getting increasing recognition—both in the design of factories, in DP/MIS work, and now, in OA. Professor Louis Davis, of UCLA, has pioneered the use of "Sociotechnical Analysis" for the design of technical support systems in factories. Boland (1978) contrasted the use of "traditional" and "interactive" design methods for DP/MIS design in a hospital, and my colleagues and I have built an interactive design methodology for OA systems. Exhibits I and II draw some contrasts between traditional and interactive design processes.

Traditional systems design, where the systems analyst comes in and asks some directive questions about what you do and how you do it, tends, philosophically, to move toward standardizing people's behavior. There is a tendency to treat things in the same way, no matter what the person is doing. The system controls the people, typically, in traditional system design. The information sources in the system are usually put within it or high up in the human organization, rather than given to those who operate it. It emphasizes repetitive elements and it seeks predictable performance. It avoids changing itself. Once a software system has been debugged and is running it seems we just don't like to change it, if technology systems design can be avoided. It looks to transfer standard design elements, so that what worked over in the warehouse should also work in the factory. It tends to punish nonconformity. If this sounds bureaucratic—that's probably fair. Traditional systems design has always taken place in largely bureaucratic organizations, and I'm not just referring to public sector organizations. All large organizations are bureaucratic to some degree and so it's no accident that traditional systems design mirrors and matches that.

Exhibit I
The Traditional System Design

Emphasizes:

- Standardization of behavior
- System controls the people (Centraliz.)
- Search for repetitive elements
- Seeks predictable performance
- Avoids changing itself
- Transfers of standard design elements
- Punishment of nonconformity

  Sounds bureaucratic? It is.

Interactive design has a couple of key elements. First of all, it usually takes as one of its tenets that different folks are going to require different strokes. If this is the case, we want to identify the subunits in the organization that are going to have to be treated differently. The accounting department might have vastly different automated office needs from the marketing department, for example. A key element in doing interactive design, as opposed to traditional design, is to locate those boundaries. How many different groups are there, that are going to have to be treated separately in our analysis, in order to fit technology to their unique pattern of needs? That is what I mean by boundary location; it is identifying what the different units are, and then treating them differently. Once that has been done or is in process, we must look at their functions, their goals, and especially, their languages. Jargons make a big difference; we usually try to separate jargon groups in the support pattern, if we can. External relations are critical in designing an office system. If a system is designed that does not allow the groups to deal with their external relations effectively, they will be crippled.

When we summarize all of this, we come up with what we've termed a custom design, which caters to the uniqueness of different organizational subunits. The trick for the analyst, then, is to figure out what those differences are. We've developed ways of doing that through interviews and questionnaires.

Exhibit II
Interactive Design

Key elements:

1. Identify separable subunits
   ("Boundary location")

   - Functions
   - Goals
   - Languages
   - External relations

   "Custom" design = caters to uniqueness

2. Scope parent organization

   - Goals
   - Constraints
   - External environment
   - Investment in current structure, style, philosophy

Emphasizes:

   - Fits technology to ongoing processes—tolerates uniqueness.
   - People control system (decent.)
   - Seeks high payoff processes
   - Supports outstanding performance
   - Allows revision, iteration
   - Transfers design *approach,* not identical elements
   - Tolerates people, subunit variations

   Sounds utopian? Maybe.

Interactive Design:
Sociotechnical Implementation

"Re-Freezing"

   - Redesign of jobs, roles
   - Redesign of social support system
   - Redesign of recruitment, selection, training

What is done in interactive design is to treat technology as a variable. Fit it to the ongoing processes and you tolerate uniqueness. Try to make it possible for people to control the system, rather than having the system control the people. Interactive design looks for high payoff processes, wherever they are, not just for repetitive work. A high payoff process might be a crash proposal that has to be gotten out sometime in the next six months. We could get a lot of high technology to assist us with that process, and we would get a high payoff if we got it done in four months instead of six. It might be a unique process, but we know the capability of automated office equipment can be adapted to many things in fairly short order.

It would support outstanding performance, rather than just looking for mediocre performance. Dick Walton, at the Harvard Business School, has spent a lot of his time designing and building what he calls high commitment work systems. They are characterized by the people in the system being very highly involved in its success. I think we could build a high commitment office system, if we use this interactive design concept and put the equipment at the disposal of the people, rather than making them serve the equipment. Interactive design allows revision and interaction. You usually don't come up with a perfect design the first time out, whether you are using traditional or interactive design. It transfers a design approach, but not identical elements.

We are going to use the same methods to find out what others need, but what we do for them may be very different. This may be utopian, but we have done it in a couple of instances, and it seems to work pretty well. The structure for interactive design is fairly standard, interestingly enough. This structure is adapted from Lou Davis' work on sociotechnical systems design (see Table 3). He uses it largely for designing factories. We have been using this same structure for office system design. We usually have a steering committee of top managers whose work is going to be affected. We have a design team that consists of both client representatives, technical specialists, organizational specialists and a responsible manager. From time to time, you are going to call in specialists who have expertise that the other design team members don't have—expertise, for example, in filing and retrieval. You will need DP and MIS specialists, if you are going to build an integrated office system. You have to know how you connect to what they already have. You need flow analysts. We find that it's not enough

Table 3
Structure for Interactive Design

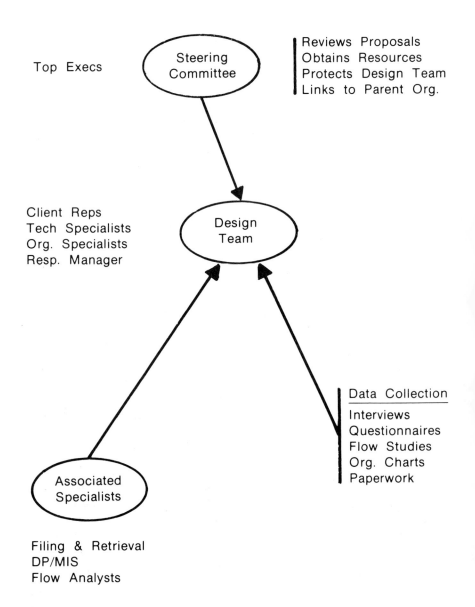

Top Execs

Steering
Committee

Reviews Proposals
Obtains Resources
Protects Design Team
Links to Parent Org.

Client Reps
Tech Specialists
Org. Specialists
Resp. Manager

Design
Team

Associated
Specialists

Data Collection

Interviews
Questionnaires
Flow Studies
Org. Charts
Paperwork

Filing & Retrieval
DP/MIS
Flow Analysts

simply to describe each of the organizational subunits; you also have to know what the work flow looks like, into and out of those, in order to design a decent computer-based message system.

Another aspect of interactive design, which will be absolutely critical in the office of the 80s, is the process of refreezing. Let's say that we go through a number of iterations on the design and it's working in a particular location. What that is going to mean, then, is that job descriptions have to be changed to fit what people are now doing. The roles that people play, in relation to each other, are also going to have to be shifted, gradually, to be more in line with the way the automated system works. We also have to redesign a social support system. We do that by having team meetings with the secretarial staff who are going to be interacting with an office system; we show them some tentative designs and ask, "Do you see any problems? Once we adopt a new pattern, what is it going to do to the people, and how can we anticipate that to minimize the damage and maximize the advantages that we can get from this?"

We also find that we have to redesign the whole recruitment, selection and training process for office people, in order to run an automated office—this is another aspect of "re-freezing." I've had a lot of trouble with personnel departments of companies that I have worked for, because they don't want to redo the whole job classification system. That's a lot of work for them. But if you don't do that, you'll find your secretaries becoming angry, because they're now doing, say, 50% managerial work. They want to get paid for the work they're now doing, if their managers are delegating substantial amounts of work to them. We find that by providing personnel departments with, for example, sample job descriptions, sample job ladders, sample promotion paths to look at and use as a model, that they're much more willing to make the necessary changes.

Refreezing a design is just as important as coming up with a good one in the first place. What I mean by refreezing is building the infrastructure to match the new organizational structure that you built.

My dream, at the moment, is to build an interactive design laboratory, because what we have left out of this equation so far is: what is the equipment itself, and how does it get designed. I have deep suspicions that most equipment design takes place very informally. The equipment designer says, "Gee, I think I could build a machine that would do x; I wonder if anybody could use that?" I'm not sure how much equipment design is actually based on real knowledge of offices and how they differ. I would like to build a laboratory someday, in which I have equipment designers working with secretaries, saying, "Hey, try this and let me know how it works, and I'll be back tomorrow and we'll change it, if it isn't working for you." I think we can build more user-friendly office environments, if we had a closer interaction between designers and users, than we now have.

My conclusion for all this, which I offer very diffidently, is that, unless we adopt new design philosophies and methods, it's very likely that the automated office of the 80s is going to see the same kind of alienation, noncommitment, and discontent as we saw in the automatic factories of the 60s and 50s.

The people who are at this conference will be responsible for making that not happen. I think we can make interactive design happen. We can create humanistic office systems, if we realize how important that is, and if we develop the organizational skills to go along with technical expertise.

REFERENCES

1. Boland, John. "Traditional and Interactive Approaches to System Design." *Management Science,* May 1978.

2. Cohen, M.D., James G March and Johan D. Olsen. "A Garbage Can Model of Organizational Choice." *Administrative Science Quarterly,* 1972, 17, 1-25.

3. Davis, Louis. "Job Design and Productivity: A New Approach." *Personnel,* March 1957, 418-430.

4. Keen, Peter and Michael Scott-Morton. *Decision Support Systems.* Cambridge: Addison-Wesley, 1980.

5. Thompson, James D. *Organizations in Action.* New York: McGraw-Hill, 1967.

CHAPTER 6

DO CURRENT ELECTRONIC OFFICE SYSTEM DESIGNERS MEET USER NEEDS?

Roger Pye and Ian Young
Communications Studies and Planning Ltd.
21 Great Titchfield Street, London England

INTRODUCTION

The introduction of office automation systems represents a major departure in office practices. At present, most office workers use only very primitive technologies—typically only the telephone, calculator, and, if a typist or secretary, a typewriter. Other attempts to gain wide acceptance of new technologies in the 1960s (Management Information Systems) and 1970s (Video conferencing) have been expensive and embarrassing failures. A concept as broad and ambitious as office automation cannot afford these mistakes. It is essential to ensure that systems meet users' needs and so have a reasonable chance of market success.

To ensure that an office automation system meets users' requirements, three issues should be addressed:

1. Service identification
   - what existing human activity is intended to be replaced or supplemented?

- what steps does that activity entail?
- will the new service automate existing steps or the complete activity?

2. Product design
   - hardware
   - software
   - user interfaces

3. Service implementation
   - introduction to users
   - involvement in design
   - training
   - support
   - feedback through evaluation

Design and implementation of services or systems that lack a sound conception, i.e., that identify poorly with users' expressed or latent needs, is a poor investment. Hence this paper will concentrate on the primary (identification) issue. Information used to identify a service likely to be successful can also be used to help product design and provide a comparison for evaluative purposes.

This paper will review methods of identifying useful facilities. The text will concentrate on methods; findings will be shown in tables and figures, and discussed during the presentation. However, it must be emphasized that many of the reported studies have as yet reached only a preliminary phase; results are often drawn from non-representative surveys used for methodological development and should be treated with caution.

DIFFERENT APPROACHES

Research and analytic techniques are well developed for the purpose of traditional market research and economic forecasting. The market researcher can test out the probable reception for a new form of breakfast cereal by measuring attitudes towards the product and comparing these, within designated market segments, with the attitudes towards established products. The economist can extrapolate the annual growth in consumption of consumer durables from the pattern evident over the preceding decade, and from the multivariate regression equation which best describes the relationship between a set of predictive variables (e.g., growth in household income) and the predicted or dependent variable (growth in buying washing machines).

Both these sets of methods and techniques share the common ground that the object of prediction already has a history from which patterns of variation in past success can be extracted. The breakfast cereal may be new, but the majority of its potential purchasers will already be regular purchasers of some existing form of breakfast cereal, and so will be making only minor changes in their behavior if they purchase this new product instead of their prior choice.

When we come to the fields of new developments in electronic office systems, however, the picture changes. Manufacturers, service providers, carriers, policy-makers, and investors all want accurate predictions of how a new facility will be accepted and taken up by the proposed consumers. But the research techniques of market research and econometrics are suddenly found to be lacking. The services and facilities in question, such as electronic mail, automated offices, and residential computer access information services, have no similar counterparts in existence. They are often wholly new service concepts for which there is no historic data from which to extrapolate.

In the absence, and obvious shortcomings, of previously reliable predictive methods, there has been a tendancy to resort to variations on refined speculation. The Delphi technique, loved by many futurists, is only a method of gaining consensus from a group of alleged experts who would otherwise take great delight in contradicting each other. It is, in comparison with the established market research and econometric techniques, singularly lacking in any depth of quantifiable data.

This issue of how to predict the market for totally new services from data available before the services come into effect is one which CS & P Ltd. (and its University predecessor, the Communications Studies Group) has addressed on several occasions. As the tried and tested methods of market prediction are not appropriate, it has been necessary to invent new strategies and adapt analysis techniques to gain a "best-fit" between the data available and the quantification sought.

Three broad strategies have been developed and to some extent tested in research activities by CS & P. They share, in common, information bases of the activities, choices and attitudes of potential users of new systems, but the information is elicited about services and facilities they currently use, and not hypothetical alternatives.

ACTIVITY SURVEYS

An obvious starting point for assessing user needs quantitatively is to measure present activities. Three types of study have been conducted:

- Paperwork flows and volumes;
- Use of time in offices; and
- Communication flows.

The first type of study is a common part of designing conventional ADP and manual-clerical systems. Unfortunately, little attention has been devoted to synthesizing or generalizing the results. Studies of the use of time in offices have usually been conducted by academics interested in organizational studies. Measures are, therefore, seldom adequate for the detailed design of office automation—although useful indicators are often obtained. Figure 1 shows some results (mostly of work by Rosemary Stewart) and their relevance. Studies of time-usage would be valuable when designing in detail office automation systems, provided the activity categories had more specific relevance.

Studies of communication patterns have often been conducted by geographers, other academics interested in spatial communication patterns, and people interested in the design of telecommunication systems. Results of some fairly general studies, and their relevance, are shown in Figure 2. However, the usefulness of these studies is restricted by two factors:

- aspects of communication appropriate to new systems are seldom measured; and
- no explanation of current observations is available.

CS & P (and earlier CSG) have concentrated considerable effort in resolving these shortcomings. The remaining two approaches reflect respectively on each shortcoming.

TAXONOMIC APPROACH

The taxonomic approach is ideally suited to the very early stages when a product concept is to be assessed for its impact on existing behavior. It involves deriving a taxonomy, or set of structures by which individual acts within a defined universe can be organized into identifiable and coherent groups with shared characteristics. The capabilities of new services and products to

Figure 1
Use of Time in Offices

Research Finding	Service Implication
90% of managers' time is spent communicating	For managerial acceptance communication orientation is important
60-63% of managers' time is spent in vocal communication	Few managers keen to operate keyboards, etc.
5 managerial styles exist — Emissaries — Writers — Discussers — Trouble shooters — Committee men	Possible services — mailbox systems — wordprocessing — none — none — message systems and wordprocessing
Research workers also spent much time communicating	Systems for their use should also be considered — ARPANET, etc.
Little knowledge of clerical staffs' time-usage.	System definition is difficult.

match the characteristic requirements of each group can then be assessed.

The early research of the Communications Studies Group on teleconferencing provides a comprehensive example. In a study to derive the "Description and Classification of Meetings" (DACOM), Pye et al. (1972) collected data on the activities, functions and atmospheres of over 300 business meetings. The co-occurrence of the descriptive variables of these meetings were measured by techniques of factor and cluster analysis. Factor analysis is well known and, indeed, often misused and hence maligned, but used properly, it performs the workmanlike function of identifying the major patterns of intercorrelations between the variables collected on each act. The outcome is a set of main descriptors of the acts.

Figure 2
Office Communication Patterns

Research Finding	Service Implication
Relatively small mail volumes are received each day per person	Personal "electronic mail" terminals may be hard to cost-justify
Top executives' communication is — fast — fragmented — current and ad hoc — vocal	Informal, fast message systems might be successful (ARPANET) But MIS unlikely to succeed at that level
Relatively little old communication is retrieved (1 study)	Message storage and retrieval systems may be little used
Much received mail is re-referred	Message distribution systems may succeed (DOD, etc.)
Most mail is intra-corporate.	Intra-corporate systems may be established
Message lengths have a polarized distribution	Different services may be needed for the types.
Technical staff travel more often than staff managers; they also have more diverse communications	They may be more appropriate targets than line managers
Inter-company communications centre on companies involved in transactions	Transaction systems may form a basis for development (IBM 3730)

Figure 2 (cont.)
Office Communication Pattern

Research Finding	Service Implication
Communication is more intensive in companies in uncertain environments	Systems permitting semi-structured communication may have value there
Communication's effect on output is unclear	Cost justification may be difficult
Communication patterns are complex	Designers shouldn't rely on the formal structures
Communication patterns are poorly understood	Measure, don't interview

In the case of the DACOM study, 12 factors, shown in Figure 3, appeared to give a good set of dimensions with which to describe meetings.

The cluster analysis techniques, by comparison, retain the individual acts as whole units and search for patterns of similarity between acts by virtue of their shared possession of attributes. There are several mechanisms by which these aims can be accomplished (see Wishart, 1969), but the simple divisive algorithm is the easiest to use as an explanatory example. If we assume that we have collected data on the presence or absence of a set of attributes for each of a sample of acts, the divisive algorithm will look for the attribute (A) which most evenly splits the total sample into two, a sub-sample with attribute "A" and a sub-sample of acts none of which possess attribute "A." It will then treat each of these two sub-samples as the original sample and in each will look for an attribute which evenly splits the sub-sample on the basis of the presence or absence of the attribute. The process is repeated until some stopping point is reached, such as having defined a set number of sub-groups (clusters) or having reached a set minimum size for the number of cases in a cluster.

The divisive algorithm is clearly very mechanistic and is prone to some readily identifiable problems due to the exclusivity of the clusters formed at each step in the process. Other algorithms exist

Figure 3
Description and Classification of Meetings
12 Factor Solution — Varimax Rotation, 47% of Variance

Factor	Function	Activity	Atmosphere
1	Problem discussion Discussion of ideas Problem review	Generating ideas	
2		Displaying aggres- sion, etc. Conflict Personality clashes Arguing Disagreeing	Angry Hostile Antagonistic
3	Info. seeking Query answering	Answering questions Giving/receiving info.	
4	Negotiation Assessing reactions	Bargaining Being defensive Compromising Persuasion	
5			Constructive Helpful Cooperative Friendly
6	Getting to know someone	Forming impression of others	
7	Task allocation Delegation of work Coordinating project		
8	Giving information to keep in picture	Maintaining morale	
9		Social chat	Informal
10	Presentation of report Presentation of draft Discussing report implementation		

Figure 3 (continued)
Description and Classification of Meetings
12 Factor Solution — Varimax Rotation, 47% of Variance

Factor	Function	Activity	Atmosphere
11	Policy decision-making Policy discussion		
12	Low scored variables		

to overcome these problems, but no one technique of cluster analysis is any more correct than any other. In the DACOM study, an alternative algorithm was used to generate between 10 and 15 clusters from the total sample of meetings. Results of a 12-cluster solution are shown in Figure 4.

Between them, the factor and cluster analysis technique provide complementary taxonomic descriptions of a set of meetings. To progress to modelling the market for teleconference services, it was necessary to conduct three further types of study. First, there had to be a consideration of how effectively the various services under investigation could cope with the types of meetings identified. This issue was investigated by a series of laboratory experiments on the meeting processes defined by the factor analysis. Second, the frequency of occurrence of different meeting types (clusters) had to be identified from further studies of existing meeting behavior. Together, these two stages provide a raw prediction of the proportions of existing meetings which could be handled adequately by the proposed new services. The third and final stage in the refinement of the raw predictions was to take into account cost considerations and assumptions on the general availability of teleconference terminals. The later stages of the predictive model are described in detail for teleconference services by Tyler *et al.* (1976). The results of the teleconference program are reported in Pye and Williams (1977); the market for video-conferencing appears small, only about 2% of existing meetings, while that for audio-graphic conferences is substantial, about 39% of meetings.

A second example of the use of taxonomic procedures, though this time not tied to a specific marketable telecommunication or office product, is a study of communication

Figure 4
DACOM — 12 Cluster Solution

Giving information to keep in picture.	Giving information to keep in picture. Information seeking. Discussion of ideas. Problem solving.
Presentation of report. Delegation of work. Giving information to keep in picture. Discussion of ideas. Policy decision-making. Problem solving.	Policy decision-making. NOT forming impression. NOT information seeking. NOT giving information to keep in picture.
Delegation of work. Problem solving. NOT forming impressions of others.	Conflict. Presentation of report. Delegation of work.
Negotiation. NOT conflict.	All dimensions except: Conflict Presentation of report Delegation of work
Negotiation. Conflict Policy decision-making.	Conflict. Forming impressions. NOT negotiation. NOT problem solving.
Forming impressions of others.	NO HIGH SCORES

---

patterns within a work group. (Pye *et al.,* in press.) The study, conducted as a piece of innovative research methodology, sought to examine the purpose, place, and nature of communication events within a 20 person project team in industry. Records kept of each communication relevant to a specific engineering project over an extended period (21 weeks) provided a full account of the attributes of those communications. The DACOM study treated the atmosphere of meetings and the behavioral processes involved; the prompts for "function" and "activity" did not properly distinguish those dimensions. In addition to "process," the later study sought data for each communication on who was involved in the communication, what were its subjects, goals and outcomes, how many people were involved, and who initiated the communication. The number of potential combinations of all these attributes exceeded 1½ millon. The application of a number of cluster analysis techniques to the data revealed recurrent patterns of attribute clusters.

Tables 1 to 4 show the relative frequencies of "stimulus," "participant choice," "subject," "goals," and "processes," the last being an extension of a set of categories obtained through DACOM. When cluster analysis (e.g., Figure 5, Table 5) was conducted, it was found that "stimulus" was an independent dimension and that patterns in the other variables focused on "subject" and "participant choice."

DISAGGREGATE CHOICE MODELING

The taxonomic approach described in the previous section provides a method of structuring the universe of behavioral acts from an empirical standpoint. However, as indicated, it can only provide guidelines to the choice mechanisms which determine individual utilization of new systems and services. The next step forward in the hierarchy of predictive methodologies is to take individual selection acts and seek the empirical determinants of those choices. This type of data can be used to construct models of the factors determining individual choice and hence, by grossing-up to total populations, generalized choice behavior (by the universe of users) can be predicted. It is a relatively small step to move from models predicting choice between existing alternatives, to models which will predict the choice of new service alternatives among the existing service alternatives, provided choices are modeled on "technology-free" attributes.

The first exploratory step in this direction taken at CS & P concerned user-choice between existing services for sending messages. Detailed records were kept of the content, format, destination, urgency, etc. of messages sent by different media. The analytic framework used was that of discriminant analysis, a regression technique to select variables which differentiate

Table 1
Stimulus of Communication

	N	%
Another communication	62	17.8
Continuation of previous communication	56	16.1
Information needed for task	49	14.1
Workflow failure	41	11.8
Own initiative	39	11.2
Inability to complete task	21	6.0
Task structure	21	6.0
Workflow	17	4.9
Frustration/impatience	17	4.9
Formal authority structure	14	4.0
Communication failure	5	1.4
Procedure failure	5	1.4
	347	

Table 2
Reason for Involving Participants in Communications

	N	%
Task structure	184	50.5
Authority structure	83	22.8
Source of information	63	17.3
Person stimulating communication	25	6.8
Friend/ally	4	1.1
Defined group membership	3	0.8
Source of required skill	1	0.3
	363	

Table 3
Subject of Communication

	N	%
Technical	179	44.9
Workflow	85	21.3
Contractual commitments	51	12.8
Communication	49	12.3
Procedures	32	8.1
	396	

Table 4
Goals of Communication

	N	%
Obtain action	72	21.6
Obtain information	63	18.9
Give information	45	13.5
Reduce/transfer responsibilities	36	10.9
Coordinate joint actions	27	8.1
Check own responsibilities	26	7.9
Investigate situation	23	6.9
Obtain expert advice	11	3.3
Report back	8	2.4
Increase power and authority	6	1.8
Interpret information	5	1.5
Obtain expert assistance	4	1.2
Refer information	3	0.9
	329	

Figure 5
Patterns in Communication Activity Identified by
Divide Cluster Analysis

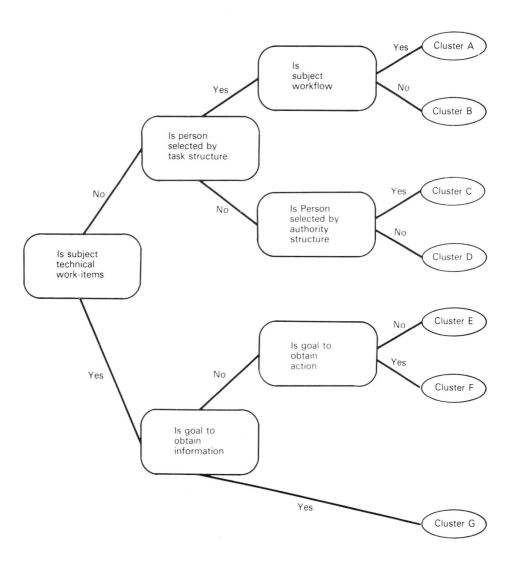

Table 5
Results of Cluster Analysis by "Divide"

Cluster	No. of members	Subject	Person	Goal	Procedure
A	40	Workflow (100%)	Task structure (100%)	Obtain action (33%)	Give/rec. info. (38%)
				Coordinate action (48%)	Report back (18%)
				Check responsibilities (13%)	Disc. gen. ideas (17%)
B	51	Communication (39%)	Task structure (100%)	Coordinate action (33%)	Give/rec. info. (78%)
		Contracts (33%)		(Outcome-action coordinated (35%)	
		Procedures (25%)			
C	60	Workflow (32%)	Authority structure (100%)	Give info. (28%)	Give/rec. info. (50%)
		Communication (25%)		Reduce resp. (23%)	
		Procedures (17%)		(Outcome-info. given (37%)	
		Contracts (23%)			
D	50		Info. source (48%)		
E	73	Technical work items (100%)	Task structure (52%)	Give info. (18%)	Give/rec. info. (29%)
				Reduce resp. (19%)	
				Investigate situation (21%)	
				(Outcome-info. given (25%))	
F	55	Techncial work items (100%)	Task structure (71%)	Obtain action (100%)	
				(Outcome-action obtained (27%))	
				Further action initiated (13%)	
		(Stimulus: Workflow (22%), failure in workflow (29%))			

Table 5 (continued)
Results of Cluster Analysis by "Divide"

Clus-ter	No. of members	Subject	Person	Goal	Procedure
G	47	Technical work items (100%)	Info. source (57%)	Obtain info. (100%)	
			Task structure (30%)	(Outcome-info. received (34%))	
		(Stimulus: Information needed for task (57%))			

significantly between the choices studied. The choices to be made were alternative available methods of sending message items: post, telex, telephone, facsimile, and internal courier or dispatch services. The output is a set of choice equations which compare the summated weighted value of individual message characteristics to predict a best choice medium. The selection of characteristics (variables) and their weighting is determined to maximize the separation between different group (media) choices and to mirror, on individual case basis, the observed choice made.

Interpretation of the six discriminant functions for seven message media are shown in Figure 6. A transformation of the discriminant functions (the classification function—Table 6) is used to assign messages to media: a message is assigned to telex, say, if its score on the classification function is higher for telex than the other media. It was found that 77% of all individual messages are correctly assigned by the algorithm. Market shares for additional media could be estimated by giving that medium coefficients according to its similarity to other media.

The benefit of this type of approach is that it identifies, from an empirical base, the attributes of importance in a decision, and the relative weights of these attributes. Hence it is possible, using these multivariate techniques, to override the absence of a specific attribute if there are other compensating factors in sufficient strength.

The second example of the use of choice-predicting techniques is taken from a fundamental study of information seeking behavior for household purposes conducted by CS & P Ltd. for the UK Post Office Telecommunications (now becoming known as British Telecommunications). The purpose of the research project was to identify the potential markets and possible required characteristics of new information media (e.g., Prestel, Viewdata, or Videotex).

Multivariate techniques were used to select predictive variables and integrate them into choice algorithms. The methodology used in this instance was the "logit" model, which has some similarity to the discriminant model but permits combinational interaction between situational variables and choice attributes. For example, a particular attribute may be more influencial in the choice under certain circumstances, e.g., the speed of the telephone when contacting a doctor in an emergency; however, significant interactions have not been found.

To use the logit model, first a sample of people are asked to score each medium on a number of attributes. Originally, 44 were used for information media, but this set was reduced to 16 on the basis of similarity of score. The logit model was then used to estimate weighting factors for attributes. The utility of using a

Figure 6
Discriminant Functions for Message Media

Function

1   Destinations internal to company, letterhead, lower word number ratio in text, "other" contents (i.e., not covered by standard categories), no urgent dispatch, signature, and contains letters and memos.

2   No letterhead or signature, internal destinations, "other" contents, prior communication with recipient and urgent dispatch.

3   Short, overseas destination, low word to number ratio, no letterhead.

4   Bulk items, no "other" contents, urgent dispatch, overseas destination, letter or memo, letterhead, high word to number ratio.

5   Directives, letter or memo, no bulk items, UK destination, moderate urgency of dispatch, quite short.

6   Letter or memo, no "other" contents, prior communication with recipient, no directives, UK destination, quite short, no letterhead or signature.

Table 6
Classification Function Coefficients to
Assign Messages to Media

Variable	Tele- phone	1st class letter	2nd class letter	Other letter	Internal van delivery	Telex	Dispatch
Internal/ external destination	19.90	20.30	20.12	21.14	12.09	18.21	21.54
U.K./overseas destination	7.16	8.45	6.34	7.64	7.20	10.16	7.06
Length	3.65	1.83	1.86	2.37	2.09	1.17	1.68
Word/number mix of text	-0.85	0.05	0.38	-0.08	1.21	0.88	-0.34
Letterhead	-4.00	5.84	4.86	4.19	1.77	-3.60	6.27
Signature	1.57	3.43	3.58	3.55	3.17	2.31	2.02
Urgency of dispatch	1.82	2.97	3.37	2.85	2.93	2.26	1.67
Prior communication with recipient	2.69	4.00	3.86	4.57	2.63	2.85	3.87
Letter/memo	-0.98	0.89	0.10	-1.91	1.32	-0.58	6.09
Bulk items	1.90	3.03	0.26	0.72	3.09	1.55	1.71
Contains directives	8.69	8.46	8.91	10.78	7.77	9.62	16.23
Contains "other" items	4.10	2.73	3.99	4.16	5.67	4.52	2.00
Constant	-29.32	-40.36	-37.22	-40.90	-25.30	-30.55	-44.75

medium is then the weighted average of its average scores. Of about 500 observed information seeking events, about 56% were correctly allocated to the medium used. However, market shares were more correctly estimated (Table 7).

Having derived models to predict individual choice behavior among existing technical alternatives, the set of choice algorithms can be modified to incorporate hypothetical and futuristic alternatives with attribute weightings estimated from the derived weightings for existing services. Table 8 shows average, and estimates scores for existing and novel media respectively. Table 9 shows how market shares are modified when these new media are

Table 7
Market Shares for Information Media

Information Using Event	Probability of IUE Being Selected Expected	Probability of IUE Being Selected Observed
Writing to someone	9%	6%
Reading	22%	29%
Phoning somebody	36%	31%
Face to face contact	33%	35%

Table 8
Attribute Scores; Means for Existing Media and Estimates for Novel Ones

Attribute	Choice Set					
	Writing	Reading	Phoning	Face to Face	View data	Hear data
Degree of color	0.56	0.73	0	0.32	0.65	0
Pictures and graphics	0.44	0.50	0	0.27	0.45	0
Audio	0	0	1.00	0.86	0	1.00
Written	1.00	1.00	0	0.52	1.00	0
Hard copy	0.70	0.38	0	0.37	0	0
Impersonal	0.48	0.69	0.48	0.32	0.70	0.60
Easy & pleasant to use	5.85	6.22	6.36	6.46	6.50	5.50
Trustworthy	4.89	4.72	5.11	5.14	5.00	4.70
An opinion	0.22	0.21	0.36	0.40	0.30	0.20
Authoritative	2.30	2.27	2.06	1.92	2.00	2.00
Up to dateness	0.93	0.96	0.91	0.92	1.00	0.95
Relevance	2.41	2.41	2.66	2.67	2.50	2.40
Familiarity	1.41	1.73	1.68	1.65	1.40	1.40
Frequency of use	0.19	0.52	0.48	0.45	0.45	0.45
Time	5.00	2.60	2.34	4.00	2.00	2.50
Cost	2.44	1.84	2.04	1.84	3.00	2.20

Table 9
Estimated Market Shares with Two New Media

Information Using Event	Probability of IUE Being Selected
to someone	7%
Reading	16%
Phoning	26%
Face to face	24%
Heardata	19%
Viewdata	7%

added. The results must be treated with caution because the database is not representative.

Movement from these individual choice algorithms to reliable predictions of new service potentials requires new data (i.e., not used to derive the choice functions) from a *representative* sample to feed through the choice model to predict media share. This sample-share can then be expanded by traditional grossing-up procedures to predict market size for new services. Figure 7 shows the structure of the model to predict market shares for information-media.

The advantages of expanding disaggregate models of individual choice to predictive models of market performance are that they:

- are more reliable predictors of general trends than extrapolation techniques;
- allow the analysis of cross-impacts between changes in existing services or the introduction of new services on existing ones;
- permit the researcher to explore which parameters of service choice will have the greatest influence on market shares; and
- can readily accommodate new service concepts where historic data for extrapolation is unavailable.

Figure 7
Structure of Market Forecasting Model System for 'Infomedia'

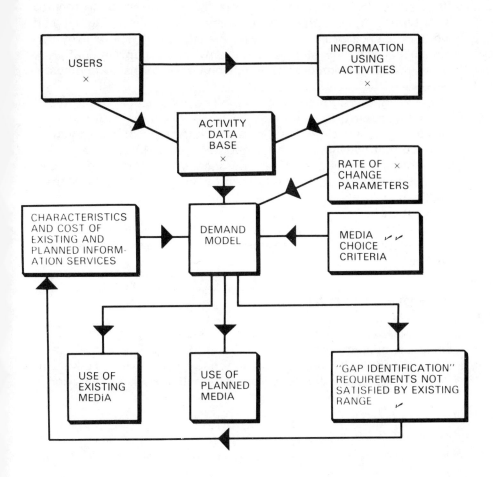

Current state of Model System

✓✓ means module is completed

✓ means module is completed provisionally, but could be improved/expanded

x means module is not yet implemented

CONCLUSION

Major uncertainties exist about the user aspects of office automation. Information handling of few worker groups is properly understood. Most attention has so far been focused on secretaries and typists, rather than more numerous or more highly paid workers: clerks, professionals, and managers. Clerical activity can almost certainly be studied adequately using conventional work measurement techniques, although better synthesis of findings is needed.

The greatest opportunity for office automation would result from improving managerial and professional productivity. Designing systems for their needs requires an understanding of their current activities, which cannot be obtained adequately using conventional techniques. The approaches outlined in this report have been successful for teleconferencing. At present, their application to aspects of office automation is incomplete and only intermediate results are available. However, we believe that completion of the work would lead to important findings able to aid in the identification and implementation of successful systems and services.

ACKNOWLEDGEMENT

This paper reports progress on research and consultancy being conducted by many CS & P staff. Particular credit is due to our colleagues Hugh Collins, Michael Tyler, and Hanko van Beinum, especially for work on information-seeking behavior.

BIBLIOGRAPHY

Pye, R. and Williams, E. "Teleconferencing—is video valuable or is audio adequate" 1977 Telecommunications Policy, pp. 230-241

Stewart, R. "Managers and their Jobs," Pan Books, London, 1970

Tyler, M., Cartwright, B., and Collins, H.A. "Interactions between telecommunications and face-to-face contact: prospects for teleconference systems," Long Range Intelligence Bulletin 9, Telecommunications System Strategy Department, British Post Office

CHAPTER 7

CRITERIA FOR USEFULNESS OF COMPUTERS IN OFFICES

John McCarthy
Computer Science Department
Stanford University

The thesis of this paper will be that there is no difficulty in getting people to use computers in offices provided the computer and its applications are genuinely useful. However, the criteria for usefulness are often not what one would imagine, and some further research is required before the real computer revolution happens.

I became interested in office use of computers in 1957, and this was one of the motivations for my research on time-sharing— the main one being use in artificial intelligence research. The first time-sharing system at Stanford was a PDP-1 in 1964. For that we provided no off-line program preparation equipment, and when we specified a display system, we insisted on both upper and lower case with a view to using the system for preparing documents as well as other applications.

OFFICE COMPUTING AT THE STANFORD ARTIFICIAL INTELLIGENCE LABORATORY

The Stanford Artificial Intelligence Laboratory received its PDP-6 computer in 1966, and it was planned to use the computer for office applications from the beginning. All displays and the printer permitted upper and lower case and a reasonable set of mathematical symbols, and we began improving on-line editors. The first Ph.D. thesis written and printed on the computer was in 1971.

Our progress in office use of the computer was mainly paced by hardware acquisition. While we could print documents from the beginning, there was no motivation to prepare them on-line as long as we were using uppercase-only teletypes for terminals. When we acquired our first display system, on-line preparation of documents began, but until we installed our 60-terminal Datadisc display system in 1971, the terminals were in a terminal room. Putting the terminals in offices, which included supplying the secretaries with terminals, was a major step. Gradually more and more Laboratory administrative files were kept on line, and the secretaries could help prepare papers. However, since it also became easier for researchers to enter and edit their own papers, there was less typing required to be done by a secretary. People differ in the extent to which they work through typists and secretaries, and an office system should provide for these differences.

Getting on the ARPA net gave a big stimulus to message sending inside the Lab as well as over the net. The E editor permitted more effective use of the displays. The POX and PUB document compilers automated many editorial aspects of document preparation. When Xerox gave us a Xerox Graphics Printer, this made possible preparing multifont documents with arbitrary character sets.

Many people work both in the Lab and at home, and their easy use of office computing requires home terminals, of which we now have a fair number.

Donald Knuth's TEX and the associated acquisition of high quality printing equipment have substantially increased the documentation use. Knuth's vigorous publicizing of TEX including the book has been at least as important as the program itself. Even mathematicians are beginning to use our computers for producing theses and papers. They have always been among the slowest to make use of computer facilities. This is because mathematics is mostly done at a high level of abstraction, and we are only beginning to develop computer programs that communicate this abstractly.

Besides the main programs associated with office use, many auxiliary programs for looking up data in files and even computing have been developed.

CONCLUSIONS FROM OUR EXPERIENCE

1. Up time of the computer and safety of its file system determine whether it will be accepted for office use.

2. Secretaries and other clerical people can use computers even without much training. Their motivation to do so requires that they have terminals on their desks and that the computer be reasonably reliable. Some amateur human engineers imagined that they might have a problem with a keyboard in which the top row of keys was displaced from standard. Like almost all of the researchers, they never noticed. For workload reasons, we have had to use many temporary secretaries from manpower agencies. This has proved unexpectedly easy. I saw one temporary typing at a terminal twenty minutes after her arrival under the supervision of a regular secretary working at another terminal in the same office.

3. Display terminals are much better and cheaper than hard copy terminals. The latter are noisy, and waste paper gets spread around. Of course, there needs to be a good accessible printer, but many people print only daily.

4. Having many display terminals, provided they have at least minimal facilities, is more important than having a few super terminals. We will shortly have a really good experimental test of this proposition, because the Computer Science Department now has perhaps 75 terminals in offices and about 15 Xerox Alto systems in terminal rooms. I am betting that people who have Datadiscs in their offices will use them rather than take their papers to a terminal room down the hall.

5. Reducing the noise level is important. A big improvement comes from eliminating typewriters, and it will probably prove worthwhile to develop less noisy keyboards.

6. If they have a proper interactive style, many programs can be used without formal documentation—whether a hard copy manual or full interactive documentation. If the program is written in a style familiar to our users and its general capabilities are known, most people will try to use it without reading the manual.

For example, punctuation of the arguments of commands must be standard: Don't require a comma in one place and a semicolon in another. "?" should always get information about the options available at the present point in the interaction.

7.   Programs should interact at a single level as much as possible. Even an experienced user often gets lost in a hierarchy of modes and submodes. Menus are bad, because as soon as a user gains the slightest experience, he hates having the screen cluttered up with changing menus. The information provided by menus and question-and-answer formats can be provided by letting the user say "?" whenever he needs to know what his options are. Worst of all are interactive programs that clear the input buffer before accepting a user's command in a new situation. The even slightly experienced user will want to type ahead, often totally ignoring what is on the screen, in order to get the program into a desired state.

8.   Keeping up with new programs and improvements in programs has proved impossible so far. People use only a part of the facilities of our interactive programs. This isn't a tragedy; everyone has his own appropriate balance of effort between learning about new features and using the old ones.

9.   Many jobs do not involve continuous use of the computer, and it is more important to meet the needs of the casual user than those of the beginner. A person will invest considerable effort in first learning how to use a computer, but if he has to learn all over again after a two-month layoff, he won't put in the effort a second time. Computer use should not be like instrument flying—requiring lessons if you haven't done it for six hours in the last ninety days.

10.   The utility of many proposed applications of computers is limited by the work required to put the information in the computer. The prize example is the proposal to use home computers to keep track of items in the pantry and warn the householder when to buy more. Even if the terminal were in the pantry, it would be too much trouble and people would forget. A bar code reader in the pantry might make it reasonable, but the geneticists may have to breed hens that lay eggs with bar codes.

SOME MORE CONTROVERSIAL CONTENTIONS

I cannot claim that these contentions have been verified by experience, because I haven't enough.

1. Executives will use computer systems provided they are genuinely useful, but when they are not useful, the complaints will often be misleading about the real reasons. An executive will always be a casual user. Therefore, the terminal must be unobtrusive and quiet; his secretary must have one too, and if he works at home, there must be a terminal at home too. In fact, the message use of a computer is most helpful out of normal working hours. I got out of bed last night, because I remembered a message I had been intending to send for a week, sent it and forgot the matter till I received the reply this morning.

Usefulness for executives will depend on how many of the people with whom they must communicate also have terminals.

Anyone who does much work at home should have a terminal at home.

2. Idiot-proofing programs is often a bad idea. It is easy for the designer of an on-line system to get into a state of mind where he regards the user as an idiot who must be prevented from making all kinds of mistakes. Indeed, the books and papers on interactive programming take this attitude. In fact, the people who write about supervising programmers take that attitude towards their charges. However, it has several disadvantages.

First, it must concentrate on the kinds of mistakes that can be detected and prevented by bureaucracy—whether it be the programmed bureaucracy of a field that allows only numeric input in a certain range or the administrative bureaucracy that requires a comment for every statement in a program. There are many situations in which the bureaucracy spends its time preventing trivial errors, while major substantive errors are ignored, because the input embodying them is "grammatical" according to the lights of the system.

Second, idiot-proofing takes time, and it often happens that the idiot-proof programs are insufficiently debugged. There is nothing as annoying as trying to get a program to accept input that it is rejecting for trivial reasons.

Third, idiot-proof programs are usually extremely inflexible and are difficult to modify to take new data into account.

Let me describe an experiment that, unfortunately, was never carried out. A certain university found its on-line registration system terribly late, full of bugs, and expensive of computer resources. The experiment was to have the clerks prepare the registration material using an ordinary editor—labelling the items in the text of the record. The files, prepared by the clerks, would then be processed by programs to get them in the desired form.

Unlike on-line input-receiving programs, the processing program could be written while the input was taking place, and if bugs showed up, they could be corrected after the fact. Even last-minute changes in the information to be included could be accommodated. The results of the data-entry could be printed and checked by supervisors or the supervisors could examine them on-line. However, the university took the "safer" path of buying another computer.

Unfortunately, the task of writing a computer program for others to use seems to bring out the latent tyrant in many people.

A STEP FURTHER OUT

There are many opportunities for expanding the usefulness of computers in offices, but many of them require the development of standardized facilities.

1. The Dialnet project. Many rival networks for interconnecting computers have been developed, but in my opinion, the possibilities of the ordinary dial telephone network have not yet been fully exploited. That network has the advantage in that it already connects all the offices in the world.

The Stanford Artificial Intelligence Laboratory is developing the Dialnet system. This consists of a telephone dialer and suitable modems connected to our computer and software implementing the Dialnet protocols. Anyone else in the world can similarly equip his computer, and users of any computer equipped with Dialnet can communicate with users of any other.

Sitting at my terminal, I will be able to type "MAIL MIKESMITH @ 202-666-6666, Mike are you free for lunch on Thursday?" Once I have done this, I can use my terminal for other purposes. My computer calls a computer at that number and tells it that it has a message for a user called MIKESMITH. He gets the message immediately if he is logged in—later otherwise. We can do this now for computers on the ARPA net, but why go through all that politics, when the telephone system is available? Dialnet can also be used for transferring files between computers.

The 1200 baud limitation of present Dialnet is important for some applications but not for messages and transfer of medium-size files like reports. If one specifies NIGHTMAIL, the telephone cost for a 9000-byte message will be only a little more than the price of a stamp.

2. National file-naming system. A major application of Dialnet or other inter-computer communication systems will be to transfer files from one computer to another. This is done now but it almost always involves specific technical arrangements between the managers of the computers. In order to transfer files freely (except as restricted by password fences), a national file-naming system is required.

3. Describing other people's files. Many programming languages contain features for describing data structures so that the compiler will generate them and compile programs that use them. However, no one such system will conquer the world and indeed, if progress is to continue, it is not even desirable that a single system be adopted. Therefore, people will always want to refer to other people's data structures.

This can be made possible by a universal system for describing existing files which can be developed using the techniques for describing grammars and data structures.

4. A standardized style of interactive programming will help people use each other's programs.

CHAPTER 8

A MAN-COMPUTER INTERFACE
ENCOURAGING USER GROWTH

Jacob Palme
Swedish National Defense Research Institute

THE HUMAN COMPUTER ENVIRONMENT

Computer Effects on User Conditions

In human society, a major problem-solving approach has always been that of making rules. A body of well-informed people analyze the problem and put on paper their best knowledge about how to handle forthcoming cases. The product of their effort is called by names such as "rule," "law," "code," "regulation" or "checklist." This problem-solving approach can be called the legal way of handling problems

Today, a new variant of the legal approach is becoming more and more common. The new approach is called "system development" and the ruling text produced is called a computer program. The users are bound by the rules laid down in the computer program in the same way as people are bound by other kinds of rules in society.

The legal approach has always had advantages and disadvantages. The advantages have been to ensure uniformity, to avoid mistakes and to disseminate knowledge and moral values. The disadvantage has been that the reality of life is always much more diversified and complex than can be understood by rules, so that the rules often do not fit the circumstances of the actual real cases met in practice.

This means that, in actual practice, rules and laws are always bent to accomodate reality. This bending of rules is often unconscious, but strict adherence to given rules will often have disastrous effects on the funtionality of an organization, as is shown, for example, by the effects of certain "go slow" strikes.

In an organization using computers, the rules built into the computer programs will, in similar ways, govern the people using the computer. The difference, however, is that a computer requires a program which is much more complete than most other rules in society. Every case must be covered, and the computer will not do anything which is not put into its program.

The system developers are thus forced to prepare much more detailed rules when these rules are to be executed by computers, than when the rules are to be executed by human beings.

When the software is ready, the computer will act as a tool for enforcing the rules built into its programs, and this tool is much more powerful in enforcing exact adherence to its rules than ordinary written rules. But since the world-view built into the software must always, by necessity, be simplified and idealized, it will not fully fit the many-facetedness of reality.

The effects of this will be that an organization using computers will often have difficulties in adjusting its behavior to special cases or a changing envrionment. The people working with the computers will find themselves restricted and hindered by the "stupidity" with which the computer adheres to its program. This will make people feel frustrated and dissatisfied, and make them perform less efficiently, since the ability to influence one's working conditions are very important to comfort and good performance.

Because a computer is such a powerful tool for enforcing rules, people with a yearning for power often use computer to enforce their will upon others. It is, therefore, easy to understand why organizations involved in a struggle for power, like the trade unions fighting to increase the power of the employees and their organizations against the employers, or big organizations with a wish to increase centralized power, are well aware of the importance of computers to hinder or aid them in achieving their goals.

But even when there is no conscious intention to use the computer as a tool for enforcing rules, the effect will often be the same. Even the most well-meaning group of people, representing all interested parties and only wishing to produce the best computer software, will often produce software which, when put into practical use, is found to be too restricting. There are several causes for this. One is that reality is so complex that it is not possible to put into a program all the special cases which will be encountered in real practice. The developers often have a false impression of their program being more complete than it really is. Another cause is that it is natural for well-meaning people to try to put their knowledge of what to do and what to avoid into the computer programs. It is natural to say things like:

"This is not good practice, do not put it into the program," or

"This person does not need that information, so the computer should not allow him/her to get the information."

In non-computer usage, technical means are sometimes used to enforce rules, like, for example, locks on doors. But mostly, rules are not enforced by such technical means. And, if we tried to use technical means to enforce all rules in society, we would encounter large problems. This is not only because the rules have to be bent to allow society to work, but also because a rule to stop certain unwanted practices will often also be simplified in a way which also causes it to make allowed practices much more difficult.

When computers are to be used, there is a tendency to wish to put all rules into the computer software—making the software allow only permitted practices and forbid all unwanted practices. This tendency will create software which is restrictive and hinders development. And it is not necessary to put all restrictive rules into the actual computer programs. It is often sufficient and much better to put only the most important rules into the program, and enforce other rules by ordinary human ways like, for example, talking to people who are breaking a rule when necessary.

It is very important not to confuse user influence during the development of a system with user influence when they are actually using the system. Both kinds of influence are important, and one cannot replace the other. Even with user influence during system development, there is still a large risk that a system is created which is found too restrictive in actual practice.

The ideal software, for the experienced user, is flexible and lets the user decide how to use the computer. The computer can, in this case, be regarded as a collection of tools. The user decides what to do by choosing which tools to apply and in which order.

Computer software often goes through several stages of development. When the software is new, its users are inexperienced and prefer software which is simple and fairly restrictive. But, as the users learn more and more, they require more and more flexibility and sophisticated functions. The software maintenance group tries to keep up with this by adding many additional functions and commands to the original software. After several years of this kind of development, the software is very complex, with a command structure which can only be mastered after long training. This is, however, no difficulty for the original users, since they have received the additions one at a time over a long time period, and people have an astonishing ability to learn how to master complex systems if learned in this way. However, to the outsider or the beginner, such complex systems can be rather frightening. C.A.R. Hoare has described the people who master these complex systems as a new kind of priesthood, understanding the magic rites (Hoare, 1975).

The same flexibility and functionality can often be achieved with a much simpler system, if rewritten from the beginning. To avoid this problem, a computer system can be designed in such a way that it is basically very flexible, and avoids restrictive rules. But there should be a top-level for inexperienced users, which is more restrictive and guides them in their use of the computer. As a user learns more, that user can step from the top-level to the more flexible base level, not as one big step, but rather in many small steps as the user learns more and more about the system.

This paper presents one approach of designing such a system with levels adjusted to users with different degrees of experience.

Human-Computer Interfaces

Assume a computer software package which is going to be used by many people. Many of them are inexperienced with computers. They need an interface, in which the computer guides them along with carefully worded questions, where they only have to answer the questions from the computer. Such an interface is simple to use for beginners, since the computer tells them what to type (Palme, 1975A).

Other users are experienced. Perhaps they have used the package for a long time. Perhaps they have other computer experience. Those users are often dissatisfied with a computer-guided interface. They feel that it takes too much time to get things done, and that their freedom is restricted. They want an interface in which they can get the computer to do what they want with short simple commands. They want the freedom to decide what to do with as few arbitrary restrictions as possible (Palme, 1975A).

Another requirement put forward by experienced users is to be able to add new facilities to the package. For example, if they need to do similar actions many times, they do not want to have to repeat the same sequence of inputs to the computer again and again. They want to add this sequence of inputs as a new facility to the package.

This could be discussed on the basis of the following diagram:

Human
satisfaction
and performance

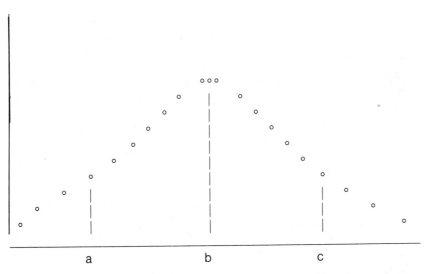

a   b   c

Requirements
put on the
human

Point **c** in the diagram represents users, who are taxed by a too advanced system. Point **a** represents users who find the work dull and tedious because of a too simple and restricted system. But this may be the same system for two different users, or even the same system and the same user at different times. Thus, the ideal system should adjust itself to the user so that all users can be as close as possible to point **b** in the diagram.

There are many software packages of the computer-guided kind for inexperienced users. There are also many packages of the kind which gives much power to the experienced users. But the ideal package should perhaps be both at the same time, be able to adjust to the experience of the user, and encourage the user to grow with the package.

THE IDEA OF GRADUAL GROWTH

Rather than two different systems, one for the novice and one for the experienced user, the system should allow for gradual growth. Gradual growth has many advantages:

- The user can move towards the advanced level in small steps, all the time feeling secure with the system before taking the next step.
- Depending on the needs of one user, the system can be advanced where this user needs it, and simple in areas which this user does not feel worth learning advanced ways of doing.
- The novice and the advanced system use the same basic routines, which saves programming effort, insures consistency after updates, and, as much as possible, will work and look alike to the novice and the advanced user.

OUR APPLICATION

This report presents this idea using a real example. The Swedish Defense needed a new system for budgeting to be used by hundreds of people all over Sweden. The system described in this report is a prototype system. The final system is under development, but may not contain all the facilities of the prototype system.

DATA BASE ORGANIZATION

The users input their budget data into the computer. This is stored in a data base. The budgets from each local government can be combined into a total budget for a region or for the whole country. One solution is to have just one big data base, with one slot for each budgetary entry. All the users access the same data base when they use the system.

Another solution is to have essentially one data base for each local budget. This allows greater freedom to the local users. They can add their own local data, which need not be seen by the regional and central authorities, since all the data in the local budgets need not be reported to higher authorities. Also, each local user can have several data bases with different parts or versions of the budget, and combine and compare them at will. However, the solution with one total data base makes it easier to centrally access and review all items in the whole budget at any time.

We choose the solution with local data bases, since one of our goals was to increase the power of the individual user.

LEVEL A: CONVERSATION LED BY QUESTIONS
AND MENUS

When new users first enter the system, they will be led along by questions and menus from the computer. Menus have the advantage compared to yes-no questions that the user has more alternatives to choose from, which gives more user power and fewer steps toward a desired user goal.

A typical interaction at this level may be:
(C: means computer, U: means user.)

    C: Do you want to?
    C: 1 Modify records in the budget
    C: 2 Add records to the budget
    C: 3 Delete records from the budget
    C: 4 Do something else
    U: 1
    C: Give name of record to be modified:

LEVEL B: HELP FACILITY

When users do not understand what the computer program is expecting, they are ripe to learn of the existence of the help facility. In our system, this can be invoked by typing a question mark (?) in response to any question from the computer. A single question mark causes a short help text to be printed which explains what the computer is expecting when the ordinary execution was interrupted by the help command.

The user has now learned two important new concepts: You can give commands to the computer instead of being led by it, and you can interrupt one sequence of operations and do something else instead.

The next command to be learned is perhaps two question marks (??), which can also be given at any time. Instead of giving a text suited to the interrupted interaction, two question marks invoke the general help facility, in which the user can get answers to all kinds of questions through a special set of menus asking what the user wants to know.

After using the help facility, the users get back to the original interaction where it was interrupted. Thus, they have encountered the idea of a subroutine call.

LEVEL C: OTHER USER COMMANDS FOR INTERRUPTION

Often, users will feel a need to interrupt the normal sequence of instructions temporarily for other reasons than to use the help facility. They may, for example, feel that the value being entered into the data base needs a special explanation, a footnote, added to it. Instead of entering the value, they can then use the "footnote" command. To distinguish commands from normal answers to questions from the computer, commands are preceded by the percent character (%). Example:

    C: Input the cost for this item:
    U: % footnote
    C: Input footnote text:
    U: This cost is extraordinarily high because of
        exchange of the main engine.
    C: —END OF %FOOTNOTE COMMAND—

C: Input the cost for this item:
U: 34000

Note that when the footnote was ready, the user returned to the question which was interrupted by the %footnote command.

The availability of footnotes is a general-purpose way of increasing the power of the user by allowing the user to add, when needed, other facts than those which fit into the specified slots in the data base.

A second example:

C: Which budget do you want to work with?
U: ?
C: You must enter the name of an existing budget, or type "NEW" if you want to start a new budget.
C: Type "%LIST BUDGETS" if you want to know which existing budgets are available.
C: —END OF HELP TEXT—
C: Which budget do you want to work with?
U: %LIST BUDGETS
C: Available budgets: REPORT BUDGET, CHARLIES BUDGET, JULY BUDGET.
C: —END OF %LIST BUDGETS COMMAND—
C: Which budget do you want to work with?
U: Report budget

In this example, the user interrupted the main question twice with interruption commands before answering the question. First, the user applied the help facility, which told the user of the %LIST BUDGETS command. The user applied this command next, to learn what budgets were available as answers to the main question from the computer, and then chose one of them as answer to the main question.

LEVEL D: PARAMETERS TO COMMANDS

At the previous level, users learned that there was a set of commands which could be given instead of the normal answer to a question from the computer. This increased the power and flexibility of the users, but they had to learn or look up the commands to use the new facility. This was thus a typical level of getting more power for users learning more about the system.

Commands can be made more flexible by adding parameters to them. Assume, for example, that a large number of different budgets were available to a user. Users might want to know which budgets of other people were available. The %LIST BUDGETS command in the previous example might be extended with parameters, so that the user could tell the computer which budget names to list:

C: Which budget do you want to work with?
U: %LIST BUDGETS for me and Charlie

In our system, parameters are preceded by keys such as "for" in the example above, and can be expressions with combining operators such as "and" in the example. For some commands, there is no key on the first parameter.

The advantage with keys on parameters is that all parameters need not be given. If a parameter is omitted, the computer can assume a default answer. For example, the level c user who only typed "%LIST BUDGETS" did not need to know that this command actually took parameters, and that the default value "me" was assumed for the omitted "for" parameter.

LEVEL E: A COMMAND-DRIVEN USER INTERFACE

Users going through the previous levels have been introduced gradually to the idea of giving commands to the computer. Until now, commands have been used only as a way of specifying interruptions from the normal flow of execution.

Whenever desired, users can move to the command level by writing the command "%BUDGOL" as answer to a question from the computer. They will then stay at the command level until they give a command to reenter the computer-led mode, such as the command "%CONTINUE," which continues in the computer-led mode where it was interrupted by the command "%BUDGOL."

The system can thus be used as a command-driven system. Instead of telling the computer what to do through answers to a series of questions and menus from the computer, the user can apply commands from the beginning.

The commands should, as much as possible, represent the same real activities which were achieved previously in a computer-led way. Often, the same words which previously were items in menus are now used as commands. To achieve this, it is important

that the commands be defined at the same time and together with the computer-led dialogue. How this can be done will be presented later in this report.
Example:

> Computer-led dialogue:
> C: Do you want?
> C: 1 Make a new budget
> C: 2 Change a budget
> C: 3 Stop
> U: 1
> C: Give budget name
> U: Test budget
>
> Command-driven dialogue:
> U: %MAKE BUDGET: test budget;

The users are never forced to give parameters to commands. If parameters are omitted, the computer is programmed to either: (a) use default values, which may depend on what the individual users have done or required previously, or (b) ask the users conversationally.
Example:

> U: %MAKE BUDGET
> C: Give budget name
> U: Test budget

This is the same conversation as before, but the user did not give any value to the parameter, and thus got a conversation which was a mixture between a command-driven and computer-led dialogue.

LEVEL F: SAVING SERIES OF COMMANDS

When the users have begun to use commands, they will soon find that they often have to repeat the same series of commands. This is the natural time to introduce the idea of saving a series of commands under the name of a new command.
Example:

> Charlies tasks
> %Look at budget: Charlies budget;
> %line: &header;
> %list tasks;

The three commands above are stored under the new command name "Charlies tasks" so that when the user gives the command "%Charlies tasks," this series of commands is performed.

LEVEL G: PARAMETERS TO USER-DEFINED COMMANDS

The users already know that parameters can be given to commands. The next level is thus natural: adding parameters to user-defined commands.
Example:

> Write tasks
> %Parameters: for &person;
> %Look at budget: &person;
> %line: &header;
> %list tasks;

If the user gives the command "%WRITE TASKS for Charlie," then this series of commands is executed with "Charlie" substituted for "&person." If the user gives the command "%WRITE TASKS" without parameters, the interpreter will automatically ask for the value of the missing parameter.

LEVEL H: MODEL LANGUAGE

Those users who wish to step even further can move to level h, learning to write simple computer programs in the model language. The series of stored commands learned in level f and g are, in fact, very simple cases of subroutines.

How should this model language work? We can make certain conjectures immediately:

- "Command" and "subroutine" are two words for the same thing. The user can invoke a subroutine by giving its name as a command.
- The statement for invoking a subroutine should have the same or similar syntax whether the command is given by the user directly or executed in a subroutine.
- All but one of the parameters to a command must be preceded by a key, since this allows users to omit parameters, and the computer still knows which parameters have been given and which have been omitted.

- The syntax should be the same or similar for commands which invoke model language subroutines and for commands which are part of the basic system.
- The model language should also be simple and easy to learn; it is probably interpreted rather than compiled.

When commands are typed at the terminal, users dislike having to type long commands. We are therefore planning to let the system accept commands typed with only enough letters to make the command distinct from other available commands. This is not implemented in the prototype system.

The system will include a simple text editor for the writing of model language routines. This editor will make routines prettier by (a) block indentation, (b) upper case for commands and keys, lower case for values, and (c) conversion of short forms of commands to the full length.

PARAMETER DEFINITION IN THE MODEL LANGUAGE

A natural way for users to define commands is to list the command as it is to be used, but with parameter names where parameter values are to be substituted. The following example shows how this is done in our system:

```
%Command: seek;
%Parameters: task &task in budget &budget;
%end of parameters;
```

This command may be invoked by writing:

U: %SEEK task 54321 in budget Charlies budget

The command may also be used without parameters:

```
U:  %SEEK
C:  Task?
U:  54321
C:  In budget?
U:  Charlies budget
```

Or the command may be given with just one parameter:

```
U:  %SEEK in budget Charlies budget
C:  Task?
U:  54321
```

Look again at how the command was defined in the model language:

    %Command: seek;
    %Parameters: task &task in budget &budget;
    %end of parameters;

The statement "%end of parameters;" will cause the interpreter to check which parameters have been defined and which are undefined, so that the questions in the dialogues above can be generated.

If the programmer wants to assume default values for omitted parameters, this is also possible:

    %Command: seek;
    %Parameters: task &task in budget & budget;
    %set: &budget := &previous.budget;
    %end of parameters;

If the variable "&previous.budget" has previously been given a value then this is used, so that "%end of parameters" does not have to ask for a value for this parameter. If, however, "&previous.budget" is undefined, then a question to the terminal is generated.

In the case where a value for the parameter "&budget" is given in the invoking command, then the "%set" statements are never executed, since there is a rule in the language which says that "%set" statements are not executed if they precede "%end of parameters" and if the variable already has a defined value.

FURTHER FEATURES OF THE MODEL LANGUAGE

Further features of the model language are similar to other programming languages. Thus, there are IF. . .THEN. . .ELSE clauses, BEGIN. . .END brackets, output and input statements, etc. Also, all commands of the system can be given in model language programs.

The basic data type of the model language is a text string of varying length. In addition to computational expressions, the language also allows text expressions like concatenation. For example, "%line 'The cost will be' &cost * &inflation;" is a statement where the text string "The cost will be " is concatenated to the value of the subexpression "&cost * &inflation."

The data types in the model language will vary with the application—in our application we have references to budgetary entries as an additional data type.

We are also considering the idea of allowing users to augment the data structure definitions in the system using the model language. For example, one user may wish to add the field "priority" to the budgetary records created by that user.

WRITING INTERACTIVE PROGRAMS IN THE MODEL LANGUAGE

To simplify the writing of interactive programs in the model language, there are two special functions in the model language for questions and menus. Here is an example of use of the question function:

```
%SET &task := %QUESTION:
   query text: Which task?
   check: %Legal task
   help: %Task help;
```

Note that the syntax of functions is very similar to the syntax of commands (=subroutine calls). Just as with commands, there are defaults when a parameter is omitted.

The parameter "legal task" is the name of a function which will take the user answer to the question as parameter and return "yes" or "no." If "legal task" returns "no," then an error message is given and the user is asked to repeat the answer to the question.

There are several such built-in check functions, for example, "%yes or no" which only accepts the two parameters "yes" and "no" and "%number" which only accepts numbers. The users may, of course, also write their own check functions.

If there is no parameter "legal task" given to the function "%question" in the model language routine, then all user answers to the question are considered legal.

The parameter "task help" is a user-defined subroutine which prints a help message to the user. This may consist of text only, but the model language programmer is free to add questions to the user to select appropriate explanations.

MODEL LANGUAGE AND BASE SYSTEM

If the software package is going to be used by many users in different places, then the integrity of the system will also become a problem. One user cannot be allowed to write model language subroutines which interfere with other normal users.

One way to achieve this, which we have chosen, is to divide the system into the two main parts: The base system and the top level, consisting of model language routines defined by the user.

The interpreter for the model language is part of the base system, and full integrity control is done at the interface between the base system and the top system, for example, when base system commands are given by users directly or in model language subroutines.

USER COMMUNICATION

All users will probably not advance through all the levels to model language programmers. This depends on their interests, ability, and use of the system. However, users need not learn to use the model language themselves to benefit from it.

Very often, one of a group of users becomes more interested and more advanced in the technical aspects of the system than the other users. They turn to this user for help when they have problems. Such an advanced user is called a "local expert" and is considered very important for the success of a computer applications system (Damodaran, 1976).

If the "local" expert" learns to write routines in the model language, then he/she can do this for the other users in the group. In this way, the model language is a vehicle for the local expert to communicate his/her knowledge to the other users.

Model language routines may also be written by a central maintenance group for individual users. One reason why central maintenance groups are so reluctant to do what people ask them to do is that a change in the system needed by one user may be detrimental to other users or even threaten the security of the system.

Since model language routines can be local to just one user, and since the integrity of the system is checked at the interface between model language routines and the base system, no one except one user is affected by the new command. This will make it easier for the central development group to create additional facilities for local users.

If one user has written a model language routine which is really useful, then other users may begin to use that routine too (this can be traced automatically by the system). Finally, the routine may be adopted for general use and included in the base system. In this way, the model language can act as a vehicle for communication between users.

On the other hand, some parts of the general system can be written in the model language. This is a good way in which the general system can be adjusted to the needs of special user groups. In our case, for example, we may have separate sets of model language routines for the army, the navy, and the air force.

A further way of generating model language routines which we are considering is to write conversational programs, which put questions to the user and then generate appropriate model language routines.

EXPERIENCE WITH THE MODEL PROPOSED

The System Development Process

The system model described above was developed in 1976 as part of the work of designing a new budgeting system to be used in the Swedish Defense. A computer program was written in two months' time by myself in the early stages of the design effort. That program incorporated all of the features described in this paper. The program was never intended for actual use—it was written very fast, using methods producing a working program but sacrificing efficiency.

This way of producing a working computer model of the system at an early stage in the development has the advantage that this model can be tested and shown to users to get their reactions at a stage where it is easy to take their requirements into consideration, since the programming of the final system has not yet begun.

In our case, this working model was very useful in gaining experience on how to design the system, but the model was used and tested mostly by the system developers and not by the future users.

The final system was then developed and tested on a small group of users in 1977. After further development, the system is now in full use by about 200 users all over Sweden.

The final system is based on the principles described in this paper but does not incorporate the model language (Levels F to H in this paper). I personally would have liked to give the users a system including a model language, but this was not done because of the cost of development and because the interpreter for the model language might make the system too complex and inefficient. (A partial cause of this may be that the model of the system developed in the beginning was very inefficient.)

System Development Problems

The structure of the system is such that the user has great freedom of deciding in which order to make certain actions. This has caused some programming difficulties. Suppose, for example, that a user circumvents the normal order of doing things and tries to make an action which requires data which were to be input at the circumvented stage. To avoid this problem, the code of every action has to be written in such a way that it checks that the necessary preconditions are fulfilled.

This way of coding the system has given other problems. If, for example, a user tried to do action B, which requires action A to be ready, the system will first take the user into Action A. The user may then again try to go to action B, and the system goes back recursively to action A again. In such cases, the users often do not understand what is happening.

Another problem occurs when users interrupt one action to do something else, then interrupt that action again and so on, adding more and more unfinished actions to an internal stack in the program. When each action is ready, the program will then go down in the stack, but the user has often forgotten what happened and does not understand what the program is trying to do.

This problem can be avoided by limiting the recursiveness of the program. If a user interrupts one action to do a small supplementary action, then the user is returned to the interrupted action again, and a full explanation is given of where the program is returning. If the user interrupts to do something big, the user is not returned to the interrupted action again, but is returned to the top level of the program.

These programming problems were no great hindrance, and the program is successfully in use.

The system development method has been different from the development of other systems. The conventional way of writing this kind of system is to have a rather large group of COBOL programmers supervised by system designers producing detailed descriptions of the program.

In our case, the whole program was produced by three programmers using the high-level language SIMULA. SIMULA, which is an extension of ALGOL, is well suited to structured programming. The system was developed and tested on a DEC System-10 computer, which has good facilities for program development and testing. Production execution is then done on a Univac 11-Series computer. This way of developing on one computer and using the system on another computer has worked very well and forced us to produce a well-defined and machine-independent program.

User Experience with the System

Our experience is that users do use the system in the way intended. New users begin with the computer-guided, menu-driven interface, but turn to the user-guided, command-driven interface after a few weeks of experience.

In the first production version now in use, there is a rather sharp limit between the menu-driven and command-driven interfaces. In the next version, this limit will be less sharp, making it easier for users to move between the levels.

One problem is that as the program grows larger, all escape commands cannot be made available with similar function throughout the program. The users will then complain when an escape command which worked in one part of the program does not work in another part.

The total experience is, however, good. The system works in the intended way, the users are satisfied and the effort is used as a model for developing new systems.

ACKNOWLEDGEMENTS

Staffan Loof made a number of important suggestions during the design of this system. The basic idea on the handling of command parameters not given by the user is partly his. Ideas came also from Erik Sandewall and Sture Hagglund. The system was tested by Lars-Ake Larsson, who provided a number of suggestions for improvements. The design of the QUESTION and MENY commands are based on ideas in SAFEIO, developed by Mats Ohlin. Mats Ohlin and Lars Enderin have helped me check the report.

The model system was developed by me, but the final system was developed by a group of three programmers, in which Lars-Ake Larson was responsible for the human-machine interface part of the program. He developed a general-purpose package in SIMULA for writing this kind of interaction, which means that he can set up a new interaction of the same kind (with a menu-driven level with defined menus and a command-driven level) in just a couple of days.

BIBLIOGRAPHY

Aaro, Ingvar, 1977: Design and Implementation of a Software System for Interactive Scientific Computing. Dept. of information processing, Royal Institute of Technology, S-100 44 Stockholm, Sweden.

Damodaran, L., 1976: The Role of User Support—Actual and Potential. Department of the human sciences, University of Technology, Loughborough, United Kingdom.

Grip, Arne, 1974: ADB-system och kommunikation. Hermods-Studentlitteratur, S-221 01 Lund 1, Sweden, 1974.

Hoare, C.A.R., 1975: Software design, a parable. In Software World, vol. 5, Numbers 9 & 10.

Marguiles, F., 1976: Evaluating Man-Computer Systems. Austrian Federation of Trade Unions, Vienna, Austria.

Ohlin, Mats, 1976: SAFE Conversational SIMULA Programs Using Class SAFEIO. FOA 1 Report C 10044.

Palme, Jacob, 1975A: Interactive Software for Humans. FOA 1 Report C10029, July, 1975. (Also available in Swedish.) (A shortened version was published in Management Datamatics, Vol. 5, 1976, No. 4, pp 139-154.)

Palme, Jacob, 1975B: A Method of Increasing User Influence on Computer Systems. FOA 1 Report C10001. (Also published in Software World, Vol. 5, No. 8, pp. 9-11, under the title "Real Time—Easing the User Task.")

Palme, Jacob, 1976: Internationell kurs om interaktion mellan mahhiska och dator. FOA 1 Rapport C 10056.

Palme, Jacob, 1977: BUDGOL-DAPU, ett system for manniska-dator-interaktion vid budgetering. FOA 1 Rapport C10076, October, 1977.

Palme, Jacob, 1979: Teleconference based Management Information Systems. To be published in the proceedings of Teleinformatics, 1979.

Stewart, T.F.M., 1976: The Specialist User. Department of Human Sciences, University of Technology, Loughborough, United Kingdom.

CHAPTER 9

AVOIDING WORKING NON-SOLUTIONS TO OFFICE COMMUNICATIONS SYSTEM DESIGN

James H. Bair
Bell Northern Research Inc.
Mountain View, California

SUMMARY

Computer-based message systems are no longer being used exclusively by computer sophisticates. The new users, primarily office workers, bring a totally different perspective to the use of digital technology. A review of lay-users' perspective reveals problems in current approaches to system design that typically result in "working non-solutions." Determining working solutions is not merely a matter of surveying potential users as they represent but one of the four divergent perceptions of the ideal system design. A design solution is proposed that facilitates convergence of the perceptions of the system chooser, user, manufacturer, and researcher. A current research effort is described which predicts, based on current attitudes and behaviors, a system design that potential users will accept and that will enhance productivity in the future.

BACKGROUND

Computer-based message systems have evolved considerably since they appeared as an adjunct to the early development of timesharing well over a decade ago. Initially, programmers adjàcent to R&D computer centers valued leaving messages for colleagues at about the level of another few lines of good code. Covert evolution of message handling software soon resulted in an awareness of a new medium of communication for white-collar workers.

Network designers and users reminisce about the almost startling discovery that the ARPA Net was being used more for messaging than for data transport and other applications for which it was designed.[1] Experienced computer users were engaged in nationwide conversations irrespective of location or hardware. We are now on the verge of another major proliferation of computer messaging represented by PLANET, ONTYME, COMET, HERMES and other personal mailbox, store and forward message systems. The potential and impact of sophisticated computer messaging as it has evolved since its earliest days is reported in two new books, *The Network Nation,* by Hiltz & Turoff[2] and *The Office of the Future,* by Uhlig, Farber, and Bair.[3]

The current proliferation of message systems represents a discontinuity in the preceding evolution. Messaging, along with other direct uses of computers, is leaving the domain of highly trained and skilled computer sophisticates, fluent in the cryptic language of machines, and appearing as a commercial product in realms where computers are more likely to be feared rather than loved. The non-sophisticated computer user has a totally different perceptual and experiential perspective than the sophisticate. This difference will not change the underlying purpose for using messaging products, but it will change the interface and performance characteristics required for acceptance.

Experience with the attempted implementation of messaging systems that did not accommodate the lay user's perspective has generally been negative. Examples abound, but it is more useful to concentrate on the nature of the user's perspective. A potential user's perspective has three fundamental, psychological components: (1) needs, (2) characteristics, and (3) expectations.

(1) User needs include both basic human needs and job requirements. The basic human needs are perhaps best characterized by Abraham Maslow.[4] In essence, Maslow explored the notion that we are motivated by needs, with certain needs having priority over others. If using a system is perceived as either enhancing a user's job security, providing additional socialization opportunities, or contributing to his esteem, in that order, there is positive motivation. If there is no perceived relationship to these needs, motivation for serious usage seems improbable. Motivation to use a system may be intuitive to system designers, but not obvious to computer non-users. Concrete portrayals of system benefits to prospective users are required that relate to job success and socialization needs. It must be remembered that the user's need is for accomplishment of his job with the computer as a means, not an end.

(2) User characteristics include the areas of sensation, attention, memory, and cognition. Most system interfaces are depraved as sensory stimuli, consisting of monochromatic, one dimensional CRT's with the resolution of drawings scratched on a sandy beach. Many systems violate memory processes by requiring a user to operationalize more than the average maximum of seven chunks of information retainable in short term memory.[5] Mnemonic aids to remembering commands and operators also seem to be ignored.

(3) User expectations are probably the most powerful influence upon the user's experience. The user brings expectations derived from use of other technologies and systems, most notably the telephone and typewriter. Overt telephone failure is almost non-existent, with inefficiencies relegated to operator error and caller unavailability—problems external to the technology. Typewriters do fail, but are easily replaced, repaired, or ignored. In both cases, the technology behaves in a *predictable* manner, fitting a model easily learned by the user. Reliability, responsiveness, and performance as advertised, without surprises, are imperative to avoid negative reactions.

To date, unfortunately, we are far from realizing systems designed in keeping with these components of the user's perspective, although such designs have been described.[6] At the least, users experience frustration and stress caused by the behavior of systems that should be as operational as the telephone, but are not. Subsequently, even adventuresome users can reject further usage and skepticism of future technological innovations spreads.

SYSTEM DESIGN PROBLEMS

The Current Design Process

Correction of any situation requires identification of the problem areas; unfortunately, the whole of current design practice appears at fault. But the fault is only apparent if we align ourselves with the *user's* values and perspective. The traditional design is driven by the highly technical, precise, and demanding computer and engineering sciences. To produce good programmers our educational system begins infusing them with the utmost of empirical rationality at an early age. A new way of thinking and problem solving is inculcated, derived from the abstract tools of mathematics and engineering. At the end of four to six years, this educational process has forever engendered a new thought process which is brought to bear on design. Collectively, a culture with its own language is created—the rigorous, logical, domain of programming languages and input-output devices.

In this culture, the questions posed do not arise from user needs for the most part, but rather from technology potential: "What neat thing can I get my software to do?" The result of competent effort is a system that functions well for the programmer-designer. Of course, accommodating the user is merely a matter of adding some user support—documentation, training, and an introduction to computers for good measure. The end result typifies message systems and other office systems today: *a working non-solution.*

The resultant system typically can be demonstrated and shown to perform in some way, for example, delivering and managing messages. However, the lay-user is confronted with operational opacity, undecipherable error conditions and error messages, and a plethora of control characters, function keys, and arbitrary steps that must be followed unconditionally. The learning process threatens the user's ability to meet basic needs (including job requirements) by consuming time for learning and operation. This same time loss has negative bottom line impact. To meet the basic needs of users, a system must be transparent to operate, minimizing time loss, and consistent with performance expectations.

Determining User Needs—Divergent Perceptions

Perhaps design problems would be readily solvable if the solution were merely to meet "user needs." However, there are four very different perceptions that confound even the most user-oriented design approach: (1) what the system chooser will buy, (2) what the user says he needs, (3) what industry can develop, and (4) what will actually increase user effectiveness.

(1) The system chooser is the buyer or decision maker in an institution acquiring a service. His criteria are primarily economic, including a limited investment per person, a predetermined rate of return, and a defined amortization period. Very often, up-front economic constraints prohibit investment in design and support that are fundamental to achieving critical mass (e.g., having enough users) and long range visibility.

(2) A classic misconception is that the user can tell designers what he needs. No different than life in general, the process of self-diagnosis is woefully inadequate as the sole determinant of needs. Certainly, users must be polled and seriously regarded in selecting opportunities for system application, but super-human powers of predicition should be left to others. A user cannot anticipate the form of a technology totally unknown to him; energy is much better spent determining the user's values and criteria for success in the context of his current work environment.

(3) Even if the user could anticipate the optimum design of useful technology, industry currently would have difficulty delivering the product. In numerous consulting studies, the author has found the currently available systems could not meet the chooser's or the user's criteria. Perhaps we were seeing industry's reaction to user demands which resulted in a situation where neither user requirements or industry capability were met, almost a "Catch 22" effect. Industry, dominated by the working non-solution approach, perceives users' needs in light of the current capabilities of *mass-produced* technology. For example, if the user wants an integrated telecommunications system for voice and data, he most likely will get a telephone interconnect switch that requires parallel wiring for any digital transmission with users. Or, for office automation, he likely will get a word processor which uses special purpose hardware for mechanized typing in total disregard for actual office functions; in other words, a mass produced non-solution. The limitation is not the potential of industry, but industry's perception of system design, an idea vividly presented by Morton, et al.[7]

(4) The convergence of the foregoing three perspectives does not yet address the most important question: What will increase user effectiveness? Plagued with two subproblems, how to measure effectiveness changes and how to determine the causal relationships to design variables, this perspective remains a frontier for design related research. In an overview of a measurement methodology for electronic office systems,[8] the author proposes a conceptual model of the variables that must be measured, methods of measurement, and the measurement controls that must be followed. Some of the results of measurement, particularly the causal relationships for improved efficiency are reported in other publications.[9,10] A surprising conclusion from this work is that users cannot judge what will improve their effectiveness. Measurement of different design factors must be done indirectly, regardless of whether the factors are cursor control or the functional capabilities of a message system.

For example, users generally appear to resist buying or using the "mouse" cursor control device. However, years of research and use at Stanford Research Institute[11] and elsewhere[12] have shown very significant improvements in the efficiency of editing and other interactive CRT tasks using the mouse. The improvement is so great that it appears worth any effort to add the mouse to present workstations or obtain a license. A second example is the difference between initial user perceptions of required functional capabilities of message systems and their perceptions after several months of experience. Invariably, the desire for a simple system with few commands for sending short messages gives way to dissatisfaction with the restricted service and a demand for extended capabilities such as document production.

In both examples users could not explicitly define the interface design or the capabilities and services they require to increase their effectiveness. Other examples show the limitations of user's subjective assessments of their needs. Observational studies of the time spent in daily office activities continually surprise subjects who subjectively anticipated far different results. Two findings were notably unbelievable by users: 75% of managerial time is spent in communication activities,[13] and 20% of clerical time is spent waiting for work.[14]

Thus, user's perceptions must be taken as only one of four perspectives of system design, and do not reflect valid changes in effectiveness. However, the user's perspective as stated above is a very important component in design success. User's perceptions can provide an understanding of expectations of system characteristics, and provide the basis of user participation in design, both critical for successful system implementation and acceptance.

A SYSTEM DESIGN SOLUTION

Design from a Model of the End-User

The design process must incorporate the four perspectives into a working solution that begins with measuring and analyzing the behavior of users, choosers, and designers, and then overlaying the results on technological feasibility. There are basically seven steps leading to a prototype system.

1. Survey User Expectations. Determine the subjective anticipation of pre-users and characterize the potential for accepting technological innovation in their work life.

2. Measure User Needs. Apply work flow analysis, work measurement techniques and psychological instruments to representative office operations and laboratory simulations to gather data about what actually will impact user effectiveness.[8, 15]

3. Use Psycho-social Characteristics. Use the literature on human performance and laboratory studies of human-computer systems as guidelines for specific design features such as cursor control, and command language consistency.[16]

4. Establish Functional Requirements. Map a progression of functional capabilities from initial implementation through system maturity for introduction to users; for example, a simple messaging capability could be followed by a personal management information system.

5. Use Efficiency Data. Design the interface, and work methods and procedures based on time-and-motion studies of simulated human-computer communication scenarios.

6. Specify Systems Features. Specify each feature based on weighted valuations from efficiency and effectiveness results, psycho-social characteristics, and user acceptance potential.

7. Overlay Functional and Feature Specification on Technology. Carefully revise the tentative design into feasible packages to be introduced incrementally as technological development permits. This emphasizes deliverables that are

reliable, responsive, packaged into non-intrusive hardware, and when they can be delivered.

This brief description of the seven steps is intended to draw attention to the user behavior-driven design and the need for thorough end-user research prior to any development of message or other systems intended for non-computer sophisticates.

An End-User Research Methodology

Our recent work focused on an approach to the front-end of the design process (Steps 1 and 2) and is oriented toward the perspective of the user and chooser as described above. (Previous work has focused on the perspectives of industry and end-user effectiveness.) Our methodology is a comprehensive package of research methods that describes the potential for usage as well as design factors for office communication technology in an organization. As a methodology, it provides all the necessary information to conduct an on-site study. For example, the methodology includes the step-by-step procedures for administering questionnaires, introducing the study to respondents, and the reasons why each question or measurement is used. To develop an accurate base for the design process, several different research methods are used that complement each other in a coordinated package.

The methodology is intended to answer two questions: what technology will enable users to be more productive (perspective 1), and what will be accepted in the working environment (perspective 2)? No single research method will address both these questions. The productivity component requires quantitative data and a model of what improves productivity; the acceptance component relies more on subjective data. Therefore, the methodology includes both quantitative and subjective types of research methods.

The research methods have been designed with the most challenging question in mind:

> How can we predict what potential users will accept
> that will make them more productive in the *future*
> based on *current* attitudes and behaviors?

The methodology addresses this question by using research tools that do not ask a respondent questions about technology of the future, or about other things which the respondent has not experienced. All questions are in terms of past experiences or attitudes currently held.

Likewise, measurements are of current behaviors from which future behaviors can be predicted. Thus, the prediction process is done by the research team, not the respondents. A complex model (conceptual) based on years of extensive investigation of prototype office-of-the-future implementations[3] enables the best possible prediction. Basically, this works by comparing the new data to previous data. Where there are significant similarities between the data, we can predict similar levels of acceptance and effects on productivity between the current study population and previous study results.

The data gathering process in each case begins with the selection of a company representative of a market segment; for example, electronics manufacturing. After an understanding of the company is obtained from its management, a representative sample of about 200 persons is selected. The sample consists of offices where the primary activity is information processing. A set of questionnaries is given to each person. Based on the questionnaire results, 20-40 respondents are interviewed. A final rating questionnaire is given to all respondents which focuses on the technological improvements possible in the office. An optional method, the communication audit,[17] may then be used to quantitatively describe communication behaviors such as meetings, telephone calls, and memos. During the process of delivering and collecting questionnaires and interviewing, observations are made of information management procedures, working environment, and working methods.

Upon completion of the case study, the data is summarized and analyzed showing the correlation between the human, organizational, and design variables. The results will identify the *opportunities* to use advanced office systems and the *acceptance level* of the potential technological solutions. "opportunities" for use reflect user needs without relying upon the user's judgment. Knowing the "acceptance level" permits selection of the appropriate functions, features, and configuration for a target implementation date. This approach, very briefly described, facilitates the successful convergence of the design goals of the chooser, user, and industry, and the requirements for improved efficiency and effectiveness.

In conclusion, we note that the reason for being for computer communication systems is to serve users who are no longer the designers! And to quote Morton, et al.,[7] "What we know above all is that the new user is most emphatically not made in the image of the designer."

REFERENCES

1. Lukasik, S.J. "Organizational and Social Impact of a Personal Message Service," *Proceedings of the National Telecommunications Conference.* IEEE Communications Society, San Diego, Calif., December, 1974.

2. Hiltz, S. R. and Turoff, M. *The Network Nation, Human Communication via Computer.* Reading, Mass.: Addison-Wesley, 1978.

3. Uhlig, R., Farber, D. and Bair, J.H. *The Office-of-the-Future: Communications and Computers.* Amsterdam: North-Holland Publishers, 1979.

4. Maslow, A.H., *Toward a Psychology of Being.* Princeton, N.J.: Van Norstrand, 1962.

5. Bair, J.H., "Human Information Processing in Man-Computer Systems." Paper presented at the annual conference of the International Communication Association, Phoenix, Arizona, 1971. (Information Sciences Abstracts, Vol. 7, No. 2, 1972.)

6. Watson, R.W., "User Interface Design Issues for a Large Interactive System." *AFIPS Conference Proceedings,* National Computer Conference, Vol. 45, 1976, pp. 357-364.

7. Morton, J., et al. "Interacting With the Computer: a Framework," in *Teleinformatics 1979.* IFIP International Conference. Amsterdam: North-Holland Publishers, 1979, pp. 201-208.

8. Bair, J.H., "Productivity Assessment of Office Information Systems." *Proceedings of the IEEE Symposium on Trends and Applications in Distributed Processing,* National Bureau of Standards, May, 1978.

9. Bair, J.H. "Communication in the Office-of-the-Future: Where the Real Payoff May Be." *Proceedings of the International Computer Communications Conference,* Kyoto, Japan, September, 1978.

10. Bair, J.H. "A Communications Perspective for Identifying Office Automation Payoffs." Invited Paper at the New York University Symposium on Automated Office Systems, New York, May, 1979.

11. Engelbart, D.C. "Design Considerations for Knowledge Workshop Terminals." *AFIPS Conference Proceedings,* 1973 NCC, Vol. 42, pp. 221-227.

12. Card, S.K., English, W.K. and Burr, B.J. "Evaluation of Mouse, Rate-Controlled Isometric Joystick, Step Keys, and Text Keys for Text Selection on a CRT." *Ergonomics,* Vol. 21 No. 8, 1978, pp. 601-613.

13. Mintzberg, Henry. *The Natural of Managerial Work.* New York: Harper and Row, 1973.

14. Purchase, Alan. "Office of the Future." SRI International Business Intelligence Program, Guideline No. 1001, 1976.

15. Tapscott, D. "Towards a Methodology for Office Information Communications Systems Research." Paper presented to the International Workshop on Integrated Office Systems, IRIA, Versailles, France, Nov. 6-9, 1979.

16. Bair, J.H. "Design Problems and Guidelines for Human-Computer Communication in Office Automation Systems." Invited Paper, *Proceedings of EuroIFIP 1979: European Conference on Applied Information Technology.* London, England, Sept., 1979.

17. Conrath, D.W. and Bair, J.H. "The Computer as an Interpersonal Communication Device: A Study of Augmentation Technology and its Apparent Impact on Organizational Communication." *Proceedings of the Second International Conference on Computer Communications,* Stockholm, Sweden, August, 1974, pp. 121-128.

PART III

EVALUATING ELECTRONIC OFFICE SYSTEMS

CHAPTER 10

EVALUATING OFFICE AUTOMATION TECHNOLOGY: NEEDS, METHODS AND CONSEQUENCES

David W. Conrath
Department of Management Sciences
and Centre for the Evaluation of
Communications-Information Technologies
University of Waterloo
Waterloo, Ontario, Canada

INTRODUCTION

The topic of "office automation," as reading recent magazines and newspapers will attest, has become very popular. Equally obvious is the fact that the expression means many different things to many different people. One finds everything from simple "word processing" typewriters to very complex, integrated, computer based communication and information systems discussed under the rubric of "office automation" or the "office of tomorrow." Apparently there is little agreement concerning what it is that is to be automated.

Part of the problem is caused by a lack of understanding of what an office is. If we cannot define and measure an office and the activities which take place within it, there are obvious difficulties in determining what technology ought to be supplied and in evaluating the effect of that which is supplied. Since this issue seems fundamental to a discussion of office automation, this paper will focus on the means of determining what goes on in an office and how knowledge of this might assist in the specification and evaluation of office automation technology.

THE OFFICE

A Hierarchy of Activities

To meaningfully discuss an "office" we should put it in the context of an organization. Doing so permits us to see the office as a hierarchy of activities, each of which involves a different level of aggregation. There could be an argument about what should be the lowest level, but we take a rather pragmatic approach and consider the most detailed description one typically finds in an organization—the Task. The Task is a well-defined piece of work or responsibility which is assigned to a given individual, the collection of which make up his or her job. Examples are: typing correspondence, preparing the year end financial reports, and verifying the accuracy of all payroll checks. It is at the level of the task that one prepares detailed specifications for office automation technology. Without an understanding of what the task requires there is no assurance that the technology provided will assist in its execution. Thus, the task becomes a key to the concept of an office.

The aggregation of office activity which is perhaps best understood is the Job. Since most of us have jobs, we feel that we know conceptually what a job entails. It is a set of tasks assigned to a particular person. If that person's work station is to be technologically equipped, the task profile of that job must be understood.

The Task and the Job aspects of office activity consider what one does on one's own. The next levels of aggregation concern what one does with others, the *raison d'etre* of organization. The first is the group, though we must admit that one's group is far from unique.There is the authority group (a boss and his or her subordinates), the work group, and the group of people located in physical proximity. Furthermore, most of these groups can be perceived at more than one level of aggregation, particularly in larger organizations. One might find not only departments, but divisions, branches and other subunits of the organization itself.

Each, to the extent that it has implications for coordination and/or certain kinds of functional activities, may be relevant to the actual and potential use of office automation technology.

The highest level of aggregation appropriate to an understanding of an office is the organization itself. While many organizations are comprised of a number of offices, the appropriate technology for these offices is likely to be heavily dependent upon their role within the organization. Furthermore, the budget and the authority to equip an office with technology is likely to be granted at the level of the organization, particularly if significant capital expenditures are involved.

To summarize, while the detailed specification of office automation technology requires a knowledge of the tasks to be performed with that technology, such a specification cannot be done independently of an understanding of how these tasks are aggregated into jobs, and how individuals holding these jobs are aggregated into interdependent groups and organizations.

"The" Office Versus "An" Office

Looking at the office at various levels of aggregation raises an important issue with respect to the specification and use of office automation technology. At what level does one find sufficient variation in activities to require significant technological differentiation? Are we to supply different equipment, especially in terms of its software, for each different task, even if one person is responsible for several of these different tasks? Or, at the other extreme, do we provide every organization with the same, all-purpose technology? One might argue that an entire industry or nation ought to be equipped similarly, such as has been the case with telecommunications until very recently. However, given the ease with which one can tailor the software of computer based technologies, the pressure to give everyone the same things has greatly diminished.

Although one can provide variation at any level of aggregation, the issue of providing all-purpose versus use specific software cannot be ignored. Not only is it a question of systems design, but it is interdependent with targeting the market for office automation technology. The office machine industry generally works at the level of the task or job. The communications industry, on the other hand, is working at the level of the organization or the public at large. These approaches are traditional. They are not based on a careful analysis of what goes on in an office, nor on an identification of similarities and differences at various levels of aggregation of office activities and what these suggest regarding the specification of technology.

The present design and marketing philosophy seems to be one of incrementalism—changes are made to existing pieces of technology and little thought has been given to starting anew from the point of view of a fully integrated system. This may suffice as long as the customer does not demand such integration. However, once the purchaser of office technology begins to recognize the advantages of having a system rather than a set of unrelated and independent parts, the issue of an office (any office) versus the office (a specific office) will come to the fore.

EVALUATION

The Several Sides of Evaluation

Evaluation, like office automation, means different things to different people. It also means several things to us. For that reason we wish to mention four different aspects of evaluation: specification of technology, evaluation of technology in terms of meeting its specifications, measuring the impact of implemented technology, and the evaluation of the procedures of implementation. Perhaps there is a word better than "evaluation" that one could use as an umbrella for these four activities, but we can not think of one. In any case, each of the four requires a precursor. All imply that we have a knowledge of what goes on in an office, and the last three require that we know what goes on in the office.

Traditionally, the specification of technology has been left in the hands of engineers. The issue has been one of how best to use what could be built rather than to determine, a priori, what should be built. Perhaps this was acceptable when the task to be accomplished by technology was rather simple and well understood, such as the problem of transmitting a message from point A to point B. Nevertheless, the side effects of accomplishing even this goal are now being felt in terms of resource use and the effect on the office environment. Furthermore, the tasks of which we now speak are usually complex, and, except for simple clerical tasks, they are not well understood. Hence, effective specification requires an understanding of what goes on in offices so that organizational activities can be translated into their technological implications.

Specification can be viewed from two perspectives: *an* office and *the* office. In the first case evaluation is being done from the point of view of the vendor: what should be produced, what services should be supplied to satisfy user needs? A key issue is the extent to which one should produce differentiated or special purpose products. Should one create a common protocol to cover many tasks, or should one create protocols unique to a given task, or job, or job type, or organization, or industry? Answers to this line of questioning has implications for other, interdependent questions. For example, how readily can one learn to use the technology beneficially? How tolerant will the target population be in terms of learning the required procedures before abandoning the process and foregoing the use of the new technology? The greater the level of aggregation of activities for which one designs a system, the more complex that system must be to satisfy the diversity. System complexity leads to operational complexity, and the more complex is the operation, the more difficult it is to learn.

The purchaser of office automation technology is interested in *the* office—his or her office. Only to the extent that his office's activities are interdependent with the activities of other offices, does he care whether or not the system is general purpose. In fact, the bias is likely to be for at least the appearance of having a tailor-made system, one designed to do the specific jobs at hand. Thus, specification from the point of view of the potential user of office technology may be quite different from that required by the producer. While the supplier needs to appreciate the position of the user, the reverse need not hold. The user is going to be less and less willing to adapt his needs to fit what the vendor has to supply, especially in this day of programmable technology in a competitive environment.

The *evaluation of specified technology,* whether from the perspective of the supplier or the user, concerns the extent to which the technology accomplishes that which it is designed to do. While this is the most straightforward of the four evaluation procedures mentioned, evaluations of this type are seldom conducted in a rigorous fashion. Perhaps the major reason for this sad state of affairs is that those who have committed themselves (and their budgets) to a given technology don't want to find out that they have made a poor commitment. The apparent assumption is that ignorance is bliss.

Measuring the impact of implemented technology involves looking at the side effects of its use. While equipment may do everything for which it is designed, it may create other problems at both individual and organizational (inter-individual) levels. The issue here is the impact that the use of the technology has on the individuals using it, from both psychological and physiological aspects, and on the organizational relationships among those individuals. For example, the author was involved in the evaluation of an elaborate computer-based logistics system which did everything its designers said it would do, and more. The problem was that its users, lower level managers, were able to bypass the traditional hierarchy. Decisions were made by the system in response to various inputs, without the need for intervention by the top of the organizational hierarchy. Once senior management perceived that they were no longer in control, they pulled the plug. The manual system with its formal hierarchical intervention was reinstated, even though this resulted in less efficient and less timely decisions. In addition to the effect on organizational relationships, one could recount a number of effects on individuals because of lowered motivation or poor man-machine interaction.

The last item of evaluation concerns *the implementation procedure* itself. It is not enough to design something which is useful and useable in principle, because if the technology is not perceived in that vein, it will be most difficult to have it accepted. Often the problem of "misperception" is caused by a poor plan of implementation. Thus the procedures for implementation also need to be examined to determine the degree to which they are effective. This evaluation should be separated from the evaluation of the technology itself and the measure of its impact on the individuals and organization using it. Admittedly, it is difficult to untangle these three aspects of evaluation. Nevertheless, one must have a knowledge of all three to avoid reaching an erroneous conclusion regarding the effect or the impact of the technology when the problem really arose because of how it was introduced.

Common Problems of Evaluation

There are several problems which are likely to arise during the evaluation of office automation technology. Once concerns familiarity. Most people involved with office automation have had experience working in an office at one time or another. Consequently, they believe they know what an office is.

Furthermore, most feel that they know what should go on in an office. Thus, they feel quite confident in their own determinations of whether or not the new technology is functioning as it should, and whether or not there are adverse side effects. We are not suggesting that one should ignore such "insights," but rather that these should be put into context. Everyone is going to view what takes place from a particular bias, and evaluations should take these into account.

Certain biases can be rather easily identified. For example, one who had to commit himself to purchase a piece of equipment is not in a good position to say that the equipment was a bad investment or that it had serious negative side effects. To reach this conclusion would be to admit that one had made a bad decision. Few people are willing to do that.

There are other obvious biases as well. The vendor of the equipment is unlikely to admit that his equipment did not perform as it should. If the system does not perform adequately, it is because it was misused, or the organizational system for using it was all wrong, or the maintenance was improper. Likewise, the manager who obtained something for his subordinate to use has a different outlook than the subordinate who has to use it. The manager may feel that he has enabled his subordinate to avoid doing tedious tasks so that the subordinate can concentrate on more creative work. The subordinate may believe, on the other hand, that the equipment he has been given is designed to replace him. Both points of view have to be taken into account.

Another problem which arises during evaluation is distinguishing between "needs" versus "wants." By *needs* we mean those aspects of one's being or one's tasks which are fundamental to the accomplishment of the tasks—they are the basis of conditions which must be satisfied to achieve high performance. These may be capable of being expressed or, more likely, they may have to be inferred by observation or questions about what one has to do and how one goes about doing it. By *wants* we are referring to expressed desired, which may or may not be directly related to needs. One may want something, such as to live in a nice climate, that has nothing to do with one's performance *per se.* Yet wants are more readily expressed than needs, often because one doesn't recognize basic needs. This distinction is raised simply because most of what we know about what one is to do on the job is obtained by questionnaires and interviews. These more often than not are designed to obtain data about one's wants (desires) rather than one's needs.

CONDUCTING THE RESEARCH

No attempt will be made here to cover all of the various aspects of research methodology one should know in order to conduct appropriate evaluations. Nevertheless, there are some issues relevant to the specification, evaluation and implementation of office automation technology which deserve some discussion.

For one thing, little of this work can be conducted in the laboratory. While human factors issues can be isolated and studied effectively in a microcosm of the real world, a study designed to establish specifications which reflect the needs of office workers cannot be. At least at the start, one must find out what office workers do. This cannot be done in the abstract. Furthermore, evaluating the effectiveness of prototype systems, measuring the impact these have on organizational behavior at both individual and collective levels, and studying problems of implementation, all require concrete situations. Thus, the stress here is on issues related to field research.

Data to be Collected

In essence there are answers to four different kinds of questions for which one gathers field data on office work. These are:

1. What one does,
2. What one thinks one does,
3. What one thinks about what one does, and
4. What one would like to be able to do.

While the differences among the four may not appear to be great, they are significant. In particular one should be aware of the distinction between categories 1) and 2). The reason is that most of the data obtained from field research are based on responses to questionnaires. While questions are often posed to determine what it is that one does, one can only respond by stating what one thinks one does, except in the rare case where "objective" measurements of what one does are available.

The third line of questioning, that which concerns what one thinks about what one does, is based on the proposition that attitudes influence the manner in which one executes what one is supposed to do. Data on attitudes, of course, are gathered on many factors other than just one's job. Regarding the prospects for office automation technology, researchers may wish to look at attitudes toward technology, toward the physical environment in which one works, toward the company for which one works, etc. All of these may affect a person's willingness to accept and effectively use computer based technology designed to assist him or her on the job.

Answers to the fourth category of questions are obtained far more frequently than the questions are asked. The reason is that when someone is asked what he or she does, often the response is biased toward what it is that they would like to do, or at least have the questioner think that they do. There is also an opposite effect which negates some of the value of this line of questioning. The author has found that respondents working for both government and industry are amazingly unimaginative. When asked what they would like to be able to do, most indicate that what they are doing is fine and that they can't think of any better way to do it. They get so caught up in action and reaction that they appear to lose the ability to reflect about their actions and reactions.

Field Research

There are three basic ways in which one can collect data on office activities and attitudes: observation, questionnaires and interviews. We will restrict our discussion of each to its most distinguished advantages and disadvantages.

Observation, whether done automatically by machine, or recorded by a third party or the respondent, is the only way in which one can get data about what one does in fact. The automatic recording of behavior, such as that which can be provided by almost any system that is computer controlled, has the advantage of accuracy and neutrality. It is non-obtrusive and unbiased to the extent that the user is not conscious that his behavior is being recorded. This, however, raises the question of ethics. Should one record the behavior of another without the latter's awareness? The consensus of opinion today would seem to be "no." But if one is aware that his behavior is being recorded, might not this influence his behavior? The answer is "yes," and as a consequence a certain degree of objectivity is lost.

Third party observation has been the most common method of collecting behavioral data. However, its use leads to the introduction of at least two biases. First, it is virtually impossible for an observer to remain neutral. A person's likes and dislikes affect what it is that he or she perceives and records. Second, third party observers in a real world environment (not in a laboratory with one-way glass or remotely operated cameras) are almost always observed by the subject of observation. As mentioned in the previous paragraph, when one knows that he or she is being observed, one's behavior may not be that which would take place if one was not being observed. Finally, the issue of cost cannot be ignored. Observers can follow only a very few people at the same time. As a consequence, either the sample size is small or the recording costs are very high.

The author has made extensive use of self-recorded observation—asking subjects to keep a journal or diary. Obviously subject bias will be found here since the recorder is also the observed. Still, if the behavior in question is not especially value loaded and if one records an event immediately after it occurs, objectivity remains reasonably high, certainly much higher than that based on recollection after a significant period of time. There are two other advantages to the use of self-recorded instruments. One is the large amount of data that can be obtained for a given cost. The other is that this is the only method of observation which permits the collection of cognitive activity. Answers to the question why one does something are obtainable.

Drawbacks to the diary exist which cannot be ignored. If one records behaviors immediately after they occur, this is an interruption to the normal flow of activities. Clearly, this might affect behavior. For example, one might not do something at a given point in time if one had to record doing it. Also, there is the ever present question of whether the data obtained by means of a self-recorded instrument reflect what one does, or what one thinks one does.

Questionnaires provide the biggest bang for the buck. If one is solely interested in the number of responses obtainable per dollar, the use of a questionnaire is the way to go. This is also the source of the major problem. They are so easy to implement that people seldom spend adequate time in questionnaire construction (the formulation of the questions and the measures to be used for the responses) and in sample selection. The assumption often appears to be the more data the merrier, though there is a limit to the number of questions a respondent is willing to answer.

Questionnaires have other attributes in addition to ease of use and ease of processing the responses. Perhaps the greatest advantage is the breadth of things one can cover. Everything from attitudes, to desires, to concerns, to elaborate descriptions can be gathered. The depth of response is limited only by one's ability at question formulation. But as has already been mentioned, question formulation is the greatest problem. While all respondents may read the same question, they may not perceive it in the same way. Problems of semantics are very difficult to avoid, and they make the interpretation of responses far more difficult than most users of questionnaires are willing to admit. This is particularly true for open-ended questions, although they permit greater insight than do closed-ended questions.

Interviews have the benefit of dialogue. This is especially advantageous when the researcher is not exactly sure what it is that he or she seeks. A dialogue permits a development of the question to the point where it can be clearly understood by both sides, as the issues of ambiguity and misinterpretation can usually be resolved. Interviews also provide considerable flexibility. For example, if one wishes to seek different data from each respondent, and if these data are to reflect characteristics unique to each subject, such data are appropriately obtained by interview.

The author has discovered another advantage of the interview in field research. It can be used effectively as a public relations tool. A major problem of field research is the suspicion on the part of the respondents that the data which they provide may be used against them and/or that the exercise is likely to be of little value, either to the respondent or to the world at large. Issues of this sort can be discussed during an interview, and a basis for continued cooperation can be established. Thus, the interview can be seen as a two-way street, as an opportunity for providing as well as collecting information.

While interview data are useful for insight, they do not provide a good basis for formal analysis. The problem of measurement is substantial, due both to the difficulties of interpreting responses and to the lack of cross-interviewer reliability. My perception of the meaning of a given response may differ substantially from yours. If interpretations differ, how can one aggregate results across a number of individuals? Finally, the problem of cost cannot be ignored. Each hour of interview requires an hour of the researcher's time.

Field Experimentation

The advantage of laboratory experiments is the control one can exercise over the research environment. This enhances the ability to study cause and effect relationships because extraneous factors can be eliminated, or at least managed. An ideal situation would be to have a "real world" laboratory where one can control the important factors, but in an operational rather than an artificial setting. A field experiment is a step toward this ideal.

Let us assume someone wishes to study the impact of a new office automation system in a native environment. Ideally he or she would like to find two identical operational environments. The new technology would be implanted in one. The other would act as a control. To study the dynamics of the situation measurements would be made on a number of organizational behavior dimensions in each organization over time, both before and after the implementation of the office automation system in the one. If several experimental and control environments existed, one could even conduct statistical analyses.

While field experiments, such as the one suggested above, are highly desirable, they are not without their problems. There is the question of whether or not the two (or more) environments being compared are in fact sufficiently similar so that the differences which are found after the fact can be attributed to the introduction of the new technology. Not only are identical organizations essentially non-existent, but certain important factors will always be outside of the researchers' control. For example, changes in management in one or both of the organizations being studied may have a far greater influence on the behavior being measured than the technology under investigation. Thus, actual control may be quite illusory.

Again there is the element of cost. Field research is expensive. Field research in several organizations is very expensive. Often the greatest constraint is time rather than money.

GUIDELINES FOR EVALUATION RESEARCH

Start by assuming that you know nothing. This is usually not far from the truth.

Context

Field research, particularly because it is difficult to control, requires that one find out as much as possible about the context of the study. While the subject of research may be a given office automation system, its use and the impact that it will have on organizational behavior may depend as much on a number of contextual factors.

For example, what are the objectives of the organizational units under study? Are they consistent with the use of the new technology? Who is going to use the equipment? What has been their relationship with others in the organization, particularly those who have suggested that they use the equipment? What is the physical environment in which the equipment will be operated? What alternative technologies are available? Who uses them, for what, how?

If the research program includes an analysis of the impact of a new technology, base line data should be obtained on several different types of organizational relations—the authority, work flow and informal structures. These are likely to be affected by and affect the use of integrated communication-information systems. Basically, the more one knows about the context of the specification, evaluation, impact and implementation of office automation technology, the less likely one is to make erroneous conjectures about its potential and actual use.

Step-by-Step Approach

Since we are exploring a relatively new terrain, we have no sound methodological base upon which to build. Thus, it is wise to follow a step-by-step procedure, evolving methods as experience is gained from their use.

The first step should be a pilot study designed to test the acceptability of the data collection instruments and procedures to the respondents. If they appear uncooperative or have difficulty answering certain questions or making certain responses, there is little point in continuing until the reasons for these problems are discovered and resolved.

Developing unambiguous questions and obtaining cooperation are only the first steps. The next few should concentrate on the analysis of the value of the data being obtained. Are they reliable? Do they appear to explain an adequate amount of the variance in observed behavior? If the answer to either question is "no," further revisions and testing are required. One secret to the successful use of feedback from early studies is not to be too proud to admit that the early efforts may have been off track. It is so easy to fall in love with one's own creation that researchers develop blinders against criticism. People hate to admit that the investment they have made in time and energy in the development of instruments and procedures may have been for naught. A safeguard is to have experienced *"No"* men evaluate early efforts. It even helps if they are a bit on the sadistic side, because they will delight in telling one where he or she went wrong.

A step-by-step approach, while it is desirable from the standpoint of developing methodology, creates problems for data base management and analysis. This is especially true when one recognizes that questions which are asked at the beginning of a study may be quite different from those one would like to ask later on. The key is to err on the side of getting too much data rather than too little in the beginning, on defining the context too broadly rather than too narrowly. Data can always be discarded. Rarely can they be collected successfully after the fact (though many try to do so).

This suggests starting with a few in-depth studies. Not only does this enhance the ability to find variability in the data that appears to be tied to behaviors of interest, but it also provides a sound basis for answers to the question of what instruments and procedures should be used for a much larger, in-breadth study. Methods used for early, thorough studies are not going to be acceptable for the large samples which are needed for statistical analysis. Yet the early studies should be used as a basis for the latter if one is interested in valid analyses.

Data Interpretation Issues

A discussion of design and analysis leads naturally to issues involved in data interpretation. At least four deserve to be mentioned: *efficiency versus effectiveness, short run versus long run, substitution versus augmentation,* and ˜*reorganization.*

The question of *efficiency versus effectiveness* is being ignored by most of the research on office automation technology. Although a number of people pay lip service to the potential value added from such equipment, current research efforts are focused on proving that it will cut white-collar labor costs. The question is: can the new technologies help us do the same things that we are doing now, but more cheaply? This most businessmen can understand. Unfortunately, as many have discovered, it is far more difficult to support increased effectiveness. For example, what is it worth to have more readable reports? What does it add to the profit and loss statement?

This brings up the second issue, especially since cost cuts are likely to be more relevant in the short run while increases in effectiveness are realized only over the long run. But this is not the only *short run versus long run* issue. Another of significance concerns system flexibility. How much is system adaptability worth? Should system specifications and evaluation be based solely on current needs, or should they consider the trends of organizational uses? If the latter is deemed to be more appropriate, how does one study the future in today's environment? Is a step-by-step implementation program an appropriate solution, one designed to look at the dynamics of the use of technologies over time? What are the costs of such an approach?

A discussion of *substitution versus augmentation* really has to go back to the purposes or objectives of an organization. But this too ties into the issue of efficiency versus effectiveness. Substitution is generally undertaken if one can get the same output at a lower cost. Augmentation suggests value added. The first use of the term with respect to office systems was by Doug Englebart.†

Here he was thinking strictly in terms of value added, of enabling people to do things they could not do before, or certainly could not do as easily. As a consequence, the thought was that the system would augment one's skills.

Perhaps subsitiution versus augmentation is also a reflection of the level at which the equipment is to be used. One thinks of a substitution for clerks and others who are doing routine jobs, for they will not be making the decisions regarding the introduction of the technology. However, when office automation moves into the executive's office, it is hard to envision that it will be accepted on any other basis than one of augmentation. An executive is not going to purchase or lease something which will replace himself. He will use it only if it assists him, if it augments his capabilities, if it makes the job to be accomplished somewhat easier to perform, if it provides a more effective outcome.

Reorganization is raised as a problem of interpretation because most people seem to be ignoring the interdependence between organizational structure and integrated computer-based communication-information systems. Yet, there are too many examples of the introduction of information systems that failed because they were inappropriate to the existing organizational structure. Either the system has to be tailored to a given network (or an overlay of several networks), or the networks have to be

---

† Englebart, D.C., "A Conceptual Framework for the Augmentation of Man's Intellect," in *Vistas in Information Handling,* Howerton and Weeks (Editors), Spartan Books, Washington, D.C., 1963, pp. 1-29.

redesigned to conform to the design of the system. As the two go hand in hand, an effective use of office automation is likely to require some adjustments on both sides. As a consequence, behavioral and software and hardware systems design are going to have to be undertaken in concert if the latter are to be accepted.

AN EXAMPLE OF EVALUATION RESEARCH

This was a study designed to evaluate various features and the impact of a new software controlled private branch exchange. We will mention the data collection instruments and procedures used and the rationale for each. In addition we will comment on the apparent effectiveness of certain of these.

Overall Plan

Two things were of paramount importance in establishing the methods to be used. First, we had nothing to build on; we were not aware of similar studies having been undertaken elsewhere. Second, we were to study impact, and thus we wanted to know what the situation was before the equipment was installed. This entailed a before and after survey of the organizations accepting the equipment.

The first point led to two conclusions. First, we needed a pilot study of the methods and procedures before using them on the organizations to be examined over time. Second, we needed to use a wide variety of instruments and collect data on a large number of possibly relevant dimensions since we had no basis upon which to exclude them. We preferred to err on the side of inclusion rather than exclusion, provided we could get the subject organizations to cooperate. Hence, we used a variety of questionnaires, a self-recorded communications diary and a semi-structured interview, both before and after the installation of the electronic PBX.

The general procedure commenced with group sessions of about 15 people. Here we introduced ourselves and the whys and wherefores of the study. All subjects were then to complete a variety of questionnaires. These sessions lasted about an hour and one-half on the average. The following week, after having analyzed the questionnaire data, we interviewed each of the subjects. We began by asking for the reason behind certain extreme responses on the questionnaire. The next week we asked each person to keep a diary of his or her next 100 communications. During these three weeks we also collected data on the physical environment, the communication and information equipment available to each person, and the organizational authority and work flow structures.

Questionnaires

Four different kinds of questionnaires were used. The first was closed ended, the responses based on a five point Likert scale ranging from "strongly agree" to "strongly disagree." Questions covered attitudes toward communication technologies, communication situations (what would you do if. . . .) and one's job. In addition data were obtained on organizational climate and personality as measured from an interpersonal communications point of view. In each case we though that the factor might be related to how one would use telecommunications and the features attached to the new PBX. While most dimensions were correlated at a statistically significant level with communications behavior, the amount of variance explained was not great.

On the assumption that interpersonal sentiments might affect how one would wish to communicate with another, we measured them along ten dimensions among those who must communicate with each other because of their jobs. Each dimension was measured using a semantic differential scale. The findings were insignificant. Interpersonal communication behavior and interpersonal sentiments were not significantly correlated. Apparently task considerations dominated in our study.

We also used an open ended question, one looking at "critical incidents." Interestingly, even though we asked people to describe especially favorable and/or unfavorable communication experiences, particularly as they related to the use of communciations technology, not one person related an incident where technology was relevant. Every response focused on interpersonal relations.

The fourth type of questionnaire used was labeled "Interaction Analysis." Its purpose was to provide a framework within which one could describe one's job in terms of its communications content. We asked each subject to estimate the portion of work time spent in communication, with whom, about what, using what support systems. People had considerable difficulty with this form since they had not thought about their jobs before in terms of communication requirements. While the data collected were quite complete, we found that they had low cross-check reliability. On the average, less than a third of each person's communication time was corroborated by the other party. If A thought he spent 25 percent of his time communicating with B, B thought he spent only 5 percent of his time communicating with A. This is one example of the problems of recollection data.

Interviews

The first part of each interview was somewhat structured as it was based on the responses to the various questionnaires. These were processed prior to the interviews. If a person gave an extreme response, we attempted to find out why they might have differed from the others. The interviews then moved toward a general discussion of the subject's job so that we could understand better what each person did from his or her point of view. We took this oral description and asked how the job might be aided by technology, without the constraints of cost or feasibility. This latter part of the interview was usually disappointing. Most people could only think about doing their job in the way that they were doing it. Seldom did they see how it might be accomplished more efficiently or effectively.

Communications Diary

The major purposes of the diary were to obtain data on the communication networks in use in each organization and on the telecommunication features used, and to act as a check on the "Interaction Analysis." We wanted to know who was communicating with whom, for how long, by what mode of communication, using what telecommunication features, involving what interaction processes, etc. Because the cross-check reliability was found to be around 50 percent, these were the data that were used as a measure of "what one does." The diary data provided us with an interesting picture of the organization, as exemplified by the communication networks, in contrast to the formal structure.

Other Data

Everyone was located spacially with respect to all others in any given study. This led to the discovery that the greatest amount of variance in mode choice was explained by distance. While this is no great surprise—we speak in person to those who are located near us and by telephone to those who are located some distance away—physical location is usually based less on the need to communicate than on status or departmental affiliation.

CONCLUSION

If "office automation" is to bring about the revolution that so many are forecasting, it will be because the technology provided satisfies the fundamental work related needs of its users. Design to meet these needs is not going to be accomplished by haphazard approaches. The clientele, today's and tomorrow's managers, are too aware to accept equipment which doesn't do what they want and need it to do. And these needs are not going to be uncovered just by chance.

The first step to determine these needs is to gain an understanding of what goes on in an/the office. This had to be the basis for any evaluation. We discussed various methods for making this determination. The focus was on field research and the strengths and weaknesses of its various components. The ingredients we described are not particularly new, but the uses to which we suggest they be put are. Emphasis must now be placed on both the activities which go on in an office *and* how these are integrated into "organized" networks of people and equipment which are capable of accomplishing given objectives. Just as integration is the key to successfully understanding an office, so is integration the key to successfully equipping one.

CHAPTER 11

PRODUCTIVITY ASSESSMENT OF OFFICE INFORMATION SYSTEMS TECHNOLOGY

James H. Bair
Bell Northern Research
Mountain View, California

SUMMARY

There has not been an adequate assessment of the pervasive impacts of automated office information systems (AOIS). Such an assessment, particularly of the impacts of AOIS on productivity, requires a framework that defines the scope of the measurement, a model of the hypothesized impacts and benefits, and a thorough enumeration of the variables; as well as an assessment plan that organizes the standard methods into a time frame to capture all relevant variability and to isolate causal relationships. The variables are at the organizational performance level where the combined benefits of AOIS are realized or thwarted. New office systems incorporate all personnel into a unified system that may change the character of the organization; consequently, this approach is designed to capture the collective effects of changes at all levels of the organization.

INTRODUCTION

Automated office information systems (AOIS) are being explored by government and industry to such an extent that office work may be completely transformed by the mid 1980s. Most large corporations and government agencies are planning or implementing "office of the future systems." The author is aware of planned office automation prototypes that represent more than $10 million in investments. Lower capability word processing systems are being installed at an annual rate of close to $1 billion. Approximately $25,000 in capital investment is made for each manufacturing worker; the traditional investment of only $2,000 for each office worker[1] is rapidly catching up and projections place it at $10,000 by 1990. At the same time, computer technology costs are dropping at rates ranging from 20% to 40% per year, permitting greater capability for the investment.

The potential market is vast. Of the estimated 3.5 million offices in the United States, about 1.5 million are considered large enough for some form of AOIS. As Standard and Poors points out, there is plenty of room for the improvements in productivity that are claimed by system manufacturers. Indeed, improvements in productivity have been demonstrated for limited applications such as secretarial typing.[2,3,4] Discussion of the benefits and potentials of AOIS have been addressed for other areas by Uhlig[5] and special issues of trade journals such as Datamation.[6] A few assessments of AOIS implementations have been publicly reported that present limited empirical evidence of productivity improvements.[7,8]

However, there are no studies that adequately measure the impact of AOIS on productivity. There are three reasons for this: (1) the resources have not been allocated for large enough test implementations, (2) current implementations are not mature enough to provide a valid test bed, and (3) a comprehensive, valid methodology has not been developed and applied.

An assessment of the impact of AOIS is a difficult problem, and cannot be made without the support of a large institution. If an institution will make a commitment to build a valid test bed, as certain government agencies are currently planning, then the expertise and knowhow for evolving a mature implementation can be applied.[9] The development of the needed comprehensive assessment methodology is the subject of this paper.

The assessment of the large-scale and pervasive impacts of AOIS requires the development of a framework that defines the scope of the measurement, a model of the hypothesized impacts and benefits, and a thorough enumeration of the variables, as well as an assessment plan that organizes well developed methods into a time frame to capture all relevant variability and to isolate causal relationships. The variables are at the organizational level where the combined benefits of AOIS are actually realized or thwarted. Automated office information systems incorporate managers and professionals, as well as clerical personnel, into a unified system that may change the character of the organization; consequently, the methodology must capture the collective effects of changes in performance for all personnel.

FRAMEWORK DEFINING THE SCOPE OF THE MEASUREMENT

Productivity is affected by the performance of many components of an office automation system. These components differ greatly in the scope of variables that must be taken into account for meaningful productivity measurement. We have organized these components into four levels where performance at each level is dependent upon the performance of the level below it in a hierarchy of detail. The choice of a level for a field evaluation will define the variables that must be taken into account and will narrow the scope of the evaluation. The definition of levels of performance also permits a framework into which to organize the results of previously reported studies. The level of a study will indicate the validity of the results.

Level 1: Equipment Performance

Equipment performance can be determined in an isolated laboratory setting. Such a determination includes only the performance of equipment using a highly skilled operation, and does not take into account useability, ease of learning, or the management of operation. It does include reliability (failure rate), equipment error rate, execution speed, required maintenance, and equipment capabilities or features. Concerns about human factors include ergonomics (display resolution, keyboard layout, etc.) and operation effort such as the keystrokes per operation. Operation effort may be determined by time and motion studies.

Level 2: Throughput Performance

Throughput performance is dependent upon equipment performance but includes the larger context of operator performance, individual differences, work-flow control, operating methods, learning rates, and the variations in input and output. Throughput is most commonly measured by the production rate in an operational implementation, for example, the number of lines typed per day. Human factors are indirectly measured by error rate and increases in errors due to fatigue. Cost factors involve the complex tradeoff between the output per unit labor and the utilization rate that can be maintained as a result of useability and available capabilities. The effect of different features, such as display versus teletypewriter access, are measured at this level.

Level 3: Organizational Performance

Organizational performance is the result of the equipment performance, throughput performance, and personnel performance. Production typically is measured by the end-product processes that are completed on schedule. However, numerous factors affect personnel performance beyond the throughput performance of the equipment, making personnel performance much more difficult to quantify. Factors such as the attitudes, morale, management style, organizational climate, office operating procedures, and decision time must be taken into account. Performance indicators include personnel absenteeism, turnover, overtime, and labor costs. Labor costs may be determined on a per process basis or on a per unit time basis. It is necessary to establish the goals and functions of the organization and translate these into performance criteria that in essence represent the *raison d'etre* for the organization.

Organizational performance also has a qualitative dimension that is more difficult to measure. However, the ultimate judge of quality is the recipient of the end-products of the organizational unit. In office where the primary product is textual (reports, plans, papers, etc.), the management is likely to be the recipient. To measure quality, we can obtain subject judgements from the product recipients by using well developed measurement instruments from the social sciences, such as those used in marketing. Similar instruments can also be used to rate the quality of services and processes where specific products are difficult to define.

Level 4: Institutional Performance

Institutional performance refers here to the economic context of the organization's performance[10] which may cause fluctuations that must be taken into account. For example, an austerity program may decrease morale and provide inadequate resources to meet organizational goals. Lack of personnel or support services could cancel any advantages of increased processing capability. Conversely, economic conditions could place high demand and workload on the organization resulting in temporarily increased performance. The general state of the economy affects the availability of labor, materials and services, support costs, and so on. Government policies, sales, seasonal variations, and earnings all place different pressures on an organization that ultimately affect the performance of individuals. Separating effects such as these from those of the office automation system is necessary in order to determine the system's impact on productivity.

For example, most studies of word processing equipment have been at level two. Essentially, the equipment has been examined in isolation from higher level factors such as personnel management style and the needs of the organization. Thus, results that show an increase in typing production (lines per day) represent ideal circumstances, that is, what the equipment is capable of if the operator is at maximum efficiency. However, that efficiency is dependent upon management style and other more global variables from higher levels, and is typically much lower in the wider context.

MODEL OF HYPOTHESIZED IMPACTS AND BENEFITS

A model of office information processing is necessary to guide the development of assessment methodology and the assessment process. The model provides hypotheses of the impact of AOIS on the office. The impact of a complete AOIS is pervasive, affecting most organizational behavior. Because the office is a complex information system with formal and informal relationships, the hypothetical impacts must take into account the characteristics of office processes. The model is potentially extremely complex— the office is a mini-social system, where the informal personal relations can play as important a role as the formally defined responsibilities. Rather than venture too deeply into the labyrinth of the psycho-social system, the following structure identifies some characteristics of office processes, categorizes the hypothesized benefits, and identifies known impacts.

The structure of the model is dependent upon dividing what is essentially one continuous process into discrete processes. Perfect identification of discrete processes is simply not feasible, because information is flowing in offices in a relatively unpredictable manner, especially compared with industrial manufacturing processes. Hence, salient features of an office such as individuals, organizational boundaries, abrupt time delays in the information flow, and the differing purposes of the information are used to identify discrete processes.

Office processes are categorized into: maintenance or end-product processes, and individual, group, or organization processes depending upon the context. Processes occur in parallel, and clustered together, represent the various functions of the office. Functions are the organizational roles of offices, indicated by the traditional labels such as accounting, contract processing, and research. Office functions support the mission of an institution, for example, archive maintenance, banking, and air defense. Processes subsume several activities, which are the specific behaviors occurring within processes, including composing, writing, talking and typing. This structure forms a descriptive hierarchy as shown in Figure 1.

Maintenance processes differ from end-product processes in that they are ongoing and do not directly produce a product, but support the end-product processes. Maintenance processes include personnel records, accounting and inventory, and tend to be routine. End-products are identified when a completed information unit is forwarded to another group or office for continued processing or as input to other processes such as decision making. A typical kind of end-product is a report or a form, which is a discrete, traceable information unit, and tends to have unique content. The identification of end products permits the evaluation of end-product processes on the basis of the character- istics of the product, for example, timeliness, and perceived quality. Analysis of end-product processes provides a meaningful indicator of performance and will be discussed under "methods."

The classification of processes by individual, group, and organization is based on the extent of the process—whether the process involves an individual, extends to a group, or extends to some part of the organization. For example, individuals may perform numerous processes that do not extend to other persons such as making personal phone lists. Another example would be an end-product that never leaves a group of co-workers; under these circumstances, its characteristics tend to be quite different from its characteristics if it is intended for another office. To focus evaluation, it is necessary to specify a class of processes, because the variables for each class vary greatly. Individual processes include psychological factors such as cognition, perception,

Figure 1
Hierarchical Office Description

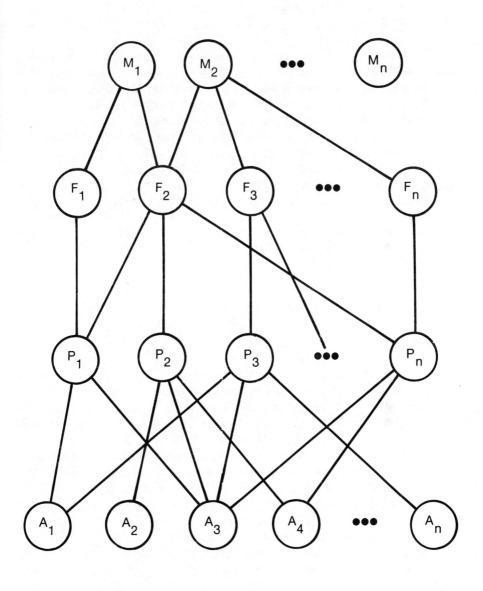

M = Missions
F = Functions
P = Processes — End and Maintenance
A = Activities

conceptualization, and personal planning, which, although they impact upon productivity, can be set aside when organizational performance is of concern. This discussion will focus on the class of organizational processes, which indirectly reflects individual and group processes.

When processes are described for the complete office system, the result represents information flow.[11] Tracing information flow shows the interdependencies between parallel and sequential processes. Information flow may be mapped into a network, showing timing constraints and bottlenecks. The information-flow network can be carried to great descriptive detail. Methods for empirically establishing information flow are described later.

A major result of describing information flow is the identification of media, e.g., written, digital, or voice. The conversion of information from one media to another represents a critical point that I call media transformation. Media transformations are bottlenecks in information flow and require inordinate resources. The reduction of media transformation is one hypothesized benefit area in the model of AOIS benefits.

Potential Benefit Areas

The impacts of AOIS may be classified into five areas of potential benefit: (1) media transformation, (2) shadow functions, (3) automation, (4) timing, and (5) control. Each of these areas represents costs savings in this model; if an impact of AOIS results in benefits in one or more of these areas, it represents improved performance to the extent of proper system implementation. The degree to which the potential improvement is realized depends upon numerous variables that are discussed later.

Media Transformation. Media transformations—changing the medium of the message—are necessary between speaking and writing, handwriting and typewriting, dictation and typewriting, phoning and writing, computer and hardcopy, local copy and mailed copy, and so on. The reduced number of media transformations is a benefit that depends upon the extent of the AOIS implementation in the organization. The more media that are automated within a single system, the fewer the transformations between different media. For example, the primary support cost in communication activity is form preparation, packaging, and mailing written correspondence. This cost would be eliminated by a mail system in a single medium as is the case with a computer mail system. Messages are typically stored as paper media organized in the omnipresent file cabinet. (See Figure 2.)

Figure 2
Example of Media Transformation for
End Product Process

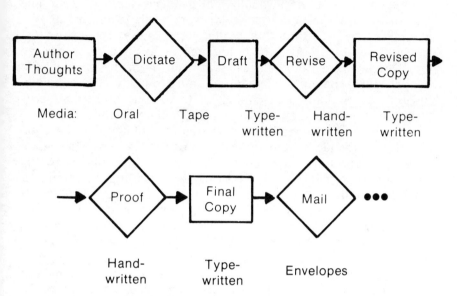

Shadow Functions. "Shadow functions" are the unforeseen, unpredicatable, time consuming activities that are associated with accomplishing any task, but do not contribute to productivity.[12] They follow workers through all daily activities, but usually are not noticed. For example, when a phone call is made, there are several potential shadow functions: a misdialed number, a busy signal, the recipient temporarily out of the office, the recipient gone for some period of time, or a bad connection. Meetings can result in a number of shadow functions, for example, delays in arrival (traffic jams, not finding the meeting location) or other delays in starting (one member of the group being late), and interruptions.

Automation. Automation benefits are derived from the replacement or elimination of manual processes by machine processes, thus eliminating the labor required. Automation benefits do not result if labor is merely involved in a different process than before automation. Automation benefits are the most obvious, but the actual labor reduction needs to be measured to show cost benefits. A number of impacts of AOIS have been shown to substitute for labor, and benefits of some of these impacts are projected by the model.

Timing. Timing benefits are derived from the direct savings resulting from reduced waiting time (labor savings), faster decisions to realize more opportunities and move capital and other business resources more rapidly. For example, secretaries are idle 18% of the avarage day, waiting for work;[13] this idleness could be minimized by AOIS in this model. Idle capital results in lost revenues, and a reduction in idle resources in a hypothesized direct benefit. Less tangible benefits result from the capability to communicate needed information more quickly, for example, through computer mail systems, or to turn around documents faster in an automated document production cycle.

Control. The benefits of increased control in an organization are closely related to timing because control is dependent upon timely information. However, the realization of control benefits requires that processes, functions, or missions be changed. Control benefits depend upon improved information flow to the things being controlled. Improvements in control are reflected by less information to effect more rapid changes. Improved control will result in fewer surprises to management, permitting better planning and less crises driven behavior.

In this model, benefits result from impacts, but not all impacts are beneficial. Impacts are derived from several years of experimental implementations of systems in laboratory and real environments.[7,8] Impacts generally fall into four categories: (1) general office support, (2) document production, (3) communication, and (4) data processing support. These categories are not mutually exclusive, but facilitate the structuring of impacts by the kind of function they are typically associated with.

To show the hypothetical benefits of AOIS, this model relates the extensive list of impacts to the benefit areas. This provides a guide to assessing the quantitative payoff from AOIS. Some impacts may appear to be benefits; however, an adequately defined relationship to organizational productivity has not yet been established. Impacts may result in benefits in more than one benefit area—the relationships are shown in the matrix in Table 1.

CAUSAL VARIABLES

The model of AOIS impact is not complete without establishing what variables cause what impacts. To have a valid assessment strategy, it is necessary first to establish the theoretical causal factors. This will ensure that the requisite implementation of equipment and procedures for impacts is established. Desired impacts are identified by the potential benefit described by the

Table 1
Exemplary Impacts of AOIS and Benefit Areas*

	Media Transformations	Shadow Functions	Benefit Areas Automation	Timing	Control
1. General office impacts					
Immediate availability of information	2	4	3	5	4
Idle time reduction	4	4		5	3
Turnaround time reduction		5		5	
Reduced work fluctuation		3		4	5
Reduced routine travel needs		3		4	2
Wider range of contacts for increased special travel		?			5
Reduced work interruptions		5		4	2
Increased flexibility in work hours		4		4	
Extended work day		4		4	
Extended work week		4		4	
Increased flexibility in work location		4	3		2
Work from home		4	3		2
Work while on travel		4	3		2
Increased management communication		3		4	5
Obsolescence of "line of sight" management		1		4	5
Increased span of control				4	5
Faster information distribution				5	
Easier communication with distant levels of management		3			5
Materials saving: paper, filespace	5		4		
2. Text processing capabilities impacts					
Immediate and automatic distribution and routing	4	4	4	5	5
Storage in same media (e.g., digital)	5	4	4		
Higher accuracy, fewer errors		5	4		
Information filtering				5	4
Power keyboarding		4	5		
Reusable text storage ("canned" text)	3	3	5	2	
Text data base storage and automated retrieval	5		5	4	
Interactive formatting online	5	4	5	2	
Automatic formatting	4	3	5		
Automatic indexing and KWIC	2		5		
Automatic Table of Contents	2		5		
Global editing (1 edit automatically repeated)	2		5		

Table 1 (continued)
Exemplary Impacts of AOIS and Benefit Areas*

Impacts	Media Transformations	Shadow Functions	Automation	Timing	Control
			Benefit Areas		
Data processing integration with text	5	3	3	3	
Automated text data base management			5		4
Automatic forms preparation and storage	4	4	5		
Direct output to photocomposition	5		4		
Graphics editing, transmission, and storage with text	5	1	4		
Automatic spelling correction	2	1	5		
Automatic archival control	4	3	5	2	3
Large size document management		2			4
Shared data bases, local and remote access	4	1		3	
Access control limited to selected groups					5
Document revision without retyping		3	5	4	
Cross reference automation (and maintenance)			5	2	
Proofreading reduction	4	3	5		
Document structure editing and viewing online	1		4	3	
High speed printing	3			4	
Automated coordination and sign-off			5	4	4
Automated production routing and scheduling		2	3	4	5
Reduced professional handwriting	5	3		2	
Lessened dependence on secretary	4	2	5	4	3
3. Communication impacts (message switching)					
Decreased face-to-face routine meetings		?		5	?
Loss of face-to-face nonverbal information	3				?
Increased rate of information transfer		3		5	
Reduced meeting scheduling		4		4	
Optimum time for composing, reading, and responding may be selected		5		3	
No interruptions of meetings		5		4	
Alternative modes of communicating					
Digital communication of text and data	5	3		2	
Remote management realistic because of combined impacts					5

Table 1 (continued)
Exemplary Impacts of AOIS and Benefit Areas*

Impacts	Media Transfor- mations	Shadow Functions	Benefit Areas Auto- mation	Timing	Control
Decrease in use of telephone and mail	4	5	3	5	1
Increased accessibility of work to others		2		5	3
Physical collocation not necessary			4		
No simultaneous activity necessary		4		5	
Added capabilities					
Permanent, searchable, stored record of messages	5	3	4	2	1
One action for general information distribution		3	5	2	1
Fast delivery at low costs	1	4	5	5	
Automatic distribution		3	5	4	2
Automatic headers		3	5		
Increased vertical and horizontal communication		2		5	5
Wider range of contacts					4
4. Data processing support impacts					
Direct accessibility of data to decision maker	4		5	5	5
Immediate access to data (no intermediary)	4			5	5
Continually updated databases		3		4	
Capability of processing text-embedded data	5				

*Benefit projection rated on a 5-point scale, 5 points = highest benefit of impact.
(Based on studies such as references 7, 8, and 25.)

model. The requisite conditions that will result in the desired impacts are represented by a certain value for each causal variable and these values are interdependent. In the case of descriptive variables, they are numeric. The list of descriptive variables and alternative values is too extensive to present here; however, a sample list is shown in Table 2.

In some cases, there is a fine line between the different variable values, for example, the difference between "textual drafts" and "typing reports" under "characteristics of application." Changes in the variable values will result in changes in the results of the quantitative measures discussed later.

Table 2
Variable Areas

1. Organization of services

2. Principal user access to services

3. Equipment type

4. Equipment interface

5. Characteristics of application

6. Workload distribution and conditions

7. Input type

8. Training method

9. Functions available as integrated part of system

10. Physical location

11. Physical environment

12. Human variables

A crucial and difficult question to answer is how do changes in these causal variables change the measurement results? For example, does the use of "multiple single stations" instead of a "centralized system" change the "job completion" rate? If we could predict the effect of changing these variables, we would have a model of office work that would obviate further research. There is little conclusive empirical data about these relationships. The variables and other aspects of the model serve as a structure from which to refine research questions and procedures for empirical studies.

MEASURES

The measures are derived from studying the equipment and office processes for those discrete units that can be counted. The units of measure are linear and interval (i.e., interval scaled) and thus can be used for direct numeric comparisons. Each measure is used at only one level of the performance framework, which shows the scope and thus the limits of the conclusions that can be based on the measure. Measures are made according to the methods described later. A sample list is presented in Table 3.

Table 3

Representative Measures at Each of Level of Performance

Level 1: Equipment performance

1. Machine error rate

2. Performance compared to manufacturer's specifications

3. Reliability (up-time)

4. Response time

5. Breakdown threshold (load at which no longer useful)

6. The number of features compared to comprehensive checklist

7. Keystrokes per machine operation

8. Cost per unit time

9. Cost per machine operation

Level 2: Throughput performance

1. User error rate

2. Learning rate

3. Lines per unit time

4. Pages per unit time

5. Utilization rate (function of cost per unit time)

6. Output per person hour

7. Utilities and services consumption rate

8. Operator maintenance rate

Level 3: Organizational Performance

1. End-product completion rate and labor

2. End-product turnaround time

3. Interpersonal communication rate and labor

4. Daily activities (labor determined for each activity)

5. Labor performance: absenteeism, turn over, overtime, salary changes

Table 3 (continued)
Representative Measures at Each of
Level of Performance

6. Objective attainment and goal achievement (number of times missed, rating of how close)

7. Costs: operating personnel, overhead, equipment, maintenance, supplies, amortization

8. Decision turnaround time

9. Maintenance process labor

10. Informational surprises

Level 4: Institutional Performance

1. Total labor costs

2. Capital (money cost)

3. Raw materials

4. Miscellaneous goods (depreciation) and services

5. The above four factors divided into total output = total productivity

6. General economic indicators: including GNP, inflation rate, dollar value

7. Seasonal economic indicators

ASSESSMENT PLAN

The foregoing sections establish the setting for empirical studies of the impact of AOIS on offices; this section briefly describes the assessment plan. The model of AOIS impact provides hypotheses about impact that result from certain values for the related variables. The measures can establish the variable values where they are not obvious from direct observation of the office and the AOIS equipment. Measurement must be planned to minimize interference of extraneous variables with those that support or reject the hypotheses.

However, the measurements alone are essentially static and do not reflect the changes that occur over time. In terms of time, the measurements represent a "snapshot" of conditions and do not permit the causal relationships to be established. Obviously, the array of variables at a given time must be related to those at a later time. If the variable list is comprehensive, we can say that changes in some variables are causal to other, dependent variables on the list. Isolating the specific causal relationships requires a plan (experimental design) that controls variability.

Causal relationships can be established by controlling all changes—variables—that may influence a particular causal relationship. Variable control is the most difficult problem in assessment, and this is reflected in the lack of controlled studies to date. The model hypothesizes that variations in the organization, such as management style and economic pressures, will cause variations in productivity. Variables of this kind must be controlled during a measurement period of sufficient length to permit the variables that support or reject the hypotheses to change significantly.

Although the model permits the identification of those variables that must either be held constant or monitored during the assessment, it does not specifically address extraneous variables that are introduced by the act of conducting a study. Whenever an assessment is based on changes over time, the standard extraneous variables including maturation, history, mortality, test effects, instrumentation, selection, and Hawthorne effects must also be controlled insofar as is possible. This control is possible by implementing a "field experimental design" that uses comparison groups. Because it is not necessary to maintain the experimental rigor of scholarly research, the design will be referred to as a "controlled assessment plan" that is proposed to offer enough control to assess significant changes in productivity. Further discussion of control in field studies will not be offered here—it is essentially the study of experimental procedure and research design for the social sciences.[14]

The controlled assessment plan provides the optimum control of independent and extraneous variables. It requires a minimum of three offices that are to be compared by description and measurement. Descriptive results are especially important because the individuals cannot be randomly selected, and offices vary considerably in missions and functions. Thus, individual and office differences must be analyzed as potential causal factors to any measured changes. The descriptive assessment is as important as the quantitative measurement in this plan, because description is the basis of determining the representativeness of results. Faced with the snapshot nature of measurement, it is imperative that the measurements are of representative time periods.

The three offices to be compared are: (1) the AOIS user group, (2) a similar office where performance is optimized manually, and (3) an office that is not changed. All three offices receive the same measurements according to the same schedule. Analysis of results is by a three-way comparison: between the groups at the beginning of the assessment, between the pre- and post-assessment, and between the groups at the end of assessment. The differences between group one pre-assessment and post-assessment that do not appear in the other groups are the result of the AOIS. Conclusions must be carefully drawn based on a thorough descriptive analysis of all the variables and any serendipity events during the assessment.

Differences between groups two and three from pre- to post-assessment are the result of the manual optimization of group two's performance. The influence of extraneous variables such as test effects is minimized by the identical measurement of the groups, which are matched as much as possible in the operational setting. Hawthorne effects, which tend to be high in productivity assessments, are controlled by the attention given to group two that approximates the attention resultant from system implementation for group one. Other extraneous variables, such as maturation and mortality, are monitored and, if necessary, equalized across groups during the assessment period.

The assessment period should be a minimum of six months, and ideally, one year based on the author's experience. Profound changes in working methods and habits, significant learning efforts, and system implementation problems must be overcome for valid assessment.[9] Past experience has shown that the lack of a mature system implementation interfered with valid assessment. The assessment period is intended to permit a relatively large scale system implementation to mature. Regardless of the time and the control, a large percentage change in performance is necessary for conclusive results. (See Figure 3.)

ASSESSMENT METHODS

The methods for measurement and description of the three offices include some redundancy to overcome the limitations of assessment in an operational setting. The assessment plan provides the control necessary for validity—the methods must have the sensitivity to capture changes in a small population during a constrained time period. By employing a variety of methods, including quantitative and qualitative, direct and indirect, the large set of relevant variables can be monitored for control and valid measurement of change.

Figure 3
Controlled Assessment Plan

	Pre-Assessment	Assessment Period		Post-Assessment
AOIS User Group*	Description and Measurement of Variables	Training and Implementation	Monitoring Observing Interviewing	Description and Measurement of Variables
Manually Optimized Group	Same	Organizational Development and Improvement	Same	Same
Group Not Changed	Same	No Perturbation	Observing	Same

Methods   Analysis

*Group = office between 15 and 20 persons minimum.

Because this approach is directed at level three, organizational performance, the methods do not address equipment or throughput performance, which are included only insofar as they influence organizational performance. Organizational performance is a composite of the numerous processes within an office, each of which may change. The basic assumption here, that productivity improvement is only valid if it can be demonstrated at the organizational level, requires that methods address offices, not just typing pools or the like. This section briefly describes the following methods:

Functional Analysis   Communication Audit

Equipment Feature Analysis   Work Time-Measurement

Interviews   End-Product Tracking

Organizational History   Proficiency Testing

Attitude Scaling

Functional Analysis

Description of the missions and functions of the offices being assessed is the basis for controlling these variables. The offices being compared should have similar missions and functions. The mission serves as a criterion for judging the performance of an office.

Functions also serve as criteria and, in addition, must be considered for automation potential. Low automation potential could cause little change in performance for the office using AOIS, but would not indicate a failure of the AOIS.

The analysis first identifies functions that are then weighted for automation potential and entered as the rows in a "function organization matrix." Weighting is based upon the number of benefit-weighted impacts for each function (see Table 1). The columns represent the offices being considered for assessment or being considered for comparison, and the intersection represents whether or not that function exists in that office—if the function does exist, the intersection is assigned the benefit-weighted value. The weighted column totals are indicators of overall AOIS potential.

Equipment Feature Analysis

The potential features of the equipment represent variables that have a causal relationship to AOIS impact. The AOIS impact will be affected by the number of features available, for example, underlining or multiple type fonts. We have compiled an extensive feature list based upon manufacturer specifications and analysis of ideal equipment needs. The impact of feature is represented by a "feature-impact matrix" similar to that for functions. The intersections represent a weighted project of the feature-impact relationship—a high value would indicate that the feature contributed to an impact that has high benefit.

Interviews

Interviews of all members of the offices, using highly structured and open-ended formats, will provide much of the descriptive information, including serendipity events, missions, functions, and other characteristics of the organization, and management's criteria for performance. Workflow bottlenecks, resource needs, workload patterns and pressures, and other problems affecting productivity are identified. The interview method must conform to research standards.[15]

Organizational History

The history of the organization as represented by personnel records, various logs, management information, and operating documentation provides data about a number of variables, both dependent and extraneous. Dependent variables include turnover, attendance, overtime, sick leave, promotions, raises and salary comparisons; all of these will change as a result of AOIS, according to the model. Differences in operating procedures and management must be described to control for possible extraneous differences between groups. Management style may generate interaction effects with AOIS implementation, for example, authoritarian management may be thwarted by AOIS causing disruption of management and negative impacts on productivity. The discipline of organizational behavior[16] will provide the basis for interpreting descriptive data about management performance.

Attitude Scaling

The use of attitude rating scales has been explored in the context of AOIS assessment.[17] Exclusive dependence on management and worker attitudes towards AOIS to assess impacts is controversial; however, understanding individual reactions to AOIS is imperative. Attitudes reflect morale and willingness to work, which can be influenced only in part by management directive and other incentives. Attitudes, when combined with descriptive data, provide the basis for projecting the long-range impacts of AOIS. Even during a one-year assessment period, performance may be spuriously improved. An individual's attitude indicates his psychological integration with the new work methods and technology, and his acceptance of the system. If overall negative attitudes prevail, measured gains in productivity may be lost when system use becomes routine and imbedded in the bureaucratic culture. Attitude scales are well developed as a methodology,[18] and also have been developed for measuring organizational climate.[19] The attitude scale method for this approach is indirect and not subject to the biases inherent in direct questions about attitude.

Communication Audit

Changes in communication are among the most profound predicted by the model. The communication audit method is a straightforward, well developed method[17] that captures the frequency, length, mode, communicators, and characteristics of communication between individuals, and maps communication into a descriptive network. This measurement will show the shifts from one mode to another (e.g., phone to computer mail) and changes in communication patterns (e.g., more vertical communication within the organization). Knowledge of the frequency and length of communications permits the determination of changes in quantity of communication. Because organizational theory postulates that increased communication enhances organizational effectiveness, this measurement has implications for performance beyond that of the impact model. The large amount of time and resources expended for communication by an organization are examined by this method combined with the next method, work-time measurement. For example, we can determine the amount of labor used for communication and any changes resulting from automation, as explained in detail by Bair.[20]

Work Time-Measurement

Work time-measurement (WTM) provides concrete data about the time spent accomplishing a secific activity, the smallest unit of behavior in the model. The accumulated activity times related to a specific process represent the actual labor required by that process. Thus, the person hours required to accomplish an end-product process are measurable. WTM data may be recorded through direct observation, video recording, automatic monitoring where equipment is involved, or self recording. The obtrusiveness of the observation requires that a minimum number of samples be taken rather than attempting continuous monitoring. Sampling is critical, and in office work, the variability and lack of routine make representativeness more difficult.

The method outlined here is based on direct observation and self-recording. The observer or the individual notes on a form the start and finish times of an activity, which is translated into work-time when the form is collected. The activities are predefined from a description of the particular office; the end-product process or the purpose of activities for maintenance processes is recorded by the individual. For example, the time required to type one page of draft material, to complete one phone connection, or for routine filing is recorded.

To avoid the excessive complexity that might result from recording the time required for every activity, samples are based upon representative work periods and statistical analysis. The work periods are identified from observation, interviews, and historical data. The activity times are judged representative when statistical variance and central tendency are within acceptable parameters. Acceptable, average work times for a common activity are used as nominal times for estimating the time required for each future occurrence of the same activity. In addition, data is compared to that from other studies and the nominal times that have been established for work-time measurement in offices.[21]

The cumulative activity times for each process represent the labor expenditure. Thus, the labor required to produce a specific end-product is known and can be compared under different circumstances, i.e., with and without an AOIS. The labor required for maintenance processes can also be determined per unit time, for example, the time required to handle hourly payroll charges.

Work time for processes is combined with observed data about process contingencies so that results can be presented in work flow charts.

The interfaces between contingent processes are described in the context of work flow so that the influence of one process on processes contingent upon it can be factored into the analysis. These measurements are the basis of projected gains from a reduction of shadow functions and the other benefit areas; for example, we note the work time required for attempting a phone connection and how many attempts were required before completion. Work-time measurement and information flow representation can be elaborate; however, the goal here is to obtain a reasonably accurate quantification of labor expenditure.[22]

End-Product Tracking

End-products may result from several end-product processes requiring product tracking to the finished product. End-product processes are defined by the flow of an information unit, such as a document across organizational unit boundaries. When several organizational units are involved, which is very often the case, resources from all units may be measured and combined to yield the total resources required for the product.

Proficiency Testing

It is difficult to underestimate the resources required for attaining proficient usage of AOIS by all user personnel. These resources must be considered as part of the implementation costs and amortized over the life of the system. Adequate proficiency is also a requirement of valid measurement, and therefore proficiency testing is necessary to determine when the learning curve levels. The measurement period cannot begin until this point. The tests are designed to test the user's ability to accomplish representative activities with the AOIS.[8] The user is asked to perform an artificial process under controlled conditions while interaction with the system and time are automatically monitored. The user's repertoire of features and facilities is brought out by the test. Periodic testing provides data points for learning curves. If the curves do not level for the specified activities, it is a serious commentary on the AOIS.

Participant Observation

Observation by a specially trained participant in the offices being studied is a method widely used in social science. Because of the observer's close association with the personnel and the day-to-day activities of the organization, variations that might not be detected by other methods are described. Ideally, the observer is a member of the evaluation team transplanted into the organization for the duration of the assessment. However, "confederates" can be recruited from office personnel. Results are analogous to those of a case study; however, ongoing reporting to the assessment team may provide feedback about needed corrective actions. This case study method is also intended to capture "critical incidents," that is, significant, unique perturbations of normal work that are requisite to accurate interpretation of the results of the other methods. An illustration of this technique applied to executive personnel is reported by Mintzberg.[23]

Cost-Benefit Analysis

The cost-benefit analysis method documents the cost of operation, manpower, equipment, facilities, and other capital resources. Person-power includes the personnel required and their job descriptions and salary. The future costs are projected for the anticipated life of the AOIS. The determination of both operating and AOIS costs takes into account inflation, cost of money, and economic trends. Automated office information systems costs are calculated based on amortization of the implementation and operating costs over the life of the system. These figures are then compared with labor costs (from work-time measurement samples) adjusted for projected changes. If less labor is required as a result of the AOIS, the savings will be compared with AOIS cost calculations. Other changes in efficiency and qualitative characteristics of organizational performance will be cost evaluated and combined with changes in labor costs to show the cost benefits. Scenarios are used to determine qualitative cost impact, for example, more timely information may permit faster decisions and result in opportunities for economic gain that otherwise would have been lost (c.f. Fried,[24] who describes cost benefits in the light of qualitative changes).

CONCLUSION

The evaluation of AOIS requires a comprehensive assessment approach that focuses on organizational performance. The underlying assumption here is that organizational variables will be the determining factor for productivity improvement. Limited studies of impacts to date support this assumption. The impacts tend to be in benefit areas that reflect organizational performance (media transformation, control, and timing) as much as in benefit areas that reflect individual performance (shadow functions and automation).

The relationship between benefits and impacts in the model is tenuous requiring that numerous conditions are met. The conditions are represented by certain values for the variables that are associated with AOIS technology and organizational productivity. The variables are basically of two kinds, descriptive or measurable. The problem framework that is established here defines the scope of the measures and thus the extent of the conclusions that can be based on the measures. The assessment plan is designed to "control" the extraneous and independent variables so that variables dependent upon the impact of AOIS can be measured and described (see Figure 4). The dependent variable measures directly show changes in productivity—the challenge is to demonstrate conclusively that these changes were caused by the AOIS.

This brief description of our comprehensive approach raises the question, what does it take to perform such an assessment? Assuming that the instrumentation were complete (we are working

Figure 4
Overview of the Assessment Approach

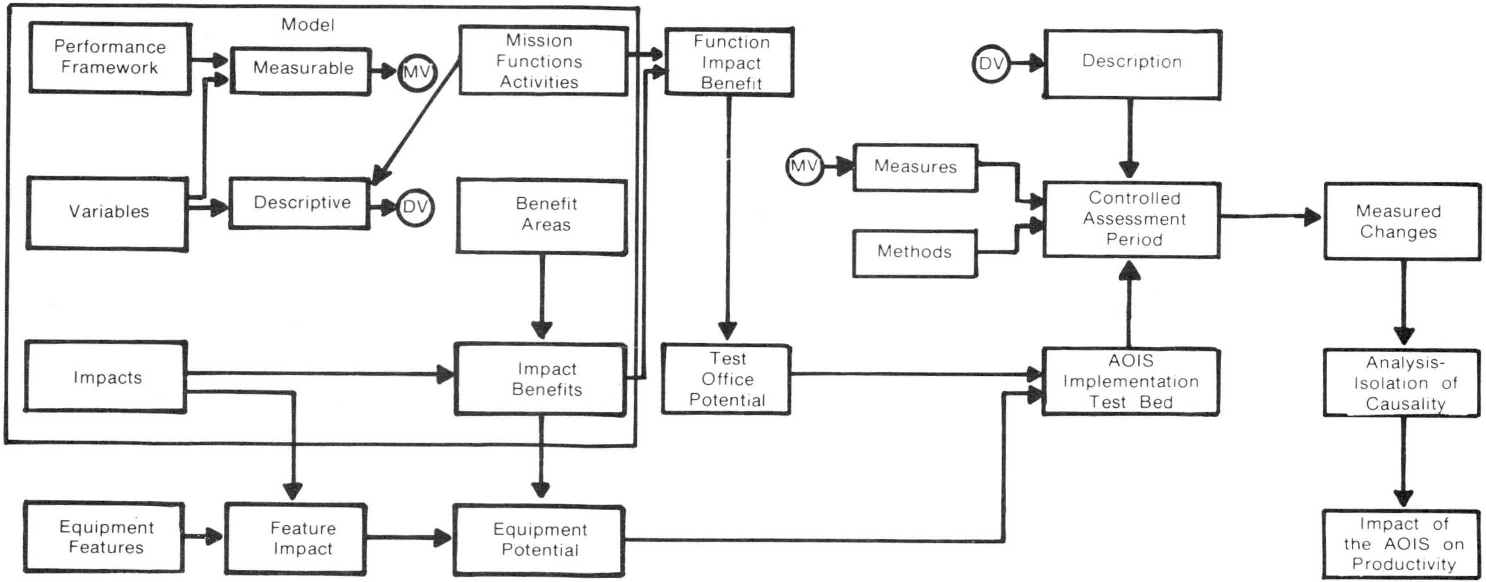

on it now), a rough estimate is between 25% and 35% of the cost of AOIS technology. This significant cost must be weighted against the gains: an institution will know if a prototype will be cost-beneficial, and perhaps even more importantly, what exactly has to be done for a particular system to work. The author has seen great disparity between a system's potential and its actual operation—this is a major reason why this assessment approach has been developed. Office automation offers phenomenal potential, but because of the vast number of variables and potential pitfalls, the probability of realizing the potential may be relatively low. This assessment approach can be to management what the sextant was to early navigators.

This work was sponsored, in part, by the Government Services Administration, National Archives and Records Service, Washington, D.C.

REFERENCES

1. Office Equipment Systems and Services: Current Analysis, *Standard & Poors Industry Surveys,* May 19, 1977.

2. Tartaglia, Benjamin. "The Economics of Word Processing," *Journal of Systems Management,* November, 1973.

3. Thomas B. Hilary. "UNICOM: A Case Study of User's Reactions to a Computer Assisted Typing Service," Communications Studies Group, University College, London, 1976.

4. O'Neal, Jeffery D. "We Increased Typing Productivity 340%," *The Office,* February, 1976, pp. 95-97.

5. Uhlig, Ronald P., "Human Factors in Computer Message Systems," *Datamation,* May, 1977, pp. 121-126.

6. *Datamation,* Special Issue: Word and Data Processing Converge, April, 1977.

7. Edwards, G. "An Analysis of Usage and Related Perceptions of NLS—a computer based text processing system," H.Q. Business Development, Bell Canada, Montreal, Quebec, October, 1977.

8. Bair, James H. "Evaluation and Analysis of an Augmented Knowledge Workshop." Final Report for Phase I, RADC-TR-74-79, Rome Air Development Center, April, 1974.

9. Bair, James H. "Strategies for the Human Use of Computer Based Systems," NATO Advanced Studies Institute on Man-Computer Interaction, Mati, Greece, September, 1976.

10. Strassman, Paul A. "Organizational Productivity, the Role of Information Technology," in *Information Processing '77—Proceedings*

IFIP World Congress, B. Gilchrist ed., Amsterdam: IFIP-North Holland, 1977.

11. Zissman, Michael D. Representation, Specification and Automation of Office Procedures, Working Paper 77-09-04, Wharton School of Business, U. of Pennsylvania, Sept., 1977, (Ph.D. Dissertation).

12. Holtzman, David L. and V. Rosenberg. "Understanding Shadow Functions, the Key to System Design and Evaluations," Paper for the Xerox Corp. Workshop on the Evaluation of Office Automation, Palo Alto Research Center, Calif. May, 1976.

13. Purchase, Alan. "Office of the Future," SRI International Business Intelligence Program, Guideline No. 1001, 1976.

14. Campbell, Donald T. and Julian C. Stanley. *Experimental and Quasi-Experimental Designs for Research,* Chicago: Rand McNally College Publishing Co., 1966.

15. Sellitz, Clare, Marie Jahoda, Morton Deutsch, and Stuart W. Cook. *Research Methods in the Social Relations.* New York, New York: Holt, Rinehart, and Winston, 1965.

16. Likert, Rensis. *The Human Organization: Its Management and Value,* NY: McGraw Hill, 1967.

17. Bair, James H. and David W. Conrath. "The Computer as an Interpersonal Communication Device: A Study of Augmentation Technology and its Apparent Impact on Organizational Communication," *Proceedings of the Second International Conference on Computer Communications,* Stockholm, Sweden, August, 1974.

18. Triandis, Harry C. *Attitude and Attitude Change.* N.Y.: John Wiley and Sons, Inc., 1971.

19. Stern, George C. *People in Context: Measuring Person-Environment Congruence in Education and Industry,* NY: Wiley, 1970.

20. Bair, James H. "Communication in the Office-of-the-Future: Where the Real Payoff May Be," *Proceedings of the International Computer Communications Conference,* Kyoto, Japan, August, 1978. (Prepublication copies are available.)

21. Huff, Walter. Measurement Techniques for Office Work from Lybrand's Office Systems Manual, SRI International Internal Working Document, 1976.

22. Morris, Peter A. and R.D. Smallwood. "An Analytical Characterization of Information Processing Organizations," Paper for the Xerox Corp. Workshop on the Evaluation of Office Automation, Palo Alto Research Center, Calif. May, 1976.

CHAPTER 12

EXPERIMENTS AND EXPERIENCES WITH COMPUTERIZED CONFERENCING

Starr Roxanne Hiltz
New Jersey Institute of Technology

ABSTRACT

EIES (The Electronic Information Exchange System) is a mini-computer based system which provides nationwide communication and information exchange capabilities. It is a research oriented system, dedicated to experimentation with and evaluation of alternative structures for human communication via computer. This paper reports selected results of operational field trials and controlled experiments. The results may be generalizable to implications for the effects of the use of such systems in the "office of the future," but the degree of generalizability is not known.

PREFACE

The research reported here was supported by grants from the National Science Foundation. The evaluation of the EIES field trials was supported by the Division of Mathematical and Computer Sciences (MCS 77-27813). The controlled experiments are supported by grant NSF MCS-00519. The Operational Trials were supported by the Division of Information Science and Technology (DSI-77-21008). The opinions and findings reported here are solely those of the author, and do not necessarily represent those of the National Science Foundation.

Many sections of this paper resulted from collaborative work with Murray Turoff. I am grateful to Kenneth Johnson, Murray Turoff and Charles Aronovitch for their participation in all phases of "experiment one"; to Julian Scher and Peter and Trudy Johnson-Lenz for their contributions to the design of the experiments; to John Howell and James Whitescarver for their software development support; and to our research assistants for their dedicated efforts in carrying out the experiments and coding questionnaires: Joanne Garofalo, Keith Anderson, Christine Naegle, Ned O'Donnell, Dorothy Preston, Karen Winters, and Stacy Simon. Nancy Rabke helped with analysis of results as well as the other phases of the experiments. For the field trials, I am indebted to Mary Ann Solimine for her assistance in project administration and data processing.

Robert Bales and Experiential Learning Systems were most cooperative in making experimental materials available for adaptation for the experiment.

The data in this paper are drawn from much longer final reports on the projects.

INTRODUCTION

Imagine the following experiment with the "office of the future." A number of spaces are equipped with a new computer based system designed to improve the effectiveness and efficiency of the communications and "paper work" which constitute the bulk of the activities of professional and managerial workers. Groups of professionals are invited to use these spaces. However, most of the groups are given no "management" in the traditional sense at all. They are not given any particular task to do; it is up to them to decide whether to set any goals. There is a nominal quarter time leader provided, but some of the leaders appear more than this, and some much less. There are no clear incentives provided, and no rules or division of labor provided iñ advance. There is written documentation for how to use the computer based communication system and equipment provided, but only a small volunteer support staff to help users who have difficulties following these somewhat incomplete directions.

Why would anyone do such a thing? It could be that they believe that the new office automation technology is a form of "magic." Give it to people and it will automatically increase their productivity and job satisfaction. And it could be that they are simply ignorant of how best to manage its use, so they introduce the technology for a kind of "trial and error" "natural experiment," to see what happens.

Now, the amazing thing is that some individuals and groups might actually evolve an effective, satisfying way of using a new technology in such a "natural experiment." And the second amazing thing is that many of the field trials of EIES (the Electronic Information Exchange System) and of other computer based communication systems resemble the "natural experiment" described.

In this paper, we will review some of the results of field trials and controlled experiments with EIES over the last five years that have implications for the effective utilization of such technologies in the "office of the future." The main themes of the paper are as follows:

1. Computerized conferencing systems *can* be effective means of communications and "working together." However, effectiveness depends largely upon an implementation which provides the proper structure for the proper task, and upon an appropriate amount and type of "management" or leadership of the group's activities on line.

2. In consciously designing a communications structure and management or leadership rights and responsibilities for a group working together on such a system, the group will have to explicitly make some choices, such as whether it wants strong central leadership or equalitarian decentralization, and whether it wants consensus/conformity or freedom/creativity.

The example used to make this point will include the results of a number of experiments which examined the extent to which group consensus can be reached in computerized conferences. These are the results of a controlled laboratory experiment which compared face to face and computerized group discussions and decision making processes and a controlled field experiment which compared four different ways of structuring or managing computer based conferences for group decision making. We will also examine a few of the results of the two year "operational trials" of EIES, the evaluation design for which included a series of three questionnaires (pre-use, follow up at six months, and post-use.)

Background

An analysis by Bair (1978, p. 733) concludes that "the greatest leverage for the benefits of office automation is in supporting the communication activities of non-clerical personnel." Based on this analysis, computer mail is judged to be "cost effective" for managerial communication. However, the data on managerial communications which serve as the basis for the analysis (Mintzberg, 1973) indicate that top managers spend the majority of their time in scheduled meetings, not in writing and receiving memoranda. Thus, it would seem that a design objective for a computer based communication system should include structures and features which support the kinds of communications that normally go on in face to face meetings, not just in mail and memoranda, in order to optimize cost effectiveness. EIES was designed to provide an integrated set of communication features, to replace some face to face meetings and provide some word processing and electronic filing, as well as electronic messages.

A Brief Description of the Nature and Purpose of EIES

The Electronic Information Exchange System (EIES) was funded to explore the use of the computer to enhance communication within geographically dispersed "small research communities," "conceived as groups of 10 to 50 individuals sharing an interest in a scientific or technological problem area" (NSF 76-45, p. 3). EIES provides a message system which enables members to send private communications to individuals or groups on the system, "conferences" which build up a permanent transcript on a topic of discussion, and notebooks where scientists may use text processing features to work on jointly authored reports. It also provides the capability for special structures to be created to handle special kinds of information or knowledge bases, or to change the interface or conduct a controlled experiment. This high level language, called "Interact" was used in the controlled experiments to administer a CAI lesson on four commands to the subjects, and then to isolate them within a simple subset of the conferencing system and deliver all instructions.

Limitations of the Findings

EIES was not originally built as a general purpose office automation system, though it is now being expanded to include features useful for such a function. Furthermore, though the users during the operational trials were professionals, they were not a cross-section of all kinds of managers and professionals, but only one subset, scientific and technical personnel. Even though the subjects for "experiment two," to be reported briefly here, were managers and staff in business and government organizations, they were using only a part of the system for a few hours for an experimental task. Thus, we do not know the extent to which any of our "experiments and experiences" are generalizable to office automation applications as a whole.

DESIGN OF THE FIRST EXPERIMENT

This experiment was basically a two by two factorial design with repeated measures. Data were collected from sixteen groups of subjects, each of which engaged in two group decision making conferences. The chief independent variable was mode of communication (Computerized Conferences, of "CC" vs. Face to Face conferences, on "FtF"). A variable of secondary interest was task type. In this article, we will look at only one of the tasks, which was a rank ordering problem with a correct solution (see Eady and Lafferty, 1975). Dependent variables included quality of decision and degree of consensus. The subjects were undergraduate and continuing education students at Upsala College, who were brought to the laboratory for the experiment. The laboratory included five separate rooms with terminals for the CC condition, and a larger room with a round table for the FtF discussions.

In computerized conferences, group members communicate by typing into and reading from a computer terminal, rather than by speaking, listening, and exchanging non-verbal gestures. Computerized conferences usually occur asynchronously—that is, participants are not on line at the same time. However, the experiments were conducted synchronously, or in "real time." In these synchronous conferences, each person types an entire entry without being interrupted, then receives communications which are waiting in the computer. The communication channel is thus missing many features of "normal" face to face communication, such as instantaneous receipt of communications and non-verbal cues (i.e., eye glance, facial expressions, tone of voice, or gestures). On the other hand, the presence of the computer in the communications loop proivdes some communications possibilities that are not available in a face to face meeting. For instance, all participants can think as long as they want without being interrupted by others, before they make their comments. All can be typing at once, rather than having to take turns speaking. The printing-reading speed is faster than speaking-listening speed (30 characters per second was used in this experiment; 120 characters per second is not uncommon). The repeat key and special characters on the keyboard can be used to easily create linguistic and graphic effects, such as the use of a whole line of exclamation points or question marks for emphasis (see Carey, 1980). The computational capabilities of the computer can be used to quickly format, analyze, and feedback a display of the decision-choices or votes of the group members. (See Hiltz and Turoff, 1978, and Johansen, Vallee and Spangler, 1979, for complete descriptions of the characteristics and applications of this medium, as well as discussions of its social impacts.)

Many persons who have not observed group decision-making processes conducted in other than face-to-face discussions tend to think that it will be difficult or impossible for members to understand and interact with one another without the various cues provided by such "back-channel" communication as facial expression. However, the existing experimental evidence indicates that this is not the case, and that indeed, most problem-solving can be done as well or better in non-face-to-face conditions. For example, Williams (1975) found that mode of communication (face-to-face vs. audio-only conference vs. closed circuit TV) had no effect on either number of ideas generated or originality and quality of ideas generated (as judged by raters). Werner and Latane (1976) compared face-to-face, TV, audio and handwritten conditions. They found that "the communications medium used for discussion tended to be less important than a partner's responsiveness in determining opinion changes and reactions to discussions. The media did not differ in their ability to convey positive images or to impart pleasure to the interaction."

Our initial hypotheses, based upon a literature search (Hiltz, 1975) and our own pilot studies (Hiltz, Johnson and Agle, 1978) were:

1. Computerized conferencing, as compared to face-to-face discussions, will probably result in more equal participation.

2. This, in turn, is likely to lead to the generation of more ideas and suggestions on how to solve a problem, and thus to a higher quality decision.

3. CC groups are less likely than FtF groups to reach total consensus in a given amount of time, since it is less likely that a single leader will emerge to push the group towards agreement.

A related factor is that the absence of non-verbal communications makes it much easier for a "deviant" group member to hold out against the other members of the group, rather than go along with the group. In the pilot studies, there were no groups in the face-to-face condition in which a 4-1 split was maintained; the deviant always reluctantly went along. In the computerized conferencing condition, there were several instances of a stable, adamant 4-1 or 3-2 split, with the deviant steadfastly holding that he or she did not agree with the rest of the members. We thus predicted that the computerized conferencing condition would be characterized by a lower probability of reaching a total consensus as compared with face to face discussions.

In a separate article (Hiltz, Turoff, and Johnson, 1980), we have reported the results for the first hypothesis. There is less tendency for a dominant person or leader to emerge in CC, for "unstructured" conferences, in which no mechanism is provided to support emergence of a designated leader. We also found that there were, in fact, no statistically significant differences in the quality of decision reached. Both face to face and CC groups improved their decision about 25% as a result of their discussions. (See Hiltz, Johnson, Aronovitch, and Turoff, 1980 for the complete details on these and other findings.)

ABILITY TO REACH CONSENSUS

For the ranking problem, consensus was measured by using Kendall's coefficient of concordance for the five "final group rankings" reported by each individual in each group. This varies from 0 for no agreement to 1.00 for perfect agreement on the placing of the fifteen items ranked by the group. The results are shown in Table 1. There is a statistically significant difference favoring face to face groups. However, substantively, the difference is not very large. All CC groups reached a reasonable amount of agreement. Some of those groups that did not reach near-total agreement seem to have run out of time; whereas all face-to-face groups completed their task within the 90 minutes allowed, many of the CC groups were cut off before they were able to finish. However, this is not the only factor. The computerized conference seems to provide little opportunity for a dominant leader to emerge to force a consensus, and an environment that is psychologically and socially more conducive to allowing persons to refuse to go along with the group when they think their decisions are better than those of the rest of the group members.

An interesting sidelight is that all of the face-to-face groups apparently *thought* that they had reached total consensus. However, in half of the groups, when individual members were

Table 1
Group Consensus on the Ranking Problem,
by Medium of Communication

Face to Face	CC
.9897	.9774
1.00	.8626
.9886	.9031
1.00	.9857
.9943	.9671
.9989	.9811
1.00	.9737
1.00	.8077

Mann-Whitney U test
$Ub=0$
$p < .01$
Note: 1.00 means perfect consensus, all five participants on all 15 items ranked.

asked to report this agreed upon decision in writing after the meeting, their versions of the decision were somewhat different. This is despite the fact that the participants usually wrote down the supposed decision on a list of the items they had with them in the conference room, and later referred to it in reporting the decision.

Quality of Decision vs. Consensus

However, consensus is not a particularly necessary or always a good goal for a group to achieve. In the case of the ranking problem, the average of the decisions in the non-consensus groups was just as good as the group decision in consensus groups. This is determined on the basis of a very low correlation (Spearman's rho of .109) between Kendall's coefficient of consensus and quality of Group decision. In fact, a detailed look at the relationship between process and outcome of communication in the two modes showed that in many cases, the type of communications process which positively contributes to consensus negatively contributes to quality of decision. Communications process was coded by using Bales Interaction Process Analysis, which breaks each spoken or typed communication into units consisting of a single thought, and then places them into one of twelve categories, such as "gives opinion" or "agrees" (see Bales, 1950). In Table 2, we see a summary of data showing the average proportion of units in each of the twelve categories for the two media, and then in column three, the correlation with quality of decision, and in column four, the appropriate correlation with degree of consensus. Among the most significant differences between the media are:

There is more agreement face to face; this is highly correlated with consensus but not with quality of decision.

Table 2
Summary of IPA Results for the Ranking Problem by Mode of Communication and Correlations with Consensus and Quality of Decision

Bales Category Average

	FTF	CC	Pearson's with Quality	Rho with Consensus
Shows:				
Solidarity	1.66	2.44	.683	-.058
Tension				
Release	7.70	1.60	-.476	.622
Agreement	13.35	6.82	.050	.766
Gives:				
Suggestions	3.56	4.89	.444	-.133
Opinion	42.99	57.80	.119	-.824
Orientation	14.58	11.81	-.408	.440
Asks for:				
Orientation	3.72	1.62	-.276	.692
Suggestions	1.14	.58	.019	.654
Shows:				
Disagreement	3.51	2.46	-.196	.258
Tension	1.52	.64	.122	.591
Antagonism	1.11	1.86	.134	.025

Critical Values for Peason's R for 16 pairs of scores
.10=.400; .05=.468; .02=.542; .01=.590

Critical Values for Spearmans' Rho, 16 pairs of scores
.10=.425; .05=.506; .01=.665

There is more opinion giving in CC. This is very negatively associated with the ability to reach consensus, but has a weak positive relationship with quality.

There is much more joking and laughing ("tension release") in FtF. This is positively related to consensus and negatively related to quality of decision.

A management or professional group cannot maximize consensus and quality in its decision at the same time—it has to make a choice. Appropriate structures can be provided to result in equalitarian participation and lots of opinions, or strong leadership and a higher probability of at least nominally reaching complete consensus. Of course, it is much easier to implement such structures on a computer system than in face-to-face meetings.

Table 3 shows the results of implementing such a structure. The CC groups in the "human leader" condition in our second series of experiments were likely to reach 100% consensus. In this experiment, groups consisted of five managerial or staff members of actual organizations, and the problem solving exercise was conducted on portable terminals brought to the organization's location. Half of the groups, at the end of their practice, elected a human leader for their discussion, who then was given certain rights and responsibilities. Such an explicit structuring of leadership does result in high consensus. (The effects of the other variable in the experiment, computer feedback, have not yet been analyzed.)

Table 3
**Ability of Computerized Conferencing Groups with
Elected Leaders to Reach Consensus
(Kendall's Coefficients of Consensus, "Experiment Two")**

Condition=Human Leader, No Computer Feedback
1.000
1.000
1.000
1.000
1.000
.982

Mean=.997

Note: A Kendall's Coefficient of 1.00 designates perfect consensus.

Putting the two experiments together, we conclude that computerized conferences can be effective replacements for at least some face-to-face meetings, which are costly in terms of time and travel. Quality of decision is likely to be just as good. If the group wants consensus, a computer based conference can be structured to make this a probable outcome.

OVERVIEW OF EIES USAGE DURING THE FIELD TRIALS

EIES has been operative since 1967 and has grown from an initial usage rate of about 100 users and 10,000 hours of operation the first year to approximately 700 users and 60,000 hours per year. With the current hardware, this is approaching peak hour usage saturation.

The following analysis is based upon data drawn from the activity monitor and represents the accumulated activity of the members of the system as of April 1980. This includes the NSF sponsored user groups, but not those members who were dropped and replaced by others. These data also represent about 70% of total usage up to that point in time. An historical analysis of EIES data is being developed as a separate report and the analysis of the first year's operation is available in Turoff and Hiltz, (1978). The data can enable us to see the overall pattern of activity.

Total activity represented by the sample is as follows:

Category	Amount
Number of Users	724
Number of Groups	52
Number of Hours Used	76,401
Text Items Composed	202,114
Text Items Received	864,254
Average Text Item Size (lines)	12
Distribution Ratio	4.3
Number of Conferences	315
Number of Notebooks	209

The distribution ratio is the number of items received divided by the number of items composed, meaning that the average EIES item written is seen by 4.3 different individuals.

Based upon the above and other data collected, we can get a profile of the average user of EIES. (See Table 4.)

Table 4
Average User Profile

Category	Amount
Hours Used	105.5
Number of Sessions	265
Average Session Time (minutes)	24
Text Items Composed	279
Text Items Received	1,194
Items Transacted/Session	5.6
Average Input Rate (words/minute)	7.9

Subsystem	% of Items Composed	% of Items Received	Size (Lines)	Circulation Ratio
Messages	69.1	35.8	10	2.2
Conferences	22.3	60.9	14	11.7
Notebooks	8.6	3.3	19	1.6

We can thus see that the EIES operational trials represent an extensive body of experience with this new medium. We can also see that whereas people write more messages than any other type of item, they do most of their reading in the conferences.

Our findings demonstrate that there is a very wide variation in the amount of use of the system. The main predictors are motivations of the participants before they ever signed on, rather than reactions to aspects of the system, or skills such as typing speed or previous experience with computers or computer terminals. We also found a marked "evolution" in user behavior. Beginning users appreciated only a fairly limited subset of the system's features, such as the message, the group conference, and the public directory. As users gained experience, however, they found valuable a much wider range of features (see Hiltz and Turoff, 1980). The groups varied greatly in the amount of satisfaction with the system, and associated with this were differences in the amount of time which the group leader or other persons spent facilitating (managing) the group. (See Hiltz, 1980, for the complete results of this study.)

With this brief summary of some aspects of the process of using the system, we will turn to two of the "outcomes" or impact areas which are of potential interest to those interested in office automation. These are the extent to which the new medium substituted for more traditional communications media or added onto them and the extent to which using the system improved the productivity of its members.

Communications Media Substitution

One of the major assumed cost savings of computer based communications for office automation is the substitution of cheaper and/or faster means of communication for existing media, such as the telephone and travel to face to face meetings (see, for instance, Nilles et al., 1976, and Kollen, 1975).

The experience with the EIES field trials indicates that the main effect of access to such a system is to increase the total amount of communication which a person does, and secondarily to substitute electronic media for others, particularly for regular or heavy users of the computer based system. There is no one-to-one "tradeoff" involved; some users report an *increase* in other modes of communication on top of the use of the new system. This is because they begin to rely on feedback from others who are not co-located and on the availability of quick input from others when it would be useful. In other words, instead of relying solely on the resources and sources of information and people who happen to be close at hand at the office, they also have the option of drawing on an expanding network of colleagues who form part of a computer-linked working group. These new working relationships and contacts stimulate the use of telephone, mail, and personal visits to supplement the on-line communication.

The data in Table 5 show that for the EIES users, a decrease in other means of communication was somewhat more likely than an increase, especially for those who spent a hundred hours or more on line during the eighteen month period studied. Mail was most likely to decrease, followed by the telephone. Travel for personal visits was just about as likely to increase as to decrease. Thus, though such a system "could" save money by substituting for travel, our experience does not indicate that it is likely to. Finally, communication with co-located colleagues does not suffer or decrease as a result of being tied into a national communication network. In fact, in a quarter of the overall cases, it increased. What seems to be happening is that a member of the EIES network receives some information or ideas that may be useful in one of their projects, and then shares it with the co-located colleagues.

Thus, our results would indicate that an organization can probably expect some savings in long distance telephone calls as a result of implementation of a computer based communication

Table 5
Impact of Communications Media Use, by Hours on Line

Hours	Increased	No effect	Decreased	N
Telephone				
100+	17%	33%	50%	18
All	14%	63%	23%	103
Mail				
100+	22%	28%	50%	18
All	20%	45%	35%	103
Personal Visits				
100+	22%	50%	28%	18
All	13%	74%	14%	103
Co-located Colleagues				
100+	16%	84%	0	19
All	24%	72%	4%	105

Source: Post Use Questionnaire

Question: Has the use of EIES changed the amount of your use of other media in the last year? (Media checklist with Increased- No effect- Decreased as choices)

Items Included:
Telephone
Mail
Visits with researchers in other locations
Communication with colleagues at your institution or organization

system, and some improvement in the speed and amount of distribution of written materials that would otherwise be mailed. However, as long as travel budgets remain the same, there is not likely to be a decrease in the total amount of travel for personal visits or face to face meetings. However, we suspect that there is likely to be some change in the nature of the travel; when a face to face meeting is not really required, the system can be used instead, and the travel budget will be used for those trips which the employee considers more important or more attractive. We have no quantitative data to support this speculation, however.

Impacts on Productivity

There are indications from the EIES field trials that a system like this can have noticeable impacts on the productivity of professionals. The degree of such impact is of course primarily a function of how much they actually use the system.

Some of the productivity-related measures are reported in Table 6. This shows the proportion of all users and of that subset who had spent one hundred or more hours on line over the eighteen months agreeing with statements about specific types of productivity-related benefits.

The strongest effects are reported in terms of increasing the inputs which can be useful in future as well as present projects that a person is doing—ideas, leads, and useful pieces of information. Even among those who had spent less than one hour a month on line on the average during the trial period, 65% reported increases in their "stock of ideas" and 69% reported that it had provided them useful leads, references, or other information. Thus it seems that even rather casual or low levels of use can be useful to professionals. To have any noticeable impact on overall quantity or quality of work, however, fairly regular or heavy use of the system seems to be necessary. In addition, we see from Table 6 that increases in the quality of work are somewhat more likely to be reported than an increase in the quantity of work. In other words, the users did not necessarily write more papers and reports, but they had more inputs to those that they did produce, and felt that their quality improved as a result.

Conclusion

The findings reported here are drawn from much longer reports and thus are somewhat out of context. In addition, it cannot be over-emphasized that the degree of generalizability of the findings is unknown.

Organizations have seldom been willing to engage in rigorous experiments with their communications and decision making processes. Thus, in thinking about computer systems for communication, there is a tendency to take the route of merely automating existing procedures, such as introducing electronic mail to replace the letter or memo. However, our evidence suggests that the new technology does make it possible to structure communications and decision making processes in new ways, in order to optimize desired outcomes such as group consensus or quality of the product.

Table 6
Impacts of EIES on Productivity, for All Users and Heavy Users

Proportion Who "Strongly Agree" or "Agree"

Basis	Proportion	N responding
Provided Leads and Information		
All	79%	107
100+	93%	19
Increased Stock of Ideas		
All	72%	107
100+	90%	19
Increased Quantity of Work		
All	27%	107
100+	53%	19
Increased Quality of Work		
All	37%	107
100+	68%	19

Source: Post Use Questionnaire and
Monitor Statistics on Accumulated Hours of Use
Note: "100+" refers to respondents who had accumulated 100 or
more hours on line

Questions:
Respondents were asked to check a five point Likert Scale
(Strongly Agree, Agree, Neither Agree nor Disagree, Disagree,
Strongly Disagree) for the following statements:

Use of EIES has increased my "stock of ideas" that might be used
in future work.

EIES has provided me leads, references, or other information
useful in my work.

Use of EIES has increased my productivity in terms of the *quantity*
of work recently completed or underway.

We would like to combine the various research approaches we have used so far and increase the direct relationship to office automation in our next study. Ideally, it will be a six to nine month controlled field experiment. We need an organization with six to eight identical divisions doing identical jobs, such a producing a five year plan or engaging in a zero based budgeting process. Half of the divisions would carry out their tasks in their "normal" manner, without a computerized conferencing system. The other half would use the system. We could then make direct comparisons of the process and outcome of the group efforts. Any volunteers?

BIBLIOGRAPHY

Bair, James, "Communication in the Office of the Future: Where the Real Payoff May Be." Proceedings of the Fourth International Conference on Computer Communication, 733-739, 1978.

Bales, Robert, Interaction Process Analysis: A Method for the Study of Small Groups. Reading, Mass., Addison Wesley, 1950.

Carey, John, "Paralanguage in Computer Mediated Communication." Proceedings of the Association for Computational Linguistics, 61-63, 1980.

Eady, Patrick M. and J. Clayton Lafferty, "The Subarctic Survival Situation." Plymouth, Michigan: Experiential Learning Methods, 1975.

Hiltz, Starr Roxanne, Communications and Group Decision Making: Experimental Evidence on the Potential Impact of Computer Conferencing. Newark, N.J., Computerized Conferencing and Communications Center, New Jersey Institute of Technology, Research Report No. 2, 1975.
The Impact of a Computerized Conferencing System on Scientific Research Communities. Final Report to the National Science Foundation. (Forthcoming NJIT Research Report, Fall, 1980.)

Hiltz, S.R., Kenneth Johnson, and Gail Matthews Agle, Replicating Bales Problem Solving Experiments on a Computerized Conference: A Pilot Study. Computerized Conferencing and Communications Center, NJIT, Research Report No. 8, 1978.

Hiltz, S.R., K. Johnson, and M. Turoff, "Equality, Dominance, and Group Decision Making: Results of a Controlled Experiment on Face to Face vs. Computerized Conferences." Proceedings of the ICCC, 1980.

Hiltz, Starr Roxanne, Kenneth Johnson, Charles Aronovitch and Murray Turoff, Face to Face vs. Computerized Conferences: A Controlled Experiment. CCCC, NJIT, Research Report No. 12, 1980.

Hiltz, Starr Roxanne and Murray Turoff, The Network Nation: Human Communication via Computer. Reading, Mass. Addison Wesley Advanced Book Program, 1978.
The Evolution of User Behavior in a Computerized Conferencing System." Paper presented at the International Communication Association, Acapulco, Mexico, 1980.

Johansen, Robert, Jacques Vallee and Kathleen Spangler, Electronic Meetings: Technical Alternatives and Social Choices. Reading, Mass.: Addison Wesley, 1979.

Kollen, James, Travel/Communications Tradeoffs: The Potential for Substitution Among Business Travellers. Bell Canada, Business Planning Group, April 1975 report.

Mintzberg, H., The Nature of Managerial Work. New York: Harper and Row, 1973.

Nilles, Jack M., F.R. Carlson, Jr., P. Gray, and G. Hanneman, The Telecommunications-Transportation Tradeoff: Options for Tomorrow. New York: Wiley, 1976.

Turoff, M. and Hiltz, S.R., Development and Field Testing of an Electronic Information Exchange System: Final Report on the EIES Development Project. Newark, New Jersey:'Computerized Conferencing and Communications Center, New Jersey Institute of Technology, Research Report No. 9, 1978.

Werner, C., and B. Latane, "Responsiveness and Communication Medium in Dyadic Interactions." Bulletin of the Psychonomic Society, 8, 11:13-15, 1976.

Williams, Ederyn, "Coalition Formation Over Telecommunication Media." European Journal of Social Psychology, 5, 4: 5-3--507, 1975.

CHAPTER 13

PRAGMATICS AND DYNAMICS OF COMPUTER CONFERENCING: A SUMMARY OF FINDINGS FROM THE FORUM PROJECT

J. Vallee, R. Johansen, H. Lipinski and T. Wilson
Institute for the Future, U.S.A.

INTRODUCTION

In the fall of 1975, the Institute for the Future completed an exploratory study of the feasibility, applications, and social effects of the new concept of computer conferencing.[1] The study was begun in 1972 and involved three phases: (1) the development and testing of an interactive system called FORUM; (2) the expansion of this initial system, with the introduction of field tests; and (3) a systematic exploration of the effects of this medium through questionnaires, interviews, and analysis of extensive usage statistics.

Although the idea of group communication through computers goes back to the 1950s and had been pursued by The Rand Corporation, the Institute for Defense Analyses, and the Office of Emergency Preparedness in the 1960s, major study of its potential effects had to await the development of viable computer networks. The FORUM system, which began as a response-elicitation program and developed gradually into a true "conferencing" medium, was implemented as a PDP-10 assembly-language program on the ARPA network. The specific computer science problems encountered in the course of this implementation were described at ICCC two years ago[2] and need not concern us here. Instead, this article summarizes the preliminary conclusions of the project regarding several practical aspects of computer conferencing: the patterns of usage, message exchange, cost, participation, and learning associated with the medium.

The systematic exploration of these questions poses a methodological challenge, but the use of the computer also creates some unique opportunities. For every conference, a printed transcript of the public entries is automatically recorded. Furthermore, the computer itself can unobtrusively map many dimensions of the group interaction that may or may not be evident from the transcript. This mapping capability may represent the most powerful analytic tool available for any current communications medium. With it, some of the detailed coding and painstaking observation that social psychologists must typically carry out in analyzing small groups can be done automatically, without distrubing the normal communications process. Private message statistics, for example, may indicate the formation of subgroups, cliques, or coalitions. Other usage statistics allow the tracing of individual participation characteristics from one conference to another as a function of role or task. Growth curves can be derived for each conference and for each content category in a conference; these latter curves indicate if and when the conference has made a transition from the procedural questions inherent in any meeting to the solution of substantive issues.

Given such tools for analysis, our research approach was to collect a series of case histories.[3] Over the period from May 1973 to December 1974, we conducted 28 conferences with FORUM; these varied in task type from staff meetings and note exchange to crisis resolution; in length, from a few hours to four months; and in group size, from three persons to several dozen. The user groups included such organizations as the U.S. Geological Survey, Washington State Planning Office, Communications Studies Group (London), Brookhaven National Laboratory, National Institute of Social Sciences, and the Information Sciences Institute, among others.

These groups were selected on the basis of their need to communicate, their geographic location, and their composition; our primary interest was in interaction among geographically disseminated experts in varied fields. FORUM was made available at no cost to the test groups, though access to terminals was usually arranged by the user groups. This overall case study effort represented about 1,500 user hours and a total of 9,000 entries.

In the course of our analysis, we observed five basic types or "styles" of computer conferencing: the first style involves unstructured groups engaged in a multi-topic discussion, typically lasting weeks or even months; we call this style the "notepad." When a specific topic is addressed by a group interacting synchronously (simultaneously), as well as asynchronously (one user at a time) over a period of a few weeks, we recognize this pattern as a "seminar." The third style, called the "assembly," is an extension of the seminar in which a larger group addresses multiple topics which are grouped in an agenda with separate parts. Fourth, computer conferencing permits an "encounter" style in which participants are linked as a group in real time for a period of hours, possibly with role assignments as in simulation/gaming and actual crisis situations. Finally, the medium can be used in a "questionnaire" style by eliciting responses from any number of remote users; the responses are then aggregated by the computer.

Most of the interactions we observed in our case histories were in the first three styles, but we also gave a significant amount of attention to synchronous meetings and some highly structured activity of the questionnaire style. The following patterns emerged from these observations.

USE OF TIME IN COMPUTER CONFERENCING

The computer conferencing medium introduces both constraints and flexibility in the use of time. The constraints derive primarily from the limitations of computer terminals and are largely theoretical. For example, in *synchronous conferencing*, a participant's time is divided between typing, reading what the other participants have typed, and waiting. Thus, when the wait time is zero, the size of the group places an upper bound on the percent of time spent typing (and vice versa). In most communications media, there is no such limit because only one person sends messages at a time. In computer conferencing, however, all group members may type at the same time. Therefore, as participants spend a larger percentage of their time typing, the actual word transmission rate approaches a maximum word transmission rate.

In actual case histories, the percentage of time spent typing in a computer conference was much less than the theoretical maximum for the group size. In four synchronous FORUM conferences in which average group typing speed was about 26 words per minute, the participants spent less than one-third of their time typing, while the theoretical maximum was about two-thirds (Figure 1). Chapanis[4] has suggested at least one explanation for this characteristic of keyboard communication. Examining the special case of interactive problem-solving by two people using a variety of media, he has found that, in communication modes which require typing, typing time represents slightly less than one-third of the total problem-solving time. By means of detailed measurements of what the subjects were actually doing, he found that they do a great many things other than type: they make notes, think about what to say, handle objects, and search for information related to the subject matter.

The limit on percent of time spent typing applies only to synchronous interaction; this distinction between synchronous and asychronous conferencing also extends to several other measures of the use of time in computer conferencing. Consider, for example, the length of conferencing sessions (the amount of time between each joining and leaving of a conference). *The average synchronous session lasted about 25 minutes; and the average asychronous session, about half that time.* Based on the histories of 12 FORUM conferences with a total of 4,486 synchronous and asychronous sessions, there is a 53 percent chance that a session will last less than 5 minutes, a 64 percent chance that it will last less than 10 minutes, and only an 8 percent chance that it will last more than 1 hour. The average duration of a session in FORUM (synchronous and asynchronous) conferences on the ARPA network was about 19 minutes.

In synchronous conferences, we found evidence that participants felt more pressed for time and overloaded than in the other styles of computer conferencing. However, this feeling of "pressure" could be a source of energy for the intense group communication possible in such discussions. In a conference that included both synchronous and asynchronous interaction, for instance, those participants who felt pressed for time also made longer public entries.

MESSAGE EXCHANGE IN COMPUTER CONFERENCING

Synchroneity also affects message exchange rates and message lengths. In conferences in which the interaction was both synchronous and asychronous, the number of characters sent per

Figure 1
Use of Time in Four Synchronous Conferences

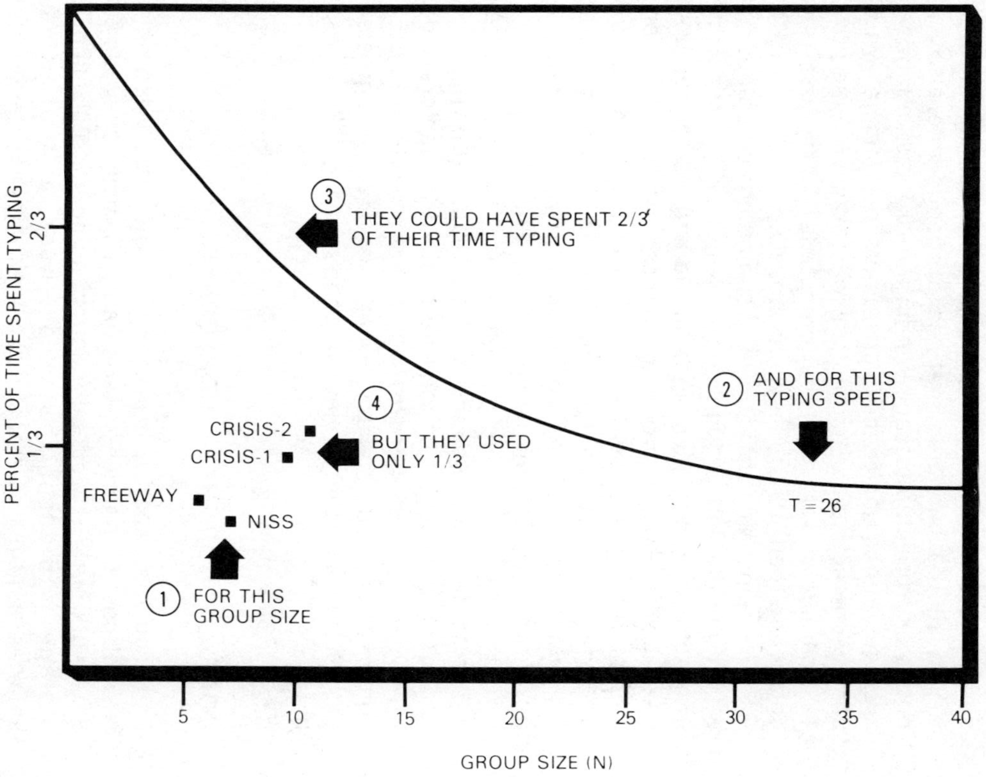

unit of time per participant was higher during synchronous interaction than during asychronous interaction. For public and private messages combined, the average exchange rate per participant was 45 characters per minute synchronously compared to 26 characters per minute asynchronously (for the three conferences for which such data were available.)

It should be noted that the exchange rate also differed for public and private message-sending. In the public mode alone, the average participant sent 33 characters per minute synchronously and 23 characters per minute asynchronously. In the private mode, 12 characters were sent per minute synchronously and only 3 characters per minute asynchronously.

The length of an entry in a computer conference, too, varied with both the mode (public or private) and the synchroneity of interaction. Public messages tended to be longer than private messages, while synchroneity produced significantly shorter public and private messages. Ignoring the effect of synchroneity, the average length of a public entry in 17 FORUM conferences (for which this information was available) was 380 characters; of a private entry, 178 characters.

In order to derive guidelines for storage requirements in future conferences, we recorded information growth for 17 FORUM conferences in terms of total number of characters sent over the total user hours. The growth for the Style 4 (synchronous) conferences (2,000 characters per user hour) was greater than the growth for all other styles of conferences (750 words per user hour).

COST OF COMPUTER CONFERENCES

The total cost of a computer conference is an aggregate of several cost components: terminal equipment, communication with a network port, network connection, computer utilization, computer storage, and administrative overhead, as well as participant salaries, editing of transcripts, training, and facilitation of the conference. Such costs are of particular interest to those who advocate the medium as a travel substitute. We therefore made direct comparisons among travel and other related costs for conferences of Styles 2 and 3. We found that the substitution of computer conferencing for travel reduced costs substantially, depending on many factors. The issue of "substitution" of one medium of communication for another is, of course, complicated;

and computer conferencing will not necessarily *replace* travel, even though it can substitute for some communication needs.[5]

WORK PATTERNS

The flexibility of asynchronous conferencing suggests an opportunity to alter the notion of "work" tied to a traditional workplace and workday. Indeed, six persons who used computer conferencing regularly over a two-year period and who had easy access to computer terminals[6] did extend their working periods outside normal office hours, with "participation peaks" occurring in the morning, afternoon, and evening.

Figure 2 shows the distribution of total participation of these six extended users of FORUM across a 24-hour period and during weekends. Nearly 40 percent of all sessions occurred outside of the 8:00-to-5:00 weekday working hours. This finding does not necessarily mean that persons with access to computer conferencing work more hours, but that the flexibility of their working hours can be increased considerably.

GROUP INTERACTION

For analyzing patterns of group interaction in computer conferencing, we have developed a "participation map" on which each conferee is represented by a rectangle on a graph, such that the sides of the rectangle are proportional to the average public and private message length ("verbosity") for that participant and the x and y coordinates of the rectangle are the number of his or her private and public messages, respectively. In the test conferences, we observed that participants were not restricted to a specific area on this map across conferences or across parts of a single conference; in fact, participants often moved across the map as a function of the conference and/or part. In a multipart conference, the participant's position relative to the group may also vary in each part.

We used participation maps to examine the relationship between participation in the public mode and that in the private mode. Comparing public and private message-sending across conferences, however, we found no significant relationship between the total number of public and private messages sent in any given conference. (A correlation coefficient of .19 was

Figure 2
Distribution of Participation of Six Users
Across a 24-Hour Period
(Based on 1,155 Sessions)

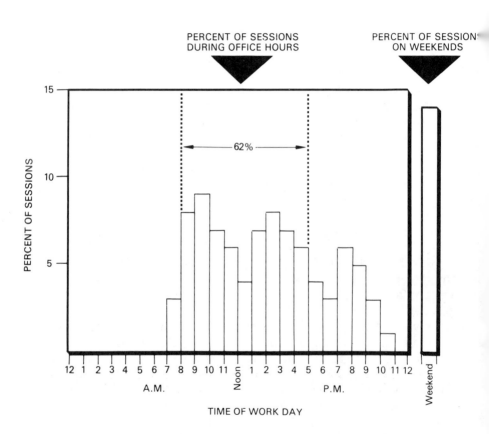

computed for public and private message-sending for 17 FORUM conferences.)

Characteristic patterns of public and private message-sending did emerge when individual roles within the group were considered. In particular, the conference facilitator and the substantive chairperson tended to be high private and public communicating via FORUM; they also make periodic procedural suggestions about the direction of the discussion. The chairpeople, on the other hand, tend to focus only on the substantive aspects of the conference from a leadership point of view.

The effect of role on participation can be seen more generally in simulation conferences in which participants were assigned different roles. In a simulation called "CRISIS,"[7] for example, participants formed clusters based on their public and private message-sending behavior; these clusters reflected their roles in the conference. Furthermore, as was shown in an analysis of their interaction according to Rales' categories for Interaction Process Analysis,[8] the message-sending patterns of participants differed across categories as a function of roles and of public/private mode.

In the analysis of participation patterns for all conferences, motivation emerged as an important factor: participants with greater motivation and with a greater professional stake sent more messages with more characters per message both publicly and privately and spent more time typing and more time online than those who were less motivated. Equally important to a positive user attitude was the reliability of the medium and the synchronous nature of the interaction. These were the critical factors in determining the participant's sense of personal interaction. Previous experience with computers, on the other hand, did not seem to be a prerequisite. In some cases, it even seemed to be a handicap to effective communication.

THE EFFECTS OF SKILL

We used a combination of monitor statistics and questionnaire responses to investigate the influence of typing skills on learning curves, use of the system, and other attitudes. We gathered participant responses to questions probing their typing ability and familiarity with computers; we found that both expressed typing ability and familiarity with computers are postively correlated with actual measures of typing rates for both

Figure 3
Participation Map for a
Synchronous Computer Conference

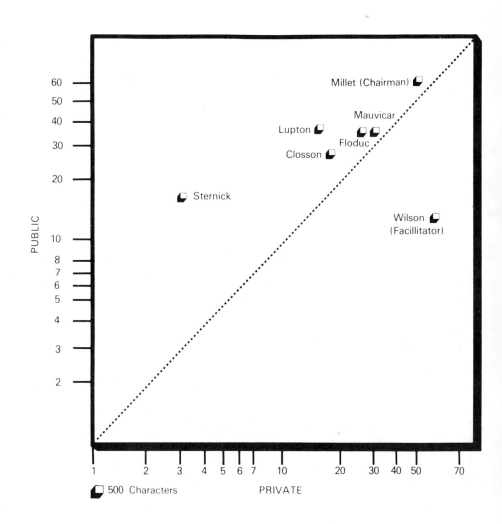

public and private entries. We also found that those participants with higher expressed typing skills remained online for a longer total time than those with lower expressed skills. However, the sample size was small: twelve participants responded and rated their own typing ability following a single conference. The correlation between their responses and time online was .60.

Learning curves were closely monitored in a single synchronous conference; and a skill rating mechanism was introduced for this conference to index nine measures of messages sent, of editing characters used, and of participant familiarity with various subcommands available within FORUM. The growth in skill for all participants over the course of the conference (with both conferencing skills and previous experience of the participants being quantified) shows that all users began at skill = 0 and reached skill > 2 after one hour (on a scale of 10 points). After 1½ hours, all users had skill > 4; after 2½ hours, their skill ratings were all higher than 6; and at the end of the conference, all users had a skill rating higher than 7.

Group learning can be quantified by analyzing the transcripts of completed conferences. We classified the content of three conferences into procedural, learning, and substantive categories. The cumulative frequency of these classes during a conference shows that issues of procedure and learning dominated the early entries of a conference, depending upon the prior training of the group, while substantive entries grew throughout the conference.

Figures 4A, B, and C show the growth of entry types in the three conferences analyzed in this fashion. In Figure 4C, issues of procedure and learning actually dominated two-thirds of the conference. In Figure 4B, the curves reflect the effect of prior training and good access to terminals, with substantive entries growing much faster than other types. In Figure 4A, procedure again dominates more than half of the conference.

Finally, in trying to understand the effect of the medium on group skills, we examined the issue of control in a crisis simulation conference, using an index of the difficulty of the group in controlling its behavior.[9] We found that, in fact, the index of difficulty of control was very comparable to that found in face to face groups analyzed by Bales and Hare.[10] While certainly not conclusive, such a finding suggests that computer conferences have some of the same characteristics as face to face meetings. Certainly, both media depend highly on the leadership and interactive skills of the participants.

Figure 4
Growth of Entry Types in Three FORUM Conferences

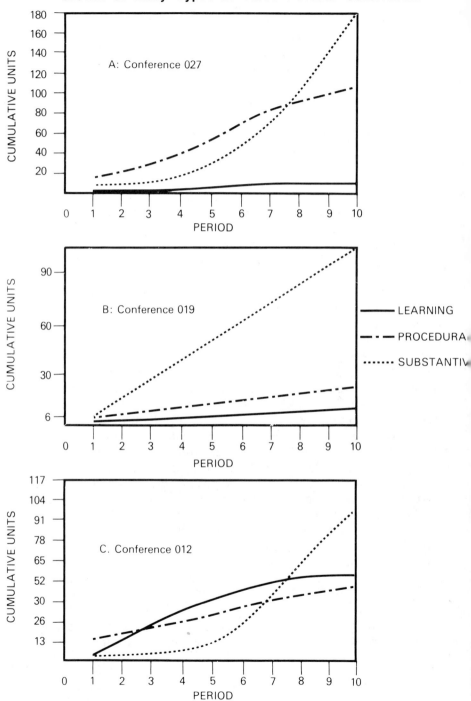

CONCLUSION

In summarizing our findings about the capabilities of computer conferencing, it is possible to project a vision of the medium as it might be used 5 to 10 years from now. Five short scenarios capture this vision:[11]

The "Notepad": When a Scientific Discipline Goes Network

In 1979, an Astronomical Resource Network (ARN) was established to link astronomers at all major universities, as well as observatories and a number of research institutions. It is estimated that approximately 100 astronomers use it daily to communicate with colleagues at remote sites, to access an astronomical data center, and to monitor flash announcements of important phenomena, such as comets and novae. ARN has redefined the nature of the discipline, strengthening communication links and increasing the collective nature of astronomical work. The field is growing more rapidly, spurred by cross-fertilization of ideas. A new power complex has certainly emerged, but it appears to be a more organic part of the discipline itself.

The "Seminar": Conferencing Unlimited, Inc.

Conferencing Unlimited, Inc., is a commercial computer conferencing service. It provides access to computer terminals and takes care of all the formalities of computer networks for short conferences and meetings among people who do not regularly use computer conferencing. The firm has no central offices; its staff are located all over the world, interconnected by international computer networks. It has serviced conferences ranging from committee meetings to topical debates by scholars to psychotherapy sessions. Even the college player draft of the National Basketball Association was organized in 1982 by Conferencing Unlimited. In short, Conferencing Unlimited has greatly extended the availability of computer conferencing and has proven that this new medium is a serious alternative for human communication.

The "Assembly": The Meeting Without Travel

From July 3 to July 6, 1983, the World Future Society held its general assembly using computer conferencing. This first major world wide meeting of scientists to use this medium was arranged in response to complaints about large conferences, stuffy panels, lack of participation, and general frustration. The chairman of the assembly noted afterward that the conference was both more authoritarian and more democractic than any previous assemblies. It was authoritarian in those sessions in which leaders exerted strong control over the proceedings, sometimes limiting comments to three lines per message or limiting the total number of questions each person could ask. It was more democratic in that more complete information was available to more people. Access to well-known persons was higher in this medium, and private messages were exchanged freely among all participants. The assembly demonstrated that a satisfying form of communication is possible without travel and that this medium should be taken seriously for more regular meetings.

The "Encounter": An International Crisis Management Network

On June 2, 1983, the United States officially joined the International Crisis Management Network. The ICMN is a worldwide network of statespeople, as well as economists, scientists, military strategists, psychologists, and other resource people who are connected to a 24-hour-a-day computer conferencing service. It has been uniquely successful in dealing with a range of worldwide crises. This success rests in the skill of ICMN members in manipulating its wealth of information—including online models and data bases—to support their proposals for solutions to crises, to evaluate the proposals of others, and to adjust their own proposals quickly. Much of the success is also due to the skill and endurance of the members who serve as organizers and facilitators of crisis conferences.

The "Questionnaire": Alaska Mineral Wealth Forecasts, Inc.

Alaska Mineral Wealth Forecasts, Inc., is a mineral forecasting service which resembles the "Delphi" concept of the 1960s. A highly trained group of mineral geologists, located all over North America, participate in weekly computer conferences to review information records about mineral properties in the files. These "conferences" are highly structured iterations of quantitative forecasts in which the probabilistic estimates supplied by each expert are mathematically aggregated to produce graphic feedback for the group. The results are supplied directly to government and private subscribers engaged in mineral exploration.

* * * * *

These scenarios are extrapolations of current technology into broader application. They are optimistic in the sense that they describe applications which are socially useful; there will certainly be negative effects as well. (Such negative and positive implications are part of a current project just begun at the Institute.) The scenarios are also somewhat conservative; they only describe conferencing styles which we have already observed. Certainly, new styles are likely to emerge if the medium becomes more broadly accepted.

As we end our initial exploration of computer conferencing, it seems likely that applications will continue to grow in number and scope. This new medium for information exchange could be applied to many practical situations where geographic dissemination and task requirements demand timely, accurate information flow among the members of a small group. Such situations are all around us—in review committees, task forces, scientific panels, research projects, and administrative groups. We now know enough about the behavior of participants to be able to recognize opportunities to make effective use of computer conferencing techniques. Several areas of uncertainty do, however, remain. In particular, the long-term effects of the medium on organizations that use it and the evaluation of its impact on the work patterns of the users have now become the main focus of our research with computer conferencing. The medium makes new types of human communication possible; evaluation of this new medium has reminded us how little is known about human communication itself.

FOOTNOTES

1. Three reports describing the study in more complete detail are available from the Institute for the Future under the title *Group Communication through Computers*. These are in three volumes: Report R-32 describes the design of the FORUM software; R-33 discusses the social evaluation, design, and preliminary results; and R-35 is the final report. This paper is a summary of the final report.

2. H.M. Lipinski and R.H. Miller, "FORUM: A Computer-Assisted Communications Medium," in *Computer Communication Today and Up to 1985,* Second International Conference on Computer Communication, Stockholm, Sweden, August 12-14, 1974.

3. It has been our view that computer conferencing could best be studied *in vivo,* and we have accordingly designed a case history method to be sensitive to the broad possibilities of the medium. This method and the rationale for its adoption are described in more detail in R-33 and R-35.

4. A. Chapanis, "Interactive Human Communication," *Scientific American,* March 1975, p. 36.

5. For a more detailed explication of the notion of travel/communication tradeoffs, see James Kollen and John Garwood, *Travel/Communication Tradeoffs: The Potential for Substitution among Business Travellers,* The Business Planning Group, Bell Canada, April 1975.

6. It should be noted that four of these users had terminals in their homes, as well as in their offices for at least part of the time under study.

7. Developed by R. Garry Shirts, Simile II, 1150 Silverado, La Jolla, California.

8. Robert F. Bales, *Interaction Process Analysis: A Method for the Study of Small Groups,* Cambridge, MA: Addison-Wesley Press, Inc., 1951.

9. This index, developed by Bales and Hare, is coded as the number of acts (i.e., complete thoughts) asking for suggestion divided by the sum of acts coded as giving suggestion and asking for suggestion.

10. Robert F. Bales and A.P. Hare, "Diagnostic Use of the Interactive Profile," *Journal of Social Psychology,* 1965, pp. 239-258.

11. These scenarios are given in full in the CONCLUSION of Report R-35.

ABOUT THE AUTHORS

Jacques Vallee is a senior research fellow at the Institute for the Future, where he directs the computer conferencing project. He was previously associated with network research at Stanford University and SRI. He is a graduate of the Sorbonne and has a Ph.D. from Northwestern University.

Robert Johansen is a research fellow responsible for the Institute's social evaluation of the medium. He has a background in evaluation research and social assessment of technology, with a Ph.D. from Northwestern University.

Hubert Lipinski is a research fellow, with primary responsibility for the design of the computer conferencing system. He holds a Ph.D. from the University of California at San Diego.

Thaddeus Wilson is responsible for the organization of field tests and development of methodologies for analyzing teleconferencing data. His background is in computer programming and data analysis.

CHAPTER 14

PROBLEMS AND FUNDAMENTAL ISSUES IN COST/BENEFIT ANALYSIS OF OFFICE AUTOMATION SYSTEMS

Peter Pin-Shan Chen
Graduate School of Management
University of California, Los Angeles

ABSTRACT

Several problems commonly found in cost/benefit analyses of office automation systems are identified. A case study involving the replacement of an existing system in a large corporation with a new office automation system is presented. The danger of excessive emphasis on cost savings justification is discussed. Finally, fundamental issues facing cost/benefit analysis of office systems are raised.

INTRODUCTION

A new frontier in the computer revolution is the automation of offices. In the past few years, office automation technologies have been advancing at an amazing pace. New office equipment, e.g., word processors, electronic mail systems, video conferencing capacities, and intelligent copiers, has been introduced and agressively marketed by numerous vendors. Many managers find it difficult to keep abreast of rapid advances and are not sure how cost effective these new technologies will be in their organizations. In particular, they would like answers to the following questions: How will these new office systems benefit their own organization? What are the associated costs of new systems? What are the costs of existing systems (manual or automated)? Are the benefits of the new systems worth the extra cost?

To answer these questions, organizations are performing cost/benefit studies of new office systems. Many of these analyses, however, are not carefully thought out. Cost figures have been challenged and invalidated when presented for management review. This not only damages the credibility of the group advocating the new system, but also may delay the introduction of important new office technologies into the organization.

The objectives of this paper are to identify the common pitfalls in cost/benefit analysis of office automation systems and to examine fundamental issues in this type of analysis. Because office automation systems are relatively new, few people have given careful thought on how to analyze costs and benefits of such systems. The problems and issues discussed in this paper will thus be useful in developing a framework for new office system cost/benefit analysis.

This paper is divided into five sections: first, the introduction; second, a case study of the cost/benefit analysis of a proposed office automation system; third, a discussion of problems with approaches that require cost savings justification; fourth, a discussion of fundamental issues in cost/benefit analysis of office automation systems and fifth, the conclusion.

ANALYSIS OF A CASE STUDY

In this section, a case study is used to analyze common problems typically overlooked in cost/benefit analysis of office automation systems. The case involves a division in a large corporation with headquarters located in New York City. The division has, in addition, five remote locations around the country. Each location has both communicating word processors and time-sharing terminals. The management of the division is considering replacing these word processors and time-sharing terminals with newly designed work stations, offering word processing, data processing and electronic mail. Currently, two configurations of work stations are available: (a) Two-user work stations for a manager and his (her) secretary, each having a terminal with a display screen, and (b) Four-user work stations for two pairs of managers and secretaries. The management of the division has requested a cost justification of the proposed system.

The cost/benefit analysis, prepared by a systems analyst, is illustrated in Tables 1, 2, and 3. Table 1 illustrates the costs for the existing system. There are nine word processors with communication capability (four in the headquarters location and one at each remote location). The purchase price for each word processor is $16,500. For nine word processors, the annual amortization cost is $21,215, using a seven-year depreciation

Table 1
The Costs of the Existing System
Alternative One

Item	Cost	Quantity	Total
Word Processors with Communication	$16,500	9	$21,215/yr.* (148,500)
Maintenance	$150/mo.	9	16,200/yr.
Facsimile†	$60/mo.	6	4,320/yr.
Time Sharing Terminals†	$135/mo.	9	14,580/yr.
Courier Mail†	$18/package	10/day	45,360/yr.
Total Yearly Cost			$101,675/yr.

Table 2
The Costs of the Proposed New System
Alternative Two - the Work Station

Item	Cost	Quantity	Total
Two User Work Station	$41,175	5	$29,410/yr.* ($205,875)
Maintenance	410/mo.	5	24,600/yr.
Four User Work Station	$57,875	2	16,535/yr.* ($115,750)
Maintenance	490/mo.	2	11,760/yr.
Facilities	$4,600	7	4,600/yr.* ($ 32,200)
Total Yearly Cost			$86,905

†In place

*7 year depreciation schedule

schedule. The annual maintenance cost is $16,200. This division also has a facsimile machine in each location.These facsimile machines are used only to transmit important alpha-numeric documents. The annual costs for the six facsimile machines is $4,320. They also have nine time-sharing terminals (for the managers) in these six locations, with an annual rental cost of $14,580. They also use a courier mail service to transport computer printouts and typed reports twice a day from the New York City headquarters to each of the five remote locations. Ten packages a day are mailed costing $45,360 per year. The total yearly cost is thus $101,675.

Table 2 presents the estimated cost for the new configuration—i.e, using the newly-designated work stations. Each of the five remote locations will get a two-user work station. Five two-user work stations will cost $29,410 a year (using a seven-year depreciation schedule), and the associated maintenance cost is $24,600 per year. In the division headquarters in New York City, four-user work stations are recommended since these managers and secretaries are in close proximity to each other. Two such work stations will cost $16,535 per year, with a maintenance cost of $11,760 per year. The facilities to support these work stations cost $4,600 per year. The total yearly cost for the new system is thus estimated to be $86,905. If the new system is adopted. the annual savings are estimated to be $14,770 per year (Table 3).

The above study was done for the management of the division. Let us take a critical look at these cost figures and see how the conclusion is sensitive to assumptions about key cost variables. A quick glance at Table 1 reveals the largest cost item is courier mail. If we were to reduce the number of packages sent to remote locations from ten to five per day, the annual cost of courier mails would be cut in half to $22,680, and the total annual cost of the existing system would become $78,995. Table 4 presents a comparison of the revised alternative 1 with alternative 2. Instead of saving $14,770 per year, the "work station" configuration will now cost $7,910 more. This division may have good reasons for sending packages to each remote location twice a day. However, it has been demonstrated that the conclusion in the above case study is *very sensitive* to assumptions that could be challenged.

Let us analyze this case study a bit further. The above cost/benefit analysis considers only the equipment and direct operating costs. Many other factors are ignored. There is no consideration of the *training* and *conversion costs* associated with

Table 3
Net Cost Savings Per Year

Alternative One	$101,675
Alternative Two	86,905
Net Annual Savings	$ 14,770

Table 4
The Result of Changing the Assumption
on the Number of
Courier Mail Packages per Day

Alternative One (5 courier mail packages a day)	$78,995
Alternative Two	$86,905
Extra Cost per Year	($ 7,910)

the new system. There are no estimates of the *time saved* by managers and secretaries due to new capabilities contained in the work stations. There is no mention of *intangible benefits* associated with the new systems. These are common faults in many cost/benefit analyses.

PROBLEMS WITH OVEREMPHASIZING THE COST SAVING ASPECT

As indicated at the end of the previous section, important costs and benefits were not included in the case study. Even if a comprehensive cost analysis had demonstrated that the new system could save millions of dollars for the organization, there might be difficulties in convincing management. The following are some reasons:

Sometimes, we are comparing "oranges" with "apples."

Comparisons of equipment and operating costs are only meaningful when both systems have the same capabilities or the less expensive system has all the capabilities offered by the more expensive system. It is difficult to judge whether a new system can save money if the new and old systems address different needs. Let us use daily-life analogies to explain this point. If we lived in a small town, we could have several choices on how to get to work: walking, jogging, bicycling, or driving a vehicle. Which way is cheapest? Obviously, walking. Which one do we prefer? Probably, most of us would prefer to drive. Why? Driving is a faster and more comfortable way to reach our destination. Cost is thus not the only factor involved in the decision. In addition, different people may prefer jogging or bicycling rather than driving as the means to get to work, as they believe the exercise involved is good for their health. In their decisions, health is a more important factor than cost or time savings.

The moral is—when comparing two systems with different capabilities, first perform a detailed feature analysis of each system and then rate the value of these features against the goals of the organization.

Many managers have had bad experiences with the cost estimates of data processing equipment and projects.

Most middle and upper level managers have insufficient knowledge of computer technology. Some even have fears of the new emerging technologies. It is therefore difficult for them to fully understand and knowledgably evaluate the differences in capabilities between different office automation systems.

More importantly, many past data processing projects cost significantly more than original estimates, and management was often burned by these experiences. They have learned from these painful experiences to be cautious of cost saving predictions on new equipment.

The cost savings argument may not be compatible with the objectives of the organization.

Not all organizations are giving high priority to cost savings. For example, the oil companies have been embarassed by enormous profits in recent years while the price of gasoline is skyrocketing. Under these circumstances, some oil companies may wish to find ways to reduce profits in order to improve their public image. In this situation, stressing the potential benefits rather than the cost savings aspect may be more acceptable to the management. However, we should keep in mind that the objectives of an organization may change as time passes and thus cost/benefit analysis should be performed based on the current objectives of the organization.

Based on the above observations, both *tangible and intangible benefits* of the new system should be studied in the cost/benefit analysis of an office automation system. The analysis should also be compatible with the organization's objectives.

FUNDAMENTAL ISSUES

A fundamental issue in the cost/benefit analysis of new office automation systems is distinguishing "efficiency" from "effectiveness." If two machines can do the same task and one is faster than the other, we say that the former is more *efficient* than the other. Usually this type of task is more structured, such as typing, and a commonly agreeable measure of performance, such as the number of words typed per minute, is available. However, many tasks in the office are not structured and thus it is difficult to measure performance. For these types of tasks, new office automation system can improve *effectiveness,* the same task using the same amount of time but with higher quality output. Both efficiency and effectiveness dimensions should be considered when analyzing the impacts of a new automation system.

A related issue is how to measure effectiveness. In some organizations, word processors did not shorten the time between initial drafting of the document and final typing because the document went through more revisions than before. We could argue that the word processor created higher quality documents. But how can we measure the quality of a document or the effectiveness of many other office tasks? Further research is needed to provide answers to these questions.

CONCLUSION

Many cost/benefit analyses of office automation systems are done hurriedly and usually are incomplete or incorrect. They typically overemphasize the cost savings aspect when the cost savings argument may not be the best way to advocate a new system to management. Many managers have had bad experiences with cost estimates of data processing projects and are suspicious of projected budgets. Sometimes two systems with different kinds of capabilities are inappropriately compared. More emphasis should be placed on the immediate and potential benefits of new office automation systems. Fundamental issues in the analysis of office systems are: (1) how to analyze the impacts of a new office automation system on office tasks in terms of efficiency and effectiveness; and (2) how to measure effectiveness. Further research is needed to address these issues.

ACKNOWLEDGEMENT

The author is indebted to Mr. Mark Lieberman. Part of the case study material in this paper is based on his talk at the Stanford Symposium.

REFERENCES

1. Lieberman, M., "Now that We've Built It, How Do We Justify It?", a talk given at Stanford University International Symposium of Office Automation, March 26-28, 1980, Palo Alto, California.

2. Mintzberg, Henry, *The Natural of Managerial Work*, Harper and Row, New York City, 1973.

3. O'Neal, J. D., "We Increased Typing Productivity 340%," *The Office*, February, 1979, pp. 95-97.

4. Uhlig, R. P., Farber, D. J., and Bair, J. H., *The Office of the Future*, North-Holland, Amsterdam, 1979, pp. 345-369.

PART IV

THE MANAGEMENT AND EVOLUTION OF ELECTRONIC OFFICE SYSTEMS

CHAPTER 15

MANAGEMENT ISSUES IN
HUMAN COMMUNICATION VIA COMPUTER

Murray Turoff

Director
Computerized Conferencing and Communications Center
New Jersey Institute of Technology

ABSTRACT

This paper discusses the process of justifying, designing, evolving and evaluating the technology of utilizing the computer to facilitate human communications. It is based upon the experience of the author in being active over the past decade implementing such systems for a variety of organizations. It emphasizes the need for an evolutionary approach to the development and evaluation of such systems within most organizations and discusses potential opportunities in the office environment. The emphasis, however, is not on automation, but on augmentation of office functions.

INTRODUCTION

There are subtle similarities between problems associated with computers and organizations that tend in many ways to make computer and information science a discipline similar to management science. One would like to think that computer and information science provides facts or natural laws in the same sense as Physics and Chemistry. However, this is not the case. Computers, like organizations, are "man made systems," which do not operate according to natural law. Rather, they operate according to some sort of working arrangement or compromise between their designers and the people who use them—the "users." Many organizations are designed the same way, and yet styles of management, specific objectives and employee behavior tend to add certain elements of uniqueness to any particular organizational body.

When we speak of office automation, management augmentation, decision support systems and/or computerized conferencing, we are referring to computer technology which has been integrated in some manner into a working human environment. Consequently, we do not have an environment where we can hope to derive natural laws from the experiences observed. What we can do is observe case studies in an uncontrolled environment and hope that some implications emerge that appear to be consistent over similar cases.

While it is possible to conduct very specialized controlled experiments in areas such as decision support systems and computerized conferencing systems (Hiltz et al., 1980) these are useful only in proving something is possible or disproving particular items of folklore. For example, the experiments on human problem solving conducted at NJIT show it is possible for human groups to reach the same quality of solution using computerized conferencing as using face to face discussions. This defeats the view held commonly by many managers that a group could not deal as well with problem solving in the electronic form as face to face. However, this provides no guarantee that the same results will be obtained in the real environment. There is no realistic way, in a working environment, that we can control factors sufficiently to force the occurence of relationships observed in the laboratory, nor can a single case study in the field be used to verify causal relationships in any scientific sense. Since most of the work in this area is largely of a case study nature, what emerges is sometimes wisdom and sometimes highly suspicious folklore. While we can approach some questions about computer and information systems in a scientific manner, these are never the questions whose answers completely decide a management issue. At best, they can provide insight for management consideration in weighing all the factors involved.

While we have supposedly evolved procedures and methodologies that guide us in the development and utilization of computer and information systems, there are many reasons why these approaches do not always work as they were envisioned. In particular, when we are dealing with a new application of computer technology, we find that the process of introducing the technology and gaining its acceptance often does not follow any rational procedures. For example, the evaluation studies of the EIES (Electronic Information Exchange System) system have shown that one of the strongest predictors of use was how much a person expected to use the system before they started use (Hiltz, 1980). Because of this the image of the technology and how it is presented to the potential user community can be highly significant in determining the system's ultimate success.

When it comes to utilizing the computer to facilitate human communications, we have the classic case of many of the right things being done for the wrong reasons and wrong things being justified on what seem to be the right rationale. This usually results from limiting our view of the potential for the technology to mere automation and to basing our actions in utilizing such systems upon our preconceptions concerning the human communication process. What we have today is a lot of confusion on what is fact, wisdom, folklore and fiction in this area. This paper attempts to provide some wisdom from the perspective of someone who has acted as a designer in a number of real world situations and has also been involved in a number of evaluation and assessment studies of the technology.

JUSTIFICATION

The process that we use to justify a system almost pre-determines the nature of the system. Unfortunately, this aspect of the decision process is usually done subconsciously. Most of the current approaches to office automation are pre-studies based upon a "substitution" rationale which often results in the introduction of systems which are automated replications of existing processes. The implications of the justification process for the nature of the system and its long term impacts on the organization are rarely made explicit. In some cases, it also works the other way: we tailor the justification process to fit the system we want to have. Neither approach occurs out of any overt dishonesty. This situation is largely a natural consequence of continued fragmentation and specialization of responsibilities on the part of management as an organization grows in size. It derives from the need to have commonly accepted procedures for justifying actions that apply across the board. This means that we are forced into largely reductionist approaches that can be uniformly applied to the particular piece of a problem a single manager is responsible for or to the collection of problems making up some global objective. With this view of the office environment, we can do things like separately treat the problem of typing from those of filing, communications, copying, data bases, decision support, management augmentation, etc.

The first consideration that usually comes to mind in the justification of a system or application of computers is economic viability. While economics has many guidelines for considering things in a more global sense, the most common approach taken in this area is one of "automation." This is perhaps the easiest and the most misleading of the economic approaches to justification. It is with us as the result of a long history of use in selling computer systems and applications on this sort of basis. It is what many analysts concerned with computer operations have been trained to do. In this process, we introduce a new computer application by presenting it as a "mere" automation of what we are doing now. The economic advantage comes from doing, supposedly, the same thing we have always done, but faster and cheaper through the use of computer technology. It is correct, in theory, when we are dealing with a closed, deterministic system. Certain systems, like one producing the payroll checks in an organization do, in fact, fit this sort of criterion over a reasonably long period of time approaching that of the life of the system. However, even systems we once thought could be justified from this perspective, such as inventory systems, have had many long term effects on organizations never considered in the original justification for such systems.

When we consider doing human communication via computer, the personification of the "automation" approach is the current popularizing of "electronic mail." The name itself is supposed to imply to the unsuspecting manager that this is an electronic form of the internal memo. It conveys a soothing message that only some typists and clerical people might be affected and that the managers and professionals and the nature of the organization itself will not be disturbed. It is a simple substitution that will result in no significant change of behavior. While it is true that we can replicate the internal memo (and do it cheaper and faster) for organizations beyond some minimum size, the key question to be addressed is what opportunities are we neglecting by not asking if the technology can provide new ways of communicating beyond the methods we are currently using. We have misdirected the design of the system by choosing to ask the wrong question. This same problem of misdirection and reductionism is reflected in the even more general "buzz words" of "office automation." It is what leads to considering word processing as the key element in office automation.

Looking at organizational communications from a more global perspective, it can be observed that over $400 billion a year goes into the salaries of office workers in this country. Well over $100 billion of that salary time is consumed by managers and professionals engaged in communication activities. In contrast, the total typing bill is less than 5 billion. What this means is that if we can improve management and professional communications by at least 5%, we would realize a savings of as much as the total typing bill in most organizations. In light of this fact, why do we place most of our effort, on the average, in the area of word processing and to a great extent ignore communications?

Doing something about the typing situation is a low level decision that on the surface does not appear to have any impact outside a local office unit. Replacing a secretary's typewriter with something a little more expensive is not a "big deal" on a small scale basis. Introducing a computer disguised as a "word processor" is easier than introducing a more general purpose computer system. Impacting the secretary raises less concern than impacting the way managers do things. Doing something about communications requires decisions affecting the whole organization, not just small parts of it.

In addition to this, we also have problems of a psychological nature. We have been communicating all our lives and have developed our own personal wisdom as to when and under what conditions we seek to use the mail, phone or face to face meeting. In a sense, we consider ourselves experts when it comes to choosing our medium of communications to accomplish some objective. Unfortunately, most of the controlled studies of communication media indicate that our wisdom is often unverifiable folklore. For example, most people believe that if they have to have a discussion with someone who may lie to them, a face to face meeting would be preferable to use of the telephone. It turns out, however, that an individual is more capable of detecting a lie over the telephone than face to face. This is because someone who is used to lying utilizes body language to convince people, subconsciously, that he is or she is telling the truth.

The various studies that have been done of small group processes show that leadership and the nature of the agreement a group may come to in a face to face meeting are far more sensitive to the talent of the leader than to the knowledge of the group that is relevant to the problem at hand. In spite of this, groups utilize face to face meetings because they believe that to be the only option. It is basically hard to conceive for an alternative communication medium because we are very used to the ones we have. It is difficult to recognize fundamental differences when we have not experienced the new form of communication. This is illustrated in some of the results of the controlled experimental work we have done comparing face to face problem solving with using computer conferencing. Small groups of five individuals who were first time users of the computer conferencing technology were able to arrive at solutions that were just as good as the solutions arrived at by the face to face groups. They used only about one-third the number of words of communications. However, on the average, they were more satisfied in using face to face and it is very possible from the data that they were less satisfied with their solution in the computerized conferencing environment.

When faced with a new communications medium, we often have to learn how to be effective using it and the rules that apply to other forms of communication may not carry over to the new one. We often forget that it took us quite a while to learn to use the telephone when we were young. Utilizing computers for communications is still foreign to most people and it is far too easy for them to view this technology as another form of fast mail and to sell it on that basis, rather than to consider the whole range of problems introduced by people having to learn new communication skills. In our own experience, while it took new users only a few hours to learn the mechanics of a computer conferencing system, the learning time on things like the communications behavior in a computer conference, with respect to things like writing style, is in the 10 to 20 hour range. Furthermore, people's attitudes toward the effectiveness of the medium for various communication tasks appear to improve with experience on the system, which is probably a result of having to experience different communications situations such as giving orders, bargaining, etc., before they can make a reasonable evaluation. We also note that for communication tasks which have emotional content, such as persuasion, those new to the technology split into two groups—those who believe it is effective and those who don't. Such views are strongly held, as contrasted to the situation where the majority is uncertain before they try the technology. It is thus very dangerous to base one's decision about the nature of a system to install on the initial views of potential users. This observation is contrary to the "text book" process for planning a new system.

The result of these considerations is that most organizations who go through elaborate justification studies usually end up with a new technology that is a slight extension or "automation" of what they are doing now. When one looks at organizations that have taken a significant leap in their use of the technology in a new area, it seems to be the case that a very different process was used to introduce the technology. The approach that seems to work involves someone going out on a limb by authorizing the development of some in-house capability on their own computer or making readily available some outside service. Then the technology is made available on a casual basis to groups who appear to have extremely demanding communications requirements. The parameters of interest here are things like the geographical spread of the group, the urgency and intensity of the communications within the group. More often than not, a group that has found a system useful in an intense and urgent communications situation will continue to use it after the unusual situation has gone away. Once a nucleus of people are seen using such a system and appearing to gain benefits from doing so, others get interested and the use of the system spreads. At least four major companies that today have many hundreds to many thousands of active professional and managerial users utilizing message and conferencing systems on a day to day basis developed their initial utilization in this way. It is also true that these were companies where terminals were already fairly plentiful and readily available to their management and professional staff.

In one example of this process, the manager of a large group of auditors was certain that the computerized conferencing technology would be of significant advantage. However, auditors are a very conservative lot to begin with. What was done was to create a system on the sly, which sat unused for approximately eight months until some 20 auditors in four offices around the country suddenly had to deal with a common audit that required them to meet face to face every two weeks. The loss of three days of time every two weeks was becoming intolerable and the computerized conferencing system was introduced to the group. They were able to cut their meetings down to once every two months for the duration of the job, and after the job was done they continued to utilize the system on a day to day basis.

The casual approach can lead to tremendous imbalances in resources and an inability to deal with the growing demand of a successful introduction. There are also numerous situations where a limited system may have an initial success, but be unable to meet the requirements necessary to extend it to a large population of users and the broader range of requirements they may have. The combination of the problem of introducing a new technology for which users have no real basis of experience and the unpredictability of the requirements that will arise once they gain the necessary experience leads to the observation that the only effective approach an organization can take in this area is an evolutionary one. What is needed besides the careful introduction of a system is a plan and the resources to evaluate the impact of the system and how it can be developed as an ongoing process in response to growing user awareness and needs.

Since its introduction in 1976, the Electronic Information Exchange System (EIES) has been designed to be an evolutionary system. It has undergone continual modification in response to an integrated evaluation and assessment program. The EIES experience now represents over 100,000 user hours and over 1,000 users who have had active access to the system ranging from six months to four years. It has had a wide diversity of groups ranging from managerial and professional groups to young teenagers, handicapped and senior citizens. We designed the software to allow individual groups to carry out significant tailoring of the system to meet their specific needs. It is the result of this and other experiences that guides the formulation of the management issues discussed in the remainder of this paper.

DESIGN

One suspects that many of us who become designers of computer systems find a certain appeal in the apparent descriptive or deductive nature of working with these systems. Utilizing a computer, one can establish a unique set of "natural" laws, which the computer would carry out without deviation. On a computer system the designer can create his or her own universe, which behaves quite explicitly according to the laws one prescribes for it.

Certainly, in the environment of batch oriented systems, a rather sharp and distinct boundary could be drawn between the computer system and the applications to which it was put. The users of such a system could be viewed by the designer as somewhat of a black box, and be represented entirely by specific items of data that they provided or sought. The computer itself was left to the designer.

The introduction of interactive terminals disturbed this rather tranquil situation somewhat, but not entirely. To date, interactive or terminal oriented systems have been largely restricted to specific functional areas such as data base retrieval, computational work, word processing, graphics, etc. In such systems it is still quite possible to replace the user with a fairly specific set of functional requirements which the computer must perform. For example, in retrieval systems one can replace the user with such refined measures as precision, recall and relevance. As a result, the designer could restrict himself to the internal workings of the information system, and leave the evaluation of impact on users to others. In such situations, the design and impact are now separable, and in the best tradition of reductionism.

Another aspect of the way the world used to be was the high hardware costs, relative to people costs, for computer systems and the frequent occurence of complete disregard of end user costs. While this has changed radically in recent years, the associated accounting and organizational measurement and performance evaluation systems still, to a large degree, ignore the impact on users of interactive systems and the evaluation of alternative systems for those same measures.

However, when we attempt to use a computer for human communications there is no possible way we can meaningfully separate the user from the design. The behavior of the user determines the behavior of the system and the design of the system can directly influence the psychology and sociology of the individuals using it. The world is no longer neat and no longer subject to demarcation by firm boundaries between the technology and the user. Superimposed upon the prescriptions of the designer are those of the users as they create their own norms within the context of a communications process. Perhaps, as a further irony, the nature of this technology is such that the designer, can to a high degree, impose a world upon users without their conscious recognition of such a process taking place. The danger here is even more significant when the designer is also unaware of this potential.

In principle, the designer should incorporate an understanding of psychology and sociology into the design of systems. Unfortunately, or perhaps fortunately, these fields offer very little knowledge on the specific questions designers are faced with. Considering the fact that we all use communications, it is rather surprising how little is actually known about the process with any scientific validity. Most current design work is literally based upon the gut intuition of either the designers or those directing the designers, rather than on established axioms of human behavior pertinent to this technology. Given such a situation, we have to recognize that the only valid approach to utilizing this technology for human communication is one where we have to integrate evaluation, feedback and evolution of the design into the system itself. This has been a significant part of the effort at the New Jersey Institute of Technology, with the operation of the Electronic Information Exchange System (EIES) since 1976. A significant amount of the design effort and the development of evaluation methodology has been with the goal of tying the design, evaluation and evolution process together (Hiltz and Turoff, 1980). It is quite clear from that work that some of the basic approaches to evaluation of an interactive design, such as usage rates, are inappropriate as pure measures of success.

People using the computer for communication expect the same simplicity and reliability of use that they obtain from a telephone. They also expect that their communications will be delivered and not lost. Often when one puts a computer system in an organization, some people have to use it because it may be the only way to get the information or analyses necessary to do their job. In such cases, the mistake is often made of taking the use of the system as a measure of user acceptance and therefore a measure of the success of the system. Whenever we have high compliance, usage is not a meaningful measure of acceptance or the performance of the design or user interface.

However, with respect to communication mode, users can decide to resort to other alternatives, such as face to face meetings, telephones and/or the mail. With the learning curves that users must go through on behavior aspects of this form of communication, the slightest unreasonable inconvenience to the user in the early stages of learning the system or in the initial introduction of the system to the user community can have a disastrous impact. This does not apply when sufficient motivation exists for the users as a whole, but in most real world situations a large percentage of the potential user population will start out as reluctant or suspicious users and it is this segment of the population that can be turned on or off by very small design mistakes. Sometimes, these inconveniences are more subtle than one would expect. Many current message systems have been designed by watching secretarial behavior in handling internal correspondence. While the designers freely state that their systems are usable by managers, we note that the way a user writes a memo exactly mimics the process whereby the secretary types a memo. First, a person is asked to fill in the title information as to whom the memo is to be sent, what the subject is and other typical title categories. Only after that is the user given the option of writing the text. This is fine for the secretary who has been given a final version of the memo by his or her boss. However, if a manager or professional is writing the memo directly, very often they will not make the final decision on how to title the memo until after they have drafted the contents. Therefore, a design that mimics the secretarial process may turn off a good many managers and inhibit their possible use of the system in the long run.

What may seem like very small considerations can have significant impacts on gaining initial user acceptance of the technology. We have found on EIES that many features that we designed to be used in a particular way, were used in very different manners by some groups. Usually this required the developing of new features which were more efficient for the particular group. For example, our voting routines were designed with the idea that a relatively small number of the comments in a conference would be votable. The average user would not be using them a lot, so they were programmed to ask very explicit questions and consequently the construction of a votable item and the taking of the votes requires about 30 seconds per item. Then one group came along that wanted hundreds of votable items in a conference all at once. The one at a time voting process for any user in this situation became too slow and tedious. Therefore, a new input routine had to be developed that allowed a lot of different votes to be entered in one operation as an alternative to the original process.

The design must be carefully segmented, so the user can learn only what he needs to learn to carry out the tasks he must perform at the moment. However, one also wants the user to be aware of the potential for doing other things and to have a general idea of the system as a whole. Arriving at a balance of these two objectives is still somewhat of an art form. If the system is only a simple message or mimic of the internal mail, no such problem exists. However, the users would never become aware of what else the technology is capable. Some of these augmentations are the subject of the following sections. What is important here is to realize that a great deal of concern has to go into the interface design and not many computer people are adequately sensitized to this consideration. They are more used to optimizing the efficiencies of the hardware and software and are frequently guilty of sacrificing interface design for the benefit of hardware and software performance. This also persuades us against trying to cram such systems into heavily loaded machines that might, under peak loading, give low priority to the responsiveness of the communication system.

STRUCTURE

The concept of structure in human communication via computer is the idea that you can utilize the computer to tailor the communication process around the particular group and its application (Hiltz and Turoff, 1978, Chapter 9). This has also been referred to as *groupware* (Johnson-Lenz, 1980) when the actions of the humans such as facilitators and leaders are included in the design. For face to face group meetings, human groups have evolved a range of structures from free discussion to parliamentary procedures to govern meetings oriented to accomplishing specific objectives and differing in such parameters as the size of the group. However, the scope of possible structures for face to face groups is far more limited than what is possible when we consider using a computer as a structuring device within a communicating group. To illustrate this, we will take a few existing examples and then reflect on the possibilities in the office environment.

The EIES system has, for example, a basic structure which provides messages, conferences and notebooks. These are now fairly typical structures; however, the details of any one message or conference system can differ considerably from implementation to implementation. With messages on EIES, for example, confirmations are stored in a large central file, as opposed to a copy of the same message being stored in each receiver's personal file space, as is common on many commercial systems. This, in particular, allows later retrieval and organization of a set of messages all dealing with the same topic or task. It also allows for indirect references and resending of messages with some assurance that everyone is seeing the same copy, even after modification. By allowing messages to stay in a common storage for up to three months after they are written, we have found that there is a sizable amount of retrieval, searching and resending that occurs in an unanticipated manner, such as when triggered by a related new task. In other words, at the time a message is initially received or sent, the individuals involved don't anticipate a need to save the item and this need occurs at a later time due to some unforecasted occurrence. If we look only at messaging, there are many features that can be included to facilitate the messaging process: future delivery, serial routing, routing with approvals incorporated, etc. All these are done manually now, but with the computer, the incorporation of these processes into the software takes the burden of tracking these functions off of the humans involved and passes it to the computer.

The basic EIES conference is a semi-free-form discussion space where a group can accumulate a transcript on a particular topic and perform numerous search options on that transcript. We have some conferences that have been active for over two years and hold thousands of comments. The conference also offers special features such as voting, in which the computer compiles and displays the votes and allows individuals to modify their votes at any time.

One common occurrence on EIES is that a group uses a conference to try to accomplish some task. After a period of time, they discover that other structures might aid them in the process. The fact that EIES provides examples of other capabilities and a diversity of communication functions brings this realization about in a very natural way. We would observe that a group given a very simple message system that only mimics their current mail process is unlikely to come to this realization if they are not already knowledgeable about computers.

One such example is the evolution of the *Politechs/Topics* system, which has actually gone through two major modifications since its creation about two years ago. The process of the gradual evolution of a system is also one we have observed as users pass new plateaus in terms of what they want to do with the system. Politechs/Topics was created for a group of state legislative science advisors. The initial group included 25 of these individuals and about 30 others who act as liaison to state legislatures from various federal agencies and professional societies. Each state legislative science advisor is responsible for answers to scientific or technical questions coming out of any legislative process (Johnson-Lenz, 1980). The topics range over a diverse set of subjects: regulations on underground high voltage transmission lines, legal definitions of death, defining antiques legally, specific toxic substances, etc. The level of activity can be 10 to 20 questions per week. The design that was arrived at through discussions with the group involved allowing any member of the exchange network to enter a three line question which would be broadcast to all the rest. Anyone could enter a one page response and anyone could decide to select the topic which would trigger delivery to that person of any current and future responses about it.

What this group has done is set up a self filtering system where they can individually choose which topics they want to track with respect to incoming responses. The level of activity is too high for them to have time to track all items. However, they also have included a key word index under the monitorship (for consistency) of one of the participants, which can be used to search for earlier items, should they become of interest to an individual later on. Also being designed now is software to allow the persons entering topics to rate the responses for their value and to transfer funds from the account of the person who entered the topic to the accounts of those who provide valuable responses. EIES currently is putting this type of software into a number of its communication structures, in order to be able to experiment with a real "information marketplace."

Each state that participates in Politechs can usually afford only one person who specializes in this area. However, through the use of EIES, each state now has available to it over 50 knowledgeable individuals. If one is talking about productivity gains, in this example we are talking about a ten fold or more increase, and not the 10% one would usually consider a significant productivity gain in most literal office "automations." While this group is somewhat unique in that it cuts across separate autonomous organizations, in any large organization one would expect numerous opportunities to share and exchange specialized knowledge according to need. Obviously, a system introduced to accomplish this in an organized way would have definite impacts on the way many professionals function within the organization and vastly increase the lateral communication channels.

One of the first conferencing systems, *Emisari* (Hiltz and Turoff, 1978, chapter 2; Renner et al., 1972), was designed to have the structure of a crisis management reporting system. While this system was implemented in 1971 for the monitoring of the Wage/Price Freeze and other crisis activities of the then Office of Emergency Preparedness, it still represents the most sophisticated example to date of a working management information system designed exclusively as a communication system. One feature of the system was a data base that could be tailored by a manager to designate which members of the system could actually enter the value of any defined data item. The system would make available to anyone retrieving the data the name of who had entered it and when they did. It would also allow any member to send messages to items of data. Therefore, a person retrieving data would be notified if there were any new messages about the data they were retrieving. This meant the individuals responsible for gathering the data, analyzing it, monitoring it or acting on it could develop their own organized discussion about that particular data, even though they were many thousands of miles apart and working very hectic schedules of 12 and 14 hours per day. For any crisis, the typical user population was about 100 professionals spread out in the ten regional OEP offices and the national office. This was only one of many unique communication features that were incorporated into the Emisari system.

When one looks specifically at the office environment, there are a host of communication structures that can be tailored to facilitate the tasks of managers and professionals. While most studies show that the average manager spends only a short time (like 10 minutes) on a vast majority of his or her daily tasks, what is often overlooked is that many single short tasks are small steps or subtasks related to a longer term activity. Two closely related structures that encompass this fact are the personal calendar of the manager or professional and the components of sub-projects making up a single project being carried on by a number of individuals. A project tracking system is one that requires inputs from a number of individuals and, in many cases, the communications in the office environment relate various tasks going on concerned with the project as a whole. Also, projects have their various deadlines, meetings and such that must go onto the individual's calendar. Most computerized project systems try to restrict themselves to quantitative information and the assorted qualitative communications dealing with the project are now handled by the usual communication alternatives. It would be far more efficient for the people involved to have one system that integrates the communications into the project flow and allows an individual access to one central file containing all the details of changes, modifications, concerns, etc. about the project. Obviously, one can also tie that into providing a personal calendar system which automatically incorporates deadlines and meetings or arranging meetings according to the information available on all the calendars.

Since 1971, the author has had the advantage of managing most software development projects he has been involved with through a computerized conferencing system. This has ranged from groups of three to twelve programmers at any one time. Given the way programmers like to come up with possible changes to a job, the ability to have a common transcript and suggestions in writing has cut down considerably on the time needed to facilitate communication in the group. More importantly, it cuts down the number of interruptions and allows the manager to schedule his or her own time better. Many times when one has checked into the project conference, one could observe that a particular programmer has already answered another with an explanation of why a suggested change would interfere with someone else's piece of the system.

Another application very typical of the office environment is a transaction tracking system. In the OEP case, a later complement to Emisari, the *Premise* system (Mckendree, 1979), allowed the definition of standard paths through the organization of certain documents. These included violations of regulations, property disposal cases, congressional correspondence, etc. One could define the steps such an item must go through, who was responsible at each step, what the alternative actions were, and what the expected delay time was in each step. When a transaction was initiated, the person having the responsibility for the first step would be notified, and when that person had completed that step they would indicate the action and add any qualitative comments to the transaction and then the computer would pass the item automatically to the next step (or person responsible for it). Once again, this cut down the bookkeeping each individual had to do in keeping track of where the item was, and the computer also provided many ways of summarizing and alerting individuals to the overall situation at any time.

Other areas that obviously include special communication structures and the merger of qualitative communications with quantitative data are budget estimation, project planning and the resource allocation process—although these today involve extensive face discussions. While we are not recommending the elimination of face to face meetings, it is felt that the number of them can be cut down tremendously with the proper communication structures. Face to face meetings can then largely focus on the issues that are not easily resolved and have surfaced as major issues through a computerized communication process.

The key element in defining a communication structure is that there is nothing in the software that is unique to the particular problem the group is dealing with. The Emisari system had nothing in it that was characteristic of the Wage/Price Freeze, therefore it was capable of being applied equally well to transportation strikes, oil shortages, fertilizer shortages, chlorine shortages and the other characteristic crises OEP had responsibility for in the 70's. This concept is the secret behind designing successful communication structures in the office environment, so they do not become outdated as the tasks of the users change with time. This leads us to the next primary concern that represents a dramatic departure from how we normally handle computer applications and systems.

EVOLUTION

The standard approach to computer applications involves very elaborate system studies that completely define the job to be done and then implementation of the total system. There may be anywhere from a few months to a few years between when the system is designed and when it is finally put into the hands of the users. Where there is a large base of experience for the type of system being developed and the behavior of the users and the system is largely predictable, this approach is feasible. However, our understanding of human communication via computer is rudimentary. We do not have the knowledge to predesign a finished system for which we can anticipate all the consequences. Extensive evaluation studies before designing and introducing such systems will only give us data on the existing operation. The views of users before they have gained experience with such systems can often be misleading. They will not tell us what new opportunities could be had or what needs the users will perceive as they gain first hand knowledge of the technology. The standard systems analysis approach is an extrapolation approach to the system planning process. In cases of basically new applications, it is far more desirable to take normative approaches, such as asking what communications processes are needed by the organization and how we could design a system that would encourage people to engage in those communication patterns. This is a much more difficult problem to tackle than asking what the current patterns are and how we can make them more efficient. However, in order to work, normative studies must be on-going planning efforts in any organization. Planning itself has never been very successful unless done on a continuous iterative basis. In this situation, where we are in effect going to be modifying the social and organizational structure of the human system, we have more potential control of the results than when we are planning the usual business actions.

In view of this, the preferred approach is to look for special situations where the individuals involved are overburdened by communications needs. With a careful examination of the existing communication patterns, these usually become obvious. Given those cases, one tries to create or provide a system that will be an aid in those situations. However, a great deal of effort should go into making the software for such a system easy to change or extend with added capabilities. While this costs a lot more for the initial software development effort, it will reduce the life cycle costs trememdously. Equally important is setting up a well designed user feedback and evaluation system and making sure the users understand that the intention is to develop the system according to the experience they have with it. To succeed here, it is crucial that one have the resources to be responsive to user requirements in a reasonably short time frame.

However, there is one key difficulty with individual user requests that should be noted. A particular user will express his needs in very specific terms. It is the task of the system designers or analysts to generalize on specific requirements so that a newly introduced capability will be a general one that services a variety of user needs and accomplishes what the computer can provide. Users seem to think that what is hard for them is hard for the computer and vice versa, when in fact, the opposite is usually true. Users, for example, will want a way to copy a message or part of a message into a new message. They will not recognize that one could also provide a capability to indirectly reference an old message in a new one so that when the new message is received by someone, the original message is retrieved at the point in time and printed out as part of the new message. On EIES, this capability is extended further to where the computer checks if the current receiver was a sender or receiver of the older message and only prints the reference to it if this is the case. This capability has proved very useful in reducing unnecessary printout of items and is only possible with a central file of messages.

At this stage in the knowledge of these systems, the only appropriate approach is the evolutionary one. Given the real world of limited resources, the major investments should be in making the system easy to change and in a responsive on-going feedback and evaluation program. Massive singleshot evaluation and design studies prior to actual experience are not recommended.

EVALUATION

One has to be careful, in this area, not to let themselves be swayed by the priests of productivity and efficiency. The big payoff in this area is in improving the quality of what people do. However, since this is a very hard thing to measure, it sometimes gets pushed to the background and people fall back on the easy things like measuring in word processing systems how many lines of text are produced.

Efficiency measures are very easy to estimate for this technology and no elaborate studying is needed. Once the size of a communicating group gets above 10, the use of the computer is cheaper than just about any other form of human communication, including face to face meetings, with no travel time or travel costs (Turoff, 1972). In fact, the current use of a dedicated mini-computer to support the operation of EIES is essentially economically competitive with the mails (Hiltz and Turoff, 1980).

One can get at quality improvements directly by very carefully designed non-threatening and confidential surveys, developed by people with experience in this particular art form. Don't let inexperienced people design surveys, the results can be very misleading.

Indirectly, one can get many measures from a good monitor of the system use. One would actually like to track the network pattern of communications over a period of time and observe if individuals are strengthening their lateral communications throughout the organization. There are various performance measures one can look at, such as the ratio of items received to sent by individuals and by groups. This ratio has some bearing when looking at this as a reward process. It is the ratio of what one receives as a result of one's efforts in entering material. We have observed that certain values seem to indicate a regular satisfied user of this technology. When it is too large, they feel overwhelmed and when it is too small they feel they are not getting enough out of the system. One would like to observe if there is more delegation of authority on an informal basis going on, since the nature of this communication medium allows significantly better accountability for actions taken. To what extent are people keeping up in the office while on the road and for what purposes are people taking terminals home to do work? Is there more call for task forces that cut across organizational lines? These are the sort of indicators of change that one is looking for.

The most telling measure of impact is the effect on user communication patterns. The design of a system to support management has to be the design of a communication system. In effect, when we design communications we are designing the social system and are redesigning the organization, whether or not we choose to admit it (Turoff, 1979). The real organizational structure of any organization is the one observed in the communications patterns of its members, regardless of what the formal organizational chart shows. The only way to evaluate a social system and its representation in a communication system is by studying an existing system. Therefore, the evaluation process and the evolution process of the system are intimately intertwined.

A counter intuitive indication of success in an on-going system is the amount of complaints gotten from users in terms of what it won't do for them. This indicates that the users not only understand the current design, but the design is such that it makes them aware of the potential the computer has for doing more for them than it is now doing. Provided the system can be evolved to respond to these requests in a timely manner, this is a healthy situation and the best confirmation of a successful operation.

We may attempt to set goals for how we would like the organization to behave, but there is no reliable way to jump from what one currently has to a system that will bring the situation about. People and the organization they represent change slowly and incrementally where human communications are involved. Only a series of small increments of change and a process of determining if the change is in the right direction can work.

OPPORTUNITIES

In the office environment, almost all communications have ties directly or indirectly to existing or potential data base structures and decision support aids. The integration of communication structures, data base structures and processing aids or models is still a wide open area for development. The Emisari experience (Hiltz and Turoff, 1978, Chapter 2) still represents the most comprehensive demonstration of this integration in a management environment. Certainly, not all organizations have the same type of crisis situations as those the Office of Emergency Preparedness was concerned with. However, the typical organization can encounter strikes, cost overruns, new competitive products, delivery delays, potential customer loss, etc. In a crisis situation timely communications is paramount and all the functions usually involve a group of people contributing data to the same situation—obtaining views, obtaining expertise, drafting contingencies, validating options, obtaining approvals and coordinating actions. While it may be desirable to introduce people to this technology when they face a crisis situation, one should design the system so it operates in the normal environment. A small group can be given training for first time use in a crisis, but for regular response to crisis type situations, the users should be familiar with the system and use it regularly.

Another function in the office environment that requires data base integration is tracking of actions, correspondence, tasks, performance of other functions, etc. A piece of important correspondence may go through a variety of different hands in order to be processed or may trigger inputs from numerous sources before it can be handled. Even the simple idea of a personal calendar can be extended into a fairly involved tracking system if it is to incorporate all the occurences in the office environment. In other words, a request to you by your supervisor to supply some information would come as both a message and as an entry in your personal calendar as to when it is due. Most simple attempts at personal calendars, which do no more than automate the person's date book and look much like the manual process, are largely doomed to failure. This is merely because it is more work and more inconvenient to enter these items at a terminal than pulling out of one's pocket a notebook and jotting it down. Therefore, there has to be a bigger reward for using a personal calendar than can be supplied by the pocket notebook. This reward would come by integrating all the other tasks flowing through the office and having one person's input result in the necessary indirect communications to other electronic personal calendars. One has to build up a critical mass of interrelated aids (e.g., electronic Rolodexes) that are tied together, in order to overcome the resistance to change, and these systems have to be designed as part of an integrated interface to reduce the effort at updating and extracting useful information.

A large number of management functions can be accomplished with the technology of human communication via computer that are sometimes prohibitively expensive or often result in failures when attempted via other communication methods. Systems, matrix and/or functional management are excellent cases in point. To be able to put together task teams from anywhere in the organization and have them work as a team either requires extensive travel or actual moving all the individuals involved to the same location for a protracted period. Attempts at using regular communications usually means long delays and poorer performance. We do know that it is possible to have geographically dispersed programming groups working on the same software, research teams working on the same research effort and lateral management groups as working committees. It would seem that there is a much wider range of possible tasks that can be carried out by a dispersed group using computerized conferencing than by phone and mail. Even those EIES user groups that hold regular face to face meetings in addition have been able to change the nature of the agenda of their meetings to be able to deal with more of the controversial points in the face to face environment.

It is also possible to have a higher degree of delegation of authority with this technology because of the increased ability to have accountability and to review decisions in a timely and organized manner. In the Emisari experience, all decisions at each of the ten regional offices were placed in a central notebook from which individual items could be retrieved and compared. Prior to the actual decision going into effect it was placed in as a tentative decision to see if it had any overlap with what might be occurring in other regional offices or if there was any immediate reaction from the national office. Another potential is the increase in the "presence of the leader" through the ability of the supervisor and his immediate staff to maintain day to day communication with a larger group of individuals.

Attempts at "zero based budgeting" have, in many cases, failed because of the significant imposition of added communications placed upon the already overburdened manager. The result, where it is employed, is usually a tradeoff among managers of a "one for me and one for you" nature, rather than the true consideration of project merits laterally across the management divisions. In fact, zero based budgeting lends itself beautifully to a mix of communications, data structuring for the budget figures and decision analysis aids such as the ones we have been experimenting with (Hiltz et al., 1980) to provide groups an analysis of their individual and collective views on priority setting.

We have had numerous examples on the EIES system of groups of up to 15 individuals jointly working on the same document and report preparation by a group is another obvious utilization of the technology. Finalizing wordings in such things as contracts is a related example of this particular function.

One of the most intriguing areas of development is the degree to which software can be designed to facilitate particular roles that humans take on. On EIES, there is special software to support a significant number of facilitation, moderation and dissemination roles taken on by specific individuals. In the management, environment there are similar analogies to this in terms of such roles as "interpersonal" (e.g., figurehead, leader, liaison), "informational" (monitor, disseminator, spokesman) and "decisional" (e.g., entrepreneur, disturbance handler, resource allocator, negotiator). Designing specific roles and role support features into the system is one of the most challenging of the design choices. It carries with it certain dangers. It is possible to design, via the computer, almost any variation from a free and open communication process to a complete dictatorship. The possibilities of going overboard in the dictatorship direction are quite numerous:

> Should a higher up be able to open others' mail if the mail is directed outside his or her organizational unit? Should a higher up be able to track the communication activity and patterns of those working for that manager? Should votes be weighed by position in the organization? Should we impose the use of standardized words and phrases? Should we provide confirmations of delivery only from subordinates or equals?

The list of possibilities for imposing control are rather large. We can use the structuring capabilities of the computer to impose a very rigid and regulated organizational structure and in fact freeze the organization in to a template or mold that is far more permanent and intimidating than the current "manual" system. In that sense, this technology is a rather unique two edged sword.

CONCLUSION

When it comes to the use of the computer for human communications, the approach in most organizations is best characterized by a poem from Carl Sandburg's "The People, Yes":

> He took the wheel in a lashing roaring hurricane
> And by what compass did he steer the course of the ship?
> "My policy is to have no policy." he said in the early months.
> And three years later, "I have been controlled by events."

The decreasing cost of the technology, the increasing costs of people's time and travel, the growing recognition of communication problems and the increased complexity of organizations leave no doubt that within the next decade almost all geographically dispersed companies will employ some form of human communication via computer. Whether these organizations will let events drag them along an uncharted course or apply some guidance to their voyage is still an open question. In the past, we have had to rely upon outside services for our methods of remote communications. This is no longer a constraint. The structuring of communications is a software technology. A computer system costing between 200,000 and 500,000 dollars can support from 1,000 to possibly 5,000 individuals in a single organization. The development and evolution of the software can be supplied by a staff of three to five professionals. This is a very different situation than is reflective of either the phone or postal system, in terms of capital investment requirements. Those that choose to rely on simulations of the internal memo or postal system will gain immediate cost displacements but sacrifice the opportunities to bring about even greater improvements in the operation of their organization. The key issue in this technology is the design of the social system making up the organization and whether or not that will be a planned process.

BIBLIOGRAPHY

Hiltz, S.R., The Effect of a Computerized Conferencing System on Scientific Communities, Draft Final Report to the National Science Foundation, 1980.

Hiltz, S.R. et al., Face to Face vs. Computerized Conferences: A Controlled Experiment, Research Report No. 12, Computerized Conferencing and Communications Center, NJIT, August, 1980.

Hiltz, S.R. and Turoff, M., The Evolution of User Behavior in a Computerized Conferencing System, to appear in the Communications of the ACM.

Hiltz, S.R. and Turoff, M. The Network Nation: Human Communication via Computer, Addison Wesley Advanced Book Program, 1978.

Hiltz, S.R. and Turoff, M., The Wired World of the Office of the Future: Applications and Impacts of Computerized Conferencing in the Multi-National Organization, Proceedings of the Fourth International Conference on Computers and Communications, Tokyo, September, 1978.

Johnson-Lenz, P. and T., Legitech/EIES: Information Exchange Among State Legislative Researchers, in Electronic Communication: Technology and Impacts, edited by Henderson & McNaughton, AAAS Selected Symposium Series 52, Westview Press, 1980.

McKendree, J., Decision Process in Crisis Management: Computers in a New Role, in Encyclopedia of Computer Science and Technology, Volume 7, edited by Belzer, et al., Marcel Dekker Press, 1977.

Renner, R.L., et al., A Management Information System Designed to Aid and Involve People, Proceedings Fourth International Symposium on Computers and Information Systems (COINS IV), 1972, Plenum Press.

Turoff, M., Party-Line and Discussion: Computerized Conferencing Systems, First International Conference on Computer Communications, Washington, D.C., 1972.

Turoff, M., On the Design of Human Social Systems: Confessions of a Designer, Irvine Conference on Social Issues and Impacts of Computing, August, 1979.

Turoff, M., The Designer's View in Electronic Communication: Technology and Impacts, edited by Henderson and MacNaughton, AAAS Selected Symposium series 52, Westview Press, 1980.

Turoff, M. and Hiltz, S.R., Structuring Communications for the Office of the Future, 1980 Office Automation Conference Proceedings, AFIPS Press, March, 1980.

Turoff, M., The Suppositions of Office Automation, Special Interest Group on Office Automation of the ACM, Newsletter, Volume 1, Number 1, March, 1980.

Turoff, M. and Hiltz, S.R., Computer Based Communication-Information Systems: Cheapest and Fastest Route to Office Automation?, Proceedings of Tele-informatics Conference, June, 1979.

Wilcox, R. and Kupperman, R., Emisari: An On-Line Management System in a Dynamic Environment, First International Conference on Computer Communications, 1972.

CHAPTER 16

OFFICE AUTOMATION: THE DYNAMICS OF A TECHNOLOGICAL BOONDOGGLE

James W. Driscoll
Assistant Professor
Industrial Relations Section
Sloan School of Management
Massachusetts Institute of Technology

For anyone who has taken the time to read these words given the title of the paper, the proposition that office automation will dramatically reshape American society within twenty years is probably assumed. Likewise, few would disagree with the assertion that the direction of office automation is largely driven by technological developments rather than responding to specific organizational or societal needs. (While most users are currently interested in office automation to reduce labor costs and improve productivity, they are seeking to take advantage of technological developments rather than guiding the form of automation.) The second fact was recently confirmed by a recent study here at M.I.T. of the current office automation efforts in nine large users (Driscoll, Sirbu, Alloway, Hammer, Harper, and Khalil 1980).

Less well-understood is presence of *choice* within any technology. There is no such thing as a technological inevitability. David Noble, a colleague here at M.I.T., has made that argument persuasively, and documented his contention in a series of compelling studies.[1] More recently, Wendy Mela and Richard Walton at Harvard Business School have supported the presence of technological choice in the specific area of concern here, namely advanced office technology.[2]

If the direction of technological development is not given, and if office automation is certainly being driven by technological developments, then who is making the choices among technological alternatives? Noble believes that technology is a means of social control in the conflict between classes within the society. The ruling (capitalist) class selects specific technologies to maximize its control over the working class. My own analysis explores some additional explanations. The purpose of this paper is to analyze the current technological path of office automation, and to demonstrate the possibility of an alternative, more humanistic path. Then, I will explore the reasons for our current path and suggest actions for interested groups in the society who prefer my proposed humanistic alternative.

THE FUTURE OF OFFICE AUTOMATION

Because of my graduate work with Larry Williams and Tom Lodahl at Cornell in the early 70's, I have been studying office automation since the early days of word processing. More recently, I have conducted my own studies of electronic mail systems and the state of the office-automation art in large users.[3] Additionally, I have participated occasionally as M.I.T.'s representative on the Office Automation Roundtable and I conduct a weekly seminar here at M.I.T. on recent developments in office automation. As my presence in this Stanford symposium suggests, I am one of the "usual suspects" when somebody rounds up a crowd of experts to discuss office automation.

Based on this reasonably informed perspective, I *detest* what I now foresee as the future of office automation.

The smart money in the technological sweepstakes now rests on two entries: *decision-support systems* and *"true" automation.* Again and again, experts tout the advantages of these "totally integrated" approaches to office automation and contrast them with the incremental advantages of word processing. But what is the inevitable result of these particular technologies which are currently being "chosen"?

Decision-support systems

As the first wave of the future, decision-support systems represent little more than the extension of the use of computers to managers (a clarification suggested by Kenan Saheen of the University of Massachusetts). A decision-support system focuses on the key decisions made by a manager or professional and tailors a computer-based system to support those decisions. Its components may vary, but typically they include a regression-based forecasting tool for analyzing alternative decisions and direct access to organizational and outside data bases for input to the analysis. A well-known system developed here at M.I.T. by John Little and his colleagues, Brandaid, helps, as I understand it, a product manager select a marketing strategy for a given product.

Decision-support systems emphasize computer support for a *few* key managers in an organization and help them to make decisions as *individuals*. The complex communications links currently being developed for boards of directors can also be conceptualized as decision-support systems. Of course, such systems neglect current research on how decisions are actually made in organizations. Decisions, most scholars now agree, are the outcome of a complex social and political process involving many people and a variety of special interests. (Graham Allison's *The Essence of Decision*, (1971), best demonstrates this position.) To the extent that decision-support systems are an attempt to rationalize this process, their implicit model of an organization emphasizes a few individuals, at high levels in organizations, making decisions with the support of technological wizardry to direct the actions of all the other people in the organization.

"True" Office Automation

The second wave of the future, "true" office automation arises from a distinction popularized by Michael Zisman, yet another M.I.T. affiliate, based on his work with Howard Morgan at Wharton (Zisman, 1978). Zisman correctly criticizes word processing and electronic mail as mere "mechanization" or the replacement of human labor with machine power. Automation, by contrast, is the exercise of discretion by machines. The computer system in true office automation *controls* office activities and exercises judgement in performing tasks according to its programmed logic. Research currently underway here at M.I.T. by Michael Hammer, Jay Kunin,

Sandy Schoiket and others at the Laboratory for Computer Sciences (along with other projects across the country) are now attempting to develop computer languages to supply the logic for such "true" automation.[4] They are attempting to discover all the structured work in offices which could be more efficiently performed by a computer system. Zisman's program for running the manuscript-review process for a journal editor is the best known example of such automation, but the current efforts are driving for the computerization of all structured tasks which possess some generalizability across offices.

What is the implication of such "true" office automation? The office of the future would maximize on machine efficiency by using the computer to gobble up the structured tasks in any office and leave people in only two roles: *bosses* and *garbage collectors.* The boss decides what tasks must be done (perhaps with the help of a decision-support system) and asks the systems analyst to prepare the program. The rest of the workforce picks up the garbage which is left over at the edges of the programmed tasks (Marvin Sirbu of the Center for Policy Alternatives at M.I.T. has elaborated this point in a recent paper).[5] Such leftovers have no internal coherence since their sole determining characteristic is that the machine couldn't do them. They do not form an integrated, purposeful whole which would engage the interest and attention of a human being. The only human control in the system resides at the top of the organization in the systems analyst or programmer and whatever collective action the lower level people can take to sabotage the system by letting the garbage pile up.

Figure 1 portrays the "office of the future" resulting from the current technological path. My assumption is that you will either like or dislike the picture depending on whether your present position makes it likely that you will be a boss/systems analyst or a garbage collector.

AN ASIDE ON WORD PROCESSING AND ELECTRONIC MAIL

The reader may quibble at my neglect of the two most popular current applications in office automation: word processing and electronic mail. I omit them because my intent is to project the future of the office given the logic of current technological development.

By the standard of future importance, word processing is widely considered irrelevant. While the largest sales volume is

Figure 1
Future of Office Automation

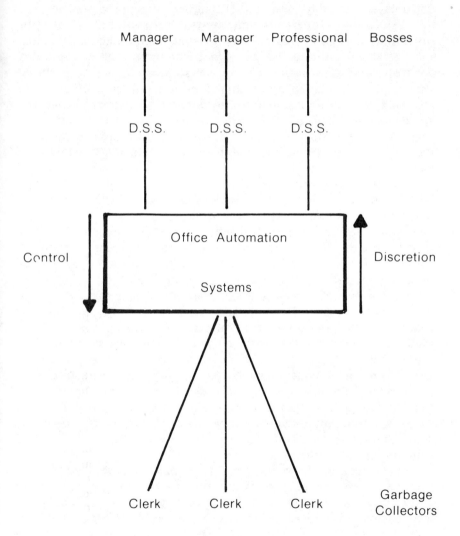

currently in stand-alone word processing systems to support secretaries, every single expert in the field (and indeed the current massive advertising campaigns from the vendors themselves) emphasizes the importance of integrated computer-based systems to support office workers. Text editing and retyping are downplayed as only one, minor feature of such a system.

Likewise, electronic mail within organizations simply substitutes computer systems for existing communications media such as the telephone. To the extent electronic mail incorporates control decisions about storing messages, forwarding them, automatic addressing and other functions, it is evolving into precisely the "true" automation envisioned by Zisman. While the mere mechanization of some office tasks, such as recording *may* save more time and money than current word processing systems, they do not represent the automation of the office which has excited so many of us.

With all that said, the evolution of word processing and electronic mail foreshadows precisely the nightmarish vision described in Figure 1. The logic of word processing has always been specialization and centralization. While the decline in product cost has made decentralized systems feasible, the vast majority of vendors and users talk about how to get as much typing as possible loaded onto a word processing machine in order to reduce the number of secretaries in an office. This logic was clear in the early days of large word processing centers, but remains today despite the pioneering efforts of Lodahl, Williams and Williams to point out the inefficiencies of such specialized systems (1979).

The consequence of such specialization in word processing has been to increase the separation between boss and secretary in the office and to create a new breed of even more menial office workers. Little improvement in the jobs of non-word processing secretaries has resulted, despite the advertising claims of the vendors about career paths for women.

This separation of secretary from boss will dominate future systems as can be seen from current discussions about inputting text to automated systems. One way or another, product designers are seeking ways to keep the boss from having to type. Menus of preprogrammed commands are presented requiring only a single keystroke for action, or an electronic "mouse" is moved across a pad to convey information, or the user simply touches the screen. In the most dramatic example, developed by Richard Bolt and his colleagues here in M.I.T.'s Architecture group,[6] the user sits in an easy chair with both hands on pressure-sensitive armrests allowing the user to "zoom" across a wall-sized projection of a desk top by pressing down with either hand.

The standard form of input for text from such high-status users, be they hunt-and-peckers, mice, pointers, or zoomers, is by dictation to a typist.

Likewise, the separation of high-skill and low skill workers is increased by the more advanced versions of electronic mail. The major applications outside the research community, where we found the most widely used systems in our recent study (Bellinger, 1980), emphasize multi-media communications among key decision makers or in support of the board of directors. Electronic mail does not appear likely to emerge as a substitute for the telephone for all office workers, rather it will only support key managers and professionals.

While these trends can be justified based on ease of user acceptance and the current cost of hardware, the leading edge of users and vendors in both word processing and electronic mail would clearly create an organization with two distinct social classes as portrayed in Figure 1.

Before exploring the reasons for that future, a few words are in order to appraise its value.

A NIGHTMARE OF COST INEFFECTIVENESS

An organizational innovation can always be appraised from two perspectives: the goals of the organization and the interests of the organization's members. Despite (or perhaps because of) their confusing connotations, the first perspective is usually called "rationality" or "economics" and the second, "politics."

A "rational" perspective

There is little reason to believe the proposed office of the future will either save money or advance organizational objectives. A recent review of word processing in the federal government painted a negative picture of the economic impact of such systems.[7] More generally, our own recent analysis of some forty studies conducted by large office automation users revealed *no* single post-implementation, economic evaluation of an office automation system (Driscoll et al., 1980). Despite the heavy emphasis that such users gave to cost savings in proposing new systems, they had never gone back to validate their claims.

Some recent attempts to cost justify office-automation systems are embarrassing from both a methodological and a managerial perspective. Frequently, the analyst will ask people on a questionnaire how much time they have saved from a new system and then multiply their response by current salary levels to estimate savings. A competent researcher would ask at least for a second, corroborating source of information and some comparison of time spent against a control group. A practical manager would want to know whether those projections ever turned up as hard dollars in a budget account which he or she could spend on something else. "Soft dollars" are viewed skeptically.

I have suggested the reasons for this disappointing economic performance of the current trend in office automation systems in an earlier paper (Driscoll, 1979). Most generally, these systems neglect the interdependent nature of office work as the product of many people and they simultaneously fail to provide any motivation for most people to work any smarter or harder in pursuit of organizational objectives. For example, decision-making is a small (and some would argue insignificant) part of a manager's job (Mintzberg, 1974). Therefore the potential impact of decision-support systems is limited. Their likely impact is further eroded by their neglect of the social and political component of decisions. Similarly, "true" office automation promises to decrease the motivation of office workers. Their motivation springs in large part from the nature of the work itself as well as from their social contacts. An emphasis on maximizing machine efficiency, specialization, and centralization destroys these two mainsprings of worker motivation.

A political perspective

The social consequences of the current technological path are, if anything, even more negative than the economics. As Figure 1 illustrates, office automation is likely to increase the distance between people at the top and the bottom of organizations. The few decision makers and systems analysts will command *more* in salaries, benefits, and differential treatment than do current managers. By contrast, the lower-level workers will find much of their work *less* interesting, have *less* chance for promotion (since the jump to decision maker is vastly more difficult), and have *less* power to demand reasonable salaries since many of their fragmented tasks can be performed by a newly hired worker with little or no training. Unless the reader advocates the overthrow of the current system of government in the United States by violent means, such a picture is distressing. It increases the likelihood of a revolution, but it contradicts our values of equal opportunity and individual mobility in the economic realm.

ALTERNATIVE TECHNOLOGICAL PATHS TO THE OFFICE OF THE FUTURE

My explanation for the likely evolution of office automation takes two parts. First, a coherence and an inertia to the current trend that provides it with stability. Second, a series of external causes first established and now maintains the direction. I will address these two points in order.

Technological path is the term I have adopted to capture the notion of internal structure.[8] A path is not a chance stroll through the forest of technological innovation. One step follows another because of the contour of the ground, the color of the soil, and markers along the way. Even so, there seems a certain direction, inevitability, and sometimes human leadership that characterizes developments in office automation.

Systems analytic is the label I use to describe the current trend in office automation. Table 1 summarizes the features of the current path and contrasts it with a largely hypothetical alternative which I have labeled "humanistic." There is little original about these distinctions. What deserves attention is the apparent clustering in the present technological path of so many wrong answers to the major questions about organizational behavior. A series of narrow, short-term perspectives characterizes the current approach.

For example, McGregor (1960) popularized the difference between optimistic and pessimistic assumptions about human nature held by managers. Successful managers tended to hold optimistic views, and his term for that constellation of assumptions has become rooted in the management literature as "Theory Y." By contrast, less successful managers more often hold pessimistic views of their fellow beings, characterized by McGregor as "Theory X." If there is an organizing framework for the present technological path, it is "Theory X" assumptions about human nature.

Designers of current office automation systems in the systems analytic path assume that people are lazy and cannot be trusted. Therefore, their systems seek to reduce skill levels required by the organization and to generate information by which operators can

Table 1
Alternative Technological Paths

	Systems Analytic	Humanistic
Assumptions about human nature	lazy, untrustworthy, need outside control	motivated, trustworthy, self-controlled
Immediate function of office automation	allow outside control, reduce skill requirements, provide information to key decision-makers	provide feedback to individual operators, utilize and increase skills and knowledge of operators
Unit of Analysis	individuals, tasks	groups, organizational units, functions
Scope of organizational objectives	efficiency	effectiveness, quality of work life
Target group	key decision makers	all organizational members
Constituency	top management	all organizational members
External effects on society	increase unemployment, threat to physical and mental health little impact on productivity	decrease unemployment, beneficial impact on mental health increased productivity

be controlled by higher level managers. The line-counter on word processors is the most obvious example.

This emphasis on measurement and control leads inevitably to the statement of objectives for the system in terms of efficiency, cost savings, and personnel reductions. Also implicit in this negative world view is the importance of the *few* motivated individuals at the *top* of the organization in setting its direction. This elite needs information, both to control the untrustworthy lot below them, and to enable the few to make the major decisions which impact organizational goals.

Unfortunately, this obsession with efficiency, cost savings, and reduction of inputs flies directly in the face of current wisdom about managerial control. Some years ago Anthony and Dearden at Harvard Business School made two critical distinctions within the management process.[9] First, they argued that managers ought to concern themselves with *effectiveness* as well as *efficiency*. Effectiveness assesses progress towards objectives while efficiency merely assesses the number of inputs required for a given level of performance. Managers too often sacrifice effectiveness in the pursuit of efficiency. This trend was apparent in our recent evaluation of office automation efforts in large users.

The second distinction advanced by Anthony and Dearden separated operational control from strategic planning. The vital role for top management is setting strategic direction, not monitoring performance of lower-level workers.

The current path of office automation thus contradicts not only the best judgement of organizational psychologists about effective management, but the dominant conception of management control as well.

The most devastating shortcoming of the current path from my perspective, however, is its repressive political overtones. Clearly, the systems currently under development cater to the approval of a few key decision makers, since that is the current decision-making structure of most large organizations. The systems designers pay little heed to the needs and interests of the large number of lower-level participants whose working lives will be affected by this technology.

In addition, current systems ignore the *external* effects of office automation beyond the boundaries of the user organization. For example, at several conferences I have heard suggestions that much of the non-automated work, such as text input, might better be performed by part-time employees in their homes or subcontracted to "service bureaus." At a time when labor economists are raising the possibility that the large supply of such lower-paid, temporary, dead-end jobs in our economy is the major cause of our chronically high unemployment, such an external effect is unconscionable for national employment policy.[10]

Likewise there are possible negative impacts on physical health from prolonged use of a cathode ray tube and unfortunate mental health implications of low-skilled, high-turnover, meaningless work.[11] However, if reactions at conferences on office automation are any indication, these health effects are among the few subjects guaranteed to induce boredom among current vendors and users.

The humanistic path, in contrast to the systems-analytical technological path, is marked by different initial assumptions about human nature and leads to quite different office automation systems. Since workers are now assumed by systems designers in the humanistic path to have the potential for self-motivation and control, the immediate purpose of an automated system is to increase the flow of information to the system operators in order to allow them to utilize and *increase* their skills and knowledge. Decisions are spread as much as possible *throughout* the organization rather than being concentrated at the top.

Wendy Mela and Richard Walton provided a delightful example of a humanistic alternative from their own research at one of my recent seminars. The designer of a product information system for a large retailer of consumer goods assumed that the purpose of the new computer system was to provide information on stock levels, advertising campaigns, and the like to the national sales manager. That key decision maker could then better deploy his sales force and advertising budget. However, the local sales managers desired a system which provided them with the same information so that these lower-level participants could make deployment decisions locally. Clearly, the computer can serve either group. A humanistic path would suggest providing the information to the local manager on the assumption that he or she wanted to act in the company's interest without the need for centralized control by the national sales manager.

A humanistic path also includes a focus on organizational *objectives* rather than inputs, since progress towards such goals is the focus of feedback to operators. Such an orientation towards *goals,* rather than inputs, inplies and reinforces the humanistic path's attention to *groups* of people rather than individuals. Goal orientation emphasizes groups because objectives usually apply to some *organizational unit* rather than individuals. The focus on individuals in the systems-analytic path results only from the need assumed by the designer to control individual behavior, not from an intrinsic need by top managers to know *how* people accomplish their objectives.

And finally, a humanistic path gives explicit recognition to the *quality-of-work-life* issues neglected by systems analysis because a wider range of motives is attributed to individuals. People are assumed, in many cases, to desire meaningful work, training, and the opportunity for advancement. Therefore an effective system must provide such potential if it is to increase productivity.

On balance, then, the humanistic path reflects current wisdom about how to best motivate and manage people at work at the same time that it creates positive rather than negative effects outside the boundaries of the user. Why then is current practice pursuing the less desirable technological path?

CAUSES OF THE SYSTEMS-ANALYTIC TECHNOLOGICAL PATH

The reasons for this domination of the systems-analytic technological path are multiple and grounded in the fabric of our society. Let me suggest psychological, organizational, and political forces at work.

Individual.

Theory X as a cosmology is as American as apple pie. Our culture and media emphasize the importance of individual efforts and the need for external checks and balances on personal self-interest. The wellspring of energy for a capitalistic economy is the individual maximizing personal interest.

In addition, engineering (and other professional) education has been taken to task for inculcating Theory X assumptions about human behavior; Chris Argyris has also pointed out the self-sustaining nature of such beliefs.[12] For example, if you believe it necessary for productivity to put people in low-skill jobs and supervise them closely, then they will never demonstrate any imagination or initiative and thus will confirm your worst suspicions.

Thus, individual systems analysts and managers in many cases bring negative views about people to the task of designing and implementing office automation systems.

Organizational.

At the organizational level, a new set of forces comes into play to support such individual tendencies. Top managers constitute the dominant group in most organizations and can be expected to direct the development of office-automation systems to support their current advantages. Money, power, and status go with current managerial jobs and, to date, relatively few managers have been willing to decrease voluntarily their share of such rewards.

From a functional perspective within organizations, office automation is, in my own experience and research, most often an extension of traditional data-processing techniques of systems development. Very rarely is a behavioral scientist or even a representative from the personnel-management or human-resources function appointed to the task force coordinating office automation. Therefore the internal bearers of the humanistic perspective advocated here are systematically neglected by current organizations.

An interesting puzzle is why organizations have not adopted the humanistic path given its advantages (at least as I have claimed for it) in terms of organizational objectives. *Some* organizations have of course taken this path with substantial success.[13] My best explanation for this widespread suboptimization is the relatively *loose* connection between the installation of computer-based systems and measures of organizational effectiveness. Recall that in our review of user research, systems designers never returned to examine the economic effects of an office automation system. In the absence of such a reality check on system design, managers and systems analysts are relatively free to pursue the biases alluded to above.

Societal.

The societal level provides perhaps the most convincing explanation for the systems-analytic path and reflects the dynamic described by Noble. In my years of attending conferences on office automation in the United States and Europe, I have encountered only *one* labor union official and he, not surprisingly, was from Sweden. In the United States, I have encountered *no* representative of government agencies (except as potential *users* of office automation). Thus, there is no systematic representation in the choice of a technological path by those interests most impaired by the current trends. Office work in the United States is largely a nonunion sector at the present time. By the time these industries (banking, finance) and occupations (secretaries, clerks, technicians) become unionized, the technology will already be in place. The German Marshall Fund is supporting my current research to assess the impact of stronger labor unions on office automation in Western Europe. To my knowledge, the Departments of Labor and Health and Welfare have done nothing on this policy issue to date.

Ours is a pluralistic, capitalistic society. So long as the major actors in the determination of technological choice are large, private firms making and using office automation, there is little reason to expect a shift to a humanistic path unless some mass conversion from Theory X to Y among managers takes place. The present sermon is an effort at such conversion.

WHAT IS TO BE DONE?

There are some obvious implications from my pessimistic analysis.

Line managers ought to insist on careful, long-term, broad-gauge economic evaluations of office-automation projects. If Theory Y is true, as I sometimes believe, then the humanistic path, somewhat counterintuitively, would benefit from *tighter* evaluations. Managers should reject systems proposals which purport to justify office automation in labor cost savings and then repeatedly return with evaluations emphasizing qualitative benefits and "soft-dollar" savings. For line managers, simply insisting on *some* follow-up would be a refreshing and effective start.

Office automation staffs, I'm afraid, emerge as the villains of this paper, despite my insistence that the causes of the problem are more widely rooted in the society. Therefore, office automation staffs ought to undertake a massive review of their current strategy to evaluate my analysis. Does the menu of future projects reflect the biases I allege towards decision support for key managers and the "true" automation of office work by the integration of multiple computer systems? Are the behavioral disciplines in fact neglected in systems design teams?

For those staffs pleading guilty or "nolo contendere," it is a trivial matter for a management-training staff to develop short workshops to convey the distinction between systems analysis and humanism. Systems analysts can gradually recognize some of their untested assumptions about human nature and see the choices possible in the design of office automation systems from a humanistic perspective. Of course, as Argyris has argued for so long, recognizing some personal assumptions is not enough to change the most fundamental and unconscious assumptions controlling behavior. For such a deep change, continued monitoring by behavioral scientists with a humanistic bent is required. Mela and Walton are developing an organizational impact statement for office automation systems to highlight the negative impacts of the systems-analytic path.

Labor unions ought to use technological paths as a guide to their organizing efforts. Employers who pursue the current systems-analytic trend in office automation will do more to increase membership among office workers than will the women's movement. In particular, individuals affected by pilot office automation projects provide a quick indication of the ripeness of an employer for organizing. Participants in pilot studies may also provide horror stories for other parts of the organization as well as a source of early members for the union's internal organizing committee.

Where a union currently holds bargaining rights for office workers, for example in the public sector in the United States, office automation should take a high priority in negotiations while there is still time to influence the organization's choice of a technological path. Unions ought to demand *notification* about all new computer systems, *participation in the design* and especially the *evaluation* of the system, and *training* for designated union officials in systems design. Such requirements are mandated by law in Norway, so counterparts in European unions provide a good source of information to American trade unionists.

The list of possible *government* actions is extensive and I have treated the possible roles for the government in improving the quality of work life in an earlier work (see Beer and Driscoll, 1977). Of pressing importance is the need for a major research effort to test my speculations about the path of technological development and its deleterious impacts on the quality of employment opportunities in the U.S.

If my fears are confirmed, then it may be necessary for the federal government to increase substantially the minimum wage and mandate substantial fringe benefits such as portable pension coverage. Such changes would bring pressure on employers to avoid the creation of low-skill, high-turnover jobs. Such external pressures would make the systems-analytic technological path less economical by eliminating the cost advantage of low-skill jobs. Of course, such measures assume that managers are turning to office automation to save money and not just to increase control over the work force.

In short, if employers are, in fact, proceeding down the systems-analytic path, then office automation provides a crucial test of the viability of our pluralistic, capitalistic system. Will enlightened employer self-interest, collective bargaining, and federal labor-market policies control the nightmarish consequences that haunt my sleep or is office automation sowing the seeds of social revolution?

FOOTNOTES

1.   David Noble, Assistant Professor of Science, Technology and Society at M.I.T., inspired the current analysis when he presented his analysis of the evolution of numerically controlled machine tools to our Industrial Relations Seminar. A complete exposition of his argument appears in *America by Design: Science, Technology, and the Rise of Corporate Capitalism* (New York: Knopf, 1977) and in "Before the Fact: Social Choice in Machine Design," 1978.

2.   Professor Richard E. Walton and Research Associate Wendy Mela at Harvard Business School, reported on their research to my Seminar on Office Automation. They are currently preparing a book on advanced office technology.

3.   The study of electronic mail is reported by two of my graduate students who, in real life, are managers for A.T.&T. and Boeing, respectively. A condensed version will be available. Hagood Bellinger, "Electronic Mail Systems: Are They Effective in the Office" (Unpublished Master's Thesis, M.I.T., 1980). Richard W. Alldredge, "Electronic Message Systems: Factors Affecting their Acceptance" (Unpublished Master's Thesis, M.I.T., 1980). The assessment of the state of the office automation art in large users is listed in the references (Driscoll, et al., 1980) and is available from the Industrial Liaison Program at M.I.T. as of June, 1980.

4.   Associate Professor Michael Hammer, Associate Director of the Laboratory for Computer Science at M.I.T. and his Research Associate, Jay Kunin, have both reported at my seminar on their efforts to develop both an office specification language and a programming language for office automation. Additional information can be obtained by writing to them directly.

5.   Dr. Marvin Sirbu, Research Associate in the Center for Policy Alternatives at M.I.T., will provide copies of this paper ("Programming Organizational Structure") upon request.

6.   A recent description of this project is available upon request from Dr. Richard Bolt, Spatial Data Management Group, Architecture Department, M.I.T.

7.   The report is available from the U.S. Government, General Accounting Office. "Federal Productivity Suffers Because Word Processing Is Not Well-Managed," April, 1979. FG MSD-79-17.

8. While I cannot specify the source of the phrase "technological path," I am reasonably certain that I did not coin the term. As noted in the text, the idea for this analysis was suggested by David Noble.

9. A full statement of these concepts about the management control process is provided by the text. Robert N. Anthony and John Dearden. *Management Control Systems: Text and Cases* (3rd ed.) Homewood, Illinois: R.D. Irwin, 1976.

10. Recent analysis suggests that unemployment is a *natural* consequence of the type of jobs in our economy. The more general conception identifies two types of jobs in our economy: primary-sector jobs with good pay, working conditions, and employment stability and secondary-sector jobs with the opposite characteristics. For an introduction to this analysis see Michael J. Piore (ed.) *Unemployment and Inflation: Institutionalist and Structuralist Views.* New York: M.E. Sharpe, 1979.

11. Unfortunately, the potential physical and mental health consequences of office automation have been little-researched. The possible effects are eye strain, back strain, radiation, boredom, and the various abuses associated with tension (accumulation of nicotine, caffein, alcohol, and other drugs; overeating, depression, high blood pressure, and suicide). My present concern is based on anecdotal evidence and the growing body of research on health consequences of negative working conditions in general. Clearly what is vital here is empirical research to test the validity of these concerns.

12. Chris Argyris has long been associated with this critique of work organizations and professional education. One starting point for the interested reader is "Double-Loop Learning in Organizations," *Harvard Business Review.* March-April 1977, Vol. 55, No. 5, pp. 111-125.

13. See Richard J. Matteis, "The New Back Office Focuses on Customer Service," *Harvard Business Review.* March-April 1979, Vol. 57, No. 2, pp. 146-159.

REFERENCES

1. Allison, Graham T., *Essence of Decision: Explaining the Cuban Missile Crisis.* Boston: Little, Brown; 1971.

2. Beer, Michael and James W. Driscoll, "Strategies for Change" in J. Richard Hackman and H. Lloyd Suttle (editors),

Improving Life at Work: Behavioral Science Approaches to Organizational Change. Santa Monica, California: Goodyear, 1977, pp. 365-453.

3. Driscoll, James W., "People and the Automated Office," *Datamation.* Vol. 25, No. 12, pp. 106-116 (November, 1979).

4. Driscoll, James W., Marvin Sirbu, Robert Alloway, Michael Hammer, William Harper and Moshen Khalil, "Office Automation: A Comparison of In-house Studies." M.I.T. Center for Policy Alternatives. Cambridge, Massachusetts, 1980.

5. Lodahl, Thomas M., L.K. Williams and Phyllis Williams, "Providing Management Support in the Automated Office." *Corporate Systems,* June, 1979

6. McGregor, Douglas, *The Human Side of Enterprise.* New York: McGraw-Hill, 1960.

7. Mintzberg, Henry, *The Nature of Managerial Work.* Harper and Row, 1973.

8. Noble, David F., "Before the Fact: Social Choice in Machine Design." Paper presented at the National Convention of the Organization of American Historians, 1978.

9. Zisman, M.D., "Office Automation: Evolution or Revolution," *Sloan Management Review.* Vol. 19, Spring 1978, pp. 1-16.

CHAPTER 17

ONCE A SYSTEM IS INVENTED, HOW DO WE GET IT INTO THE USERS' HANDS?

Everett M. Rogers
Institute for Communication Research
Standford University
Stanford, California

THE DIFFUSION OF INNOVATIONS

The objective of this presentation is to describe how new ideas diffuse among the units in a system, with implications for the diffusion of word processing equipment in a system like a university or another large system.

An *innovation* is an idea perceived as new by an individual or an organization (Rogers with Shoemaker, 1971). The idea may not necessarily be very new in an absolute or objective sense, but it is subjectively or relatively new to the individual or organization that is considering its adoption.

Uncertainty is the degree to which adequate information is lacking in a situation where an individual is faced with a decision among alternatives, such as adopting an innovation.

Diffusion is the process by which an innovation is communicated over time among the members of a system. The rate of adoption usually follows an S-shaped curve over time (Figure 1). At first, a very few units in the system adopt the innovation, and then the rate of adoption increases at an increasing rate, until there are fewer potentials remaining in a system and the rate of adoption levels off.

Evaluating an innovation through near-peers. The uncertainty that surrounds the evaluation of a new idea by an individual means that the individual's perception of the new idea is influenced not only by concrete, material aspects of the innovation but also by the individual's peers, especially if they have already adopted the new idea. In fact, interpersonal communication with near-peers about an innovation is the most important means by which most individuals evaluate an innovation, even when adequate information is also available about scientific evaluations of the innovation. In their investigation of the diffusion of a new antibiotic drug, Coleman and others (1966, p. 32) concluded: "Apparently, testing at the expert level [by pharmaceutical companies and medical schools] cannot substitute for the doctor's own testing of the new drug; but testing through the everyday experience of colleagues on the doctor's own level can substitute, at least in part."

At the heart of the diffusion process is social modeling by an individual after the behavior of a near-peer who has already adopted the innovation. The prior experience of a near-peer is the most effective way for an individual to obtain useful information to decrease uncertainty about an innovation. When the innovation represents a major cost, especially in comparison to the existing practice that it is perceived to replace (a typewriter in the case of word processors?), the degree of uncertainty is higher, and dependence upon near-peers who have experience with the innovation is even greater.

The spurt in the rate of adoption (the shaded area in Figure 1) occurs when the opinion leaders in a system adopt an innovation. *Opinion leadership* is the degree to which an individual or an innovation is informally able to influence other individuals' (or organizations') attitudes or overt behavior in a desired way with relative frequency. Opinion leaders in a system are highly accessible to their followers; they also tend to embody the norms of the system. In many systems, the very first adopters of an innovation may not be respected by the average member of the system; these innovators are too untypical in their characteristics to be perceived as useful social models for the average. But these innovators may influence the opinion leaders, who then serve as

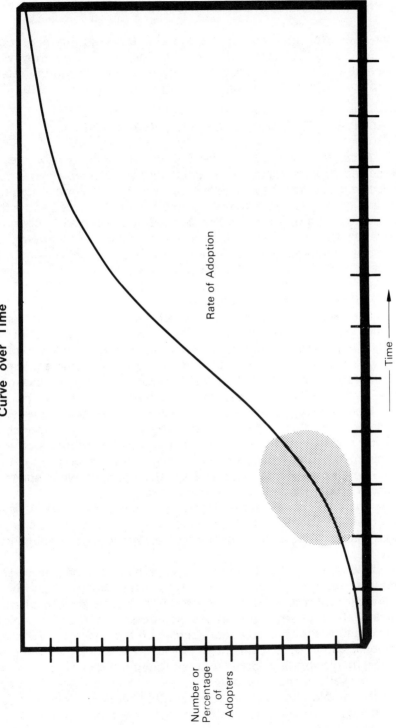

Figure 1
**The Diffusion of an Innovation in a System Follows an S-Shaped
Curve over Time**

Number or
Percentage
of
Adopters

Rate of Adoption

Time

Note: The shaded area on the curve indicates when opinion leaders adopt the innovation.

281

near-peers for the rest of the system. Most adopters of word processors at Stanford University in Fall, 1979, said they were satisfied with this innovation; this augurs well for the future rate of adoption of word processing equipment.(Marcus, 1980).

PERCEIVED ATTRIBUTES OF AN INNOVATION

Relative advantage is the degree to which a new idea is perceived as superior to the practice that it replaces. How is word processing equipment subjectively viewed by a potential adopter? As a high-priced typewriter? As a computer? These, and other relative aspects of an innovation, are learned especially from near-peers as the potential adopter gives meaning to the new idea, fitting it into other ideas that are perceived as similar. About 30 percent of the adopters of word processors at Stanford University in Fall, 1979, said that they performed a cost-analysis of the innovation prior to their adoption.

Complexity is the degree to which an innovation is perceived as difficult to understand. Site visits to an adopter are especially useful to potential adopters in determining the complexity of an innovation; over half of the adopters of word processing equipment at Stanford University in Fall, 1979, reported that site visits were very useful to them in deciding whether or not to adopt.

Compatibility is the degree to which a new idea is perceived as being consistent with the potential adopter's prior experience, beliefs, and values. For example, many potential adopters of word processors express concern about their noise, especially if they feel such noise would reqqire a special room or work space in which to use the word processing equipment.

Communicability is the degree to which a new idea is visible to potential adopters. For example, word processors are much more visible than a new accounting technique or a management tool.

Divisibility is the degree to which a new idea can be given a small-scale trial by a potential adopter. Many individuals vicariously try out an innovation through the experience of near-peers. Sellers of word processing equipment often offer to place their machines with a potential adopter on a short-term trial basis. Demonstrations by equipment sellers also allow potential adopters to try the innovation prior to their adoption decision.

Innovations that are perceived as high in relative advantage, low in complexity, high in compatibility, communicability, and divisibility, have a more rapid rate of adoption (Figure 2).

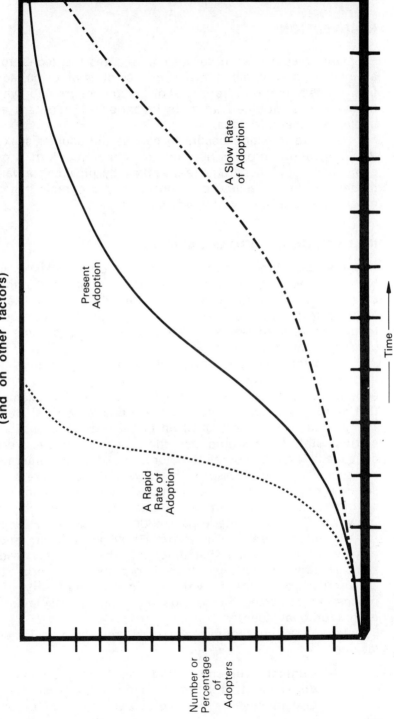

Figure 2
The Rate of Adoption of Word-Processing Equipment Depends on
How This Innovation is Perceived by Potential Adopters
(and on other factors)

A Slow Rate
of Adoption

Present
Adoption

A Rapid
Rate of
Adoption

Time ———

Number or
Percentage
of
Adopters

RE-INVENTION

Until recently, we have not fully realized the degree to which an innovation is modified in the process of its diffusion, adoption, and implementation. *Re-invention* is the degree to which an innovation is modified after its invention by adopters as they implement the new idea.

Such re-invention occurs in part as the adopter seeks to fit the innovation into his/her unique situation. Word processor companies may encourage re-invention by providing a variety of models and/or by selling components and programs that can be assembled/modified by the adopter.

INNOVATION IN ORGANIZATIONS

Because of their nature, word processors are usually adopted by an organization (or at least an organizational unit) rather than by an individual. This means that several individuals are likely to be involved in the innovation-decision. They may each perceive the innovation in a somewhat different way, and thus some kind of consensus must be reached.

More than one hierarchical level in an organization may be involved in an innovation-decision for an idea like word processing equipment (that represents a major purchase). For example, the first word processor adopted in the Stanford Medical Center (in 1977) required the approval of an office manager's boss, and his clerical staff (who would use the new equipment) were also consulted. The office of the director or the Medical Center adopted the second word processor within a year. Today, there are six or seven word processors in the Medical Center. So an innovation can spread more quickly in an organization when it diffuses "downward" through the organizational structure.

At an organizational level (or a system level), an innovation may be perceived somewhat differently than at the individual or sub-unit level. For example, there is growing concern at Stanford University about the university-wide compatibility of word processing equipment, a consideration that is less important to each individual adopter.

Less direct consequences of word processing equipment may include:

- Conflict over scheduling use of the equipment (one department at Stanford University is said to have discontinued its word processor for this reason).

- Loss of older female employees, who are not comfortable with the new equipment.
- Changing relationships among various departments in an organization because they have similar or different word processing equipment.

BIBLIOGRAPHY

James Coleman and others (1966), *Medical Innovation: A Diffusion Study.* New York, Bobbs-Merrill.

Jane E. Marcus (1980), "Survey Report: Standalone Word-Processing Systems at Stanford," *COST NEWSLETTER,* Vol. 2, No. 1.

Everett M. Rogers with F. Floyd Schomaker (1971), *Communication of Innovations: A Cross-Cultural Approach,* New York, Free Press.

CHAPTER 18
Part A

EVOLVING THE ORGANIZATION OF THE FUTURE: A POINT OF VIEW

Douglas C. Engelbart
Tymshare, Inc.
Cupertino, California

INTRODUCTION

For over two decades, I have been actively committed to the pursuit of something that I initially called "Augmenting the Human Intellect"—integrating interactive computer tools into the minute-by-minute activities of people over their whole range of think work. This paper is a two-part contribution: A "point of view" section, and a "what we've done" paper—a reprint[1], which summarizes events and results over this period. I re-named the pursuit about ten years ago, after reading Peter Drucker's discussions[2] about "knowledge workers," "knowledge organizations," and "knowledge industries." I decided that a better term would be "Augmenting the Knowledge Worker." And, from that perspective, a natural image emerged of a "Knowledge Workshop" as the place where a knowledge worker does his work—and where, if we extended his tools, his means of collaborative communication, his working methods and his organizational roles, we could speak of an "Augmented Knowledge Workshop."

As expected, my viewpoint has steadily evolved over the years: many inter-related concepts and elements gradually settled into an ever-more comprehensive and consistent framework. In recent years, my pursuit has often been identified as belonging in the emergent fields of Office Automation and The Office of the Future. In a generally useful way, this is true enough. But there are frequent, large differences—mostly stemming from differences in viewpoint. I think the major difference is that I have come to sense a much larger scale of opportunity and probable impact than I originally did. This paper attempts to summarize those aspects of my framework that relate to this issue of scale.

UNDERLYING CONCEPTS

My own perception of potential gain in human capability didn't clarify until I realized how pervasive and extensive were the things that our cultural evolution had already developed to augment our basic human capabilities. For me these developments boiled down to three main categories of "cultural invention":

> Language—how we conceptualize, attach labels and symbols, externalize, portray, model, communicate. . .

> Artifacts (physical gadgets)—tools, instruments, crutches. . .

> Methodology—procedures, methods, ways to organize people and resources. . .

For completeness, I found that I needed two other ingredients to fill out a "whole augmentation system:"

> Skills and knowledge required for humans to harness these inventions (a matter of training); and

> Attitudes, spirit, beliefs, etc. required to make the system work (a matter of indoctrination).

Note that new technology, no matter how dramatic, contributes directly only to the Artifact category. Also, consider the immense amount of invention that over the centuries has been integrated into the other categories of our knowledge-worker Augmentation System.

So, if it isn't new to be bringing technology into our Augmentation System, what then will be so remarkable about introducing the new, computer-communication technology?

Consider the four, non-technology categories as comprising a Cultural System, into which an immense amount of invention over the centuries has been integrated. Its scope, complexity, and ingenuity transcend those of any system we humans know how to develop by explicit design, and engender within me a great respect for the effectiveness of "organic" cultural evolution.

For me then, much of the answer to the above question came from one particularly important realization which emerged from this conceptual approach: elements within these different categories have a great deal of mutual effect upon one another's evolution; an innovation in the Artifacts category has almost always produced changes in the Cultural System categories—such side-effect changes will usually follow as a natural means of taking full advantage of the initial innovation's potential.

When one considers the number and degree of the changes which this emergent technology can fruitfully introduce into our Artifact category, their quantitative effect portends a qualitative impact of unprecedented degree upon the whole, five-part Augmentation System.

Perhaps this is too sketchily presented—but this type of conceptualization has been very important in shaping my viewpoint. A detailed treatment of these and other relevant concepts is presented in "Augmenting Human Intellect: A Conceptual Framework"[3] and also in "A Conceptual Framework for the Augmentation of Man's Intellect"[4]. For me, they are gaining in validity and significance every year, and still support very well the growing framework within which I perceive the possibilities and payoffs of augmentation.

A QUICK SKETCH

My viewpoint seems persistently to highlight the amount of organizational evolution that will have to be accommodated in the coming decades. This section provides some substantive imagery toward understanding what is in my mind in that regard. (These things are at the heart of our work for 15 years.)

Consider a few of the things that the knowledge-worker professional (KW-Professional) must learn to do within his augmented workshop:

compose, study and modify the proposals, memoranda, plans, budgets, etc. that are his products; (Note: "Study" means much more to us than "read.")

find earlier drafts and compare them with a current one;

send, receive, and keep track of his electronic mail;

solicit comments from his colleagues about a draft plan, then keep track of the comments and their cited passages; and

manage his "office-full" of computer-held files, notes, lists, mail, reference pieces (e.g., office procedures, contract specs, etc. against which he must work).

Consider also a knowledge-worker support person (KW-Support)—tomorrow's secretary, stenographer, records manager, documentation specialist, staff assistant, etc.

Much of their support work will involve the same assortment of basic operations as for the KW-Professional above;

and we can expect special value in their supportive assistance to be derived from their being skilled in the application of specialized computer services (e.g., data-base querying and analysis, graphic-portrayal developing, copy editing, quality-document typography, etc.).

Now consider a type of support from this technology that generally doesn't get much appreciation—a much-enhanced means for close collaboration among distributed workers. Here is what current technology can provide in this respect:

Fast, flexible electronic mail/messages: Where it is easy to formulate a short note, selectively including passages from other files, and distribute it to selected people. With a full mail service, one can send entire documents this way—including graphic illustrations. A very useful option is to have a document or message be assigned a permanent accession number and then be stored in an official archive where subsequent access is guaranteed under that accession number.

Sharable work spaces: One's working records, notes, plans, etc. can selectively be made accessible to others with a new kind of flexibility and visibility. For example, a common occurence is to send off a short, quick message saying,"Check my passage in (Jones, Draft-Plan, 3B) to see if it meets the objections you expressed in (27143-6A5)." (The first citation being to a specific passage in a private, working file; the second to a specific passage in a formally recorded, prior message or document.)

Shared-screen teleconferencing (Show-and-Tell Dialog): Consider two persons, working at a distance from one another, at their respective display screens (not necessarily the same brand of hardware, not necessarily working with the same computerized tools).

Assume that they are in telephone conversation and decide to shift to a more powerful dialog mode. Each of them elicits a conferencing set-up action from his computer, where, for instance, User A requests connection to User B for Showing, and User B requests connection to User A for Viewing.

Then on the screen at User B's workstation will be shown (as nearly as possible, depending upon the respective capabilities of their display equipment) what User A has on his screen. User B will be able to see what User A "points" to; User A can talk, point, and work in a normal fashion, doing a "show and tell" dialog with User B. At any time, User A can pass control to User B to reverse the flow of the show and tell dialog.

Assume that the interconnection processes for frequent collaborators can be preset for switching in and out of contact in a few seconds. Assume also that an almost arbitrary number of people can be connected into the conference hookup. Also, assume that there will be background, query-scheduling processes that can be used to facilitate the mutual arrangements that establish the time at which a conference session will be set up.

We can now appreciate that, besides the skills required by the Professional and Support persons to do their respective kinds of knowledge work, there will be a very important added set of skills—how to interact closely in collaborating at a new level and degree of teamwork.

Consider how capabilities such as those sketched above will affect the interplay between skilled professional specialists, and provide for the smooth integration of their respective contributions.

Their "group capability" can be so much more flexible and efficient than ever before possible that we will have to re-consider our entire set of attitudes and beliefs about human teams or other organizational units—about their possible working modes and potential effectiveness, about more effective harnessing of special human talents, about extending the critical limits of complexity and urgency for the problems that human organizations can successfully handle.

All of the above sketched scenario for an augmented organization is very real; more than this can, in fact, be supported with today's technology, and one assumes that tomorrow's offerings will at least provide as much.

QUESTIONS OF PERCEPTION

Here is a list of questions that are of special significance to my point of view:

What scale of gains do you see being derived from the adoption of this technology? (Productivity, capability, efficiency, performance. . .?)

How much change will there be in the way we work? How much change will there be in skills and knowledge required for our jobs? How much time will you as an individual probably spend learning the new skills, knowledge, and ways of working?

How much change will there be within our organizations—in structure, roles, and modes of interaction? How much time and cost will be involved in working out the major part of these organizational changes? How will this "organizational cost" compare with the cost of buying, installing, and operating the new equipment?

This list suits me because of my particular viewpoint about the Office of the Future. I happen to believe that this is the start of a very large revolution—bigger in qualitative impact than the combined effects of the printing press and the industrial revolution. In my view, the above gains and changes are going to be extremely large. Please hold this in mind as you digest what I say.

One way to help illustrate my viewpoint is to talk about "high performance" for knowledge workers and for knowledge organizations. This is what has lured me on for many years—the image of a new, much-enhanced level of capability for individual knowledge workers, and of startling gains in effectiveness for our knowledge organizations. In my framework, I much prefer to talk of "augmenting" rather than "automating" our individuals and organizations, because the principle value to me is in extending our capability for human-directed knowledge work, rather than in churning out our invoices with production-line efficiency.

Maybe they aren't fair, but these rhetorical questions convey something of my feeling: From these opportunities, do you picture a more-efficient ox cart or a more-effective vehicle (e.g., a jeep)? A more-efficient tablet-cutting chisel or a more-effective graphic writer/copier (e.g., a printing press)?

As you can see, my primary concern would better be characterized as pursuit of *The Organization of the Future* rather than of The Office of the Future.

ORGANIZATIONAL HILL CLIMBING

A useful metaphor, "hill climbing;" each knowledge organization has to relocate itself, upwards through gradient lines of new skills, knowledge, methods, and roles; struggling against the constant gravitational drag of uncertainty, the reaction to newness, the fatigue from unusual new exertions and postures, the false starts and wrong turns—*and the climbing energy can only come from within the organization.*

In my view, the only feasible approach involves an explicitly chartered, full-time, internal organizational unit whose main work is to facilitate the organization's self-development. It provides planning, coaching in hill-climbing techniques, guiding, and general facilitation; but each of the other organizational units has to do its own scrambling and sweating to set its membership into a coherent new grouping up on the next level place.

There will have to be exploratory groups that are the first to establish themselves at new levels on new parts of the hill; theirs will be much more difficult transitions than for the following groups, and the larger organization has to subsidize these exploratory probes as a general expense within its whole-organization evolutionary costs.

"Prototype" efforts seem so important, and they can't be done using minimal service systems. They have to be considered as an exploratory investment. And, consider that the process of conducting the first such prototype activities will constitute an exploratory investment in learning how to conduct prototype activities.

SOME ADMONITIONS

Do assume that everybody in the knowledge-work community within your organization will have a terminal that is connected within an organization-wide network; that every terminal can be in touch with any other; that every knowledge worker will potentially make use of service elicited from access to almost any data base or any person or any computer process in the organization.

Do assume that your organization's internal network will have communication gateways to public networks—and that almost every worker within the organization will benefit from some kind of service derived through these public networks.

Don't fight the idea of making changes in people's ways of thinking and working; look at it as an opportunity to expedite our evolution.

Don't buy on tight requirements—i.e., don't buy from the position of "I want exactly this, no more and no less." Leave expansion room.

Do assume that your organization will benefit from an explicit, conscious effort applied to the process of its evolution, for at least the next decade—and get to work upon an initial, important bit of organizational evolution, the creation of an effective, internal "evolutionary mechanism."

Do assume that the important part of the organization's evolution is the human part—the changes in skills, knowledge, methods, roles, and organizational structure. These elements take much longer to establish or change than do new hardware or software parts of the system. These latter should be employed to *support* the human-system evolution and operation.

Do realize that your human system will be strongly affected (and limited) by the hardware-software systems you buy. It is all too easy to let system acquisition wag the dog.

Do realize that you can throw away a hardware-software system, and roll in a new one; yes, they all will become obsolete and you can't keep waiting for the best one. *But,* understand that the associated changes in the human system will really be the important factors in summing up the cost vs. payoff of junking System A and installing System B.

ON MATTERS OF SCALE

The qualitative aspects of essentially every phenomenon will change as associated parameters shift in scale. Engineers long ago learned that their judgment and intuition could be drastically in error when the scale would be shifted beyond a certain range. Bridges and buildings collapsed and a Spruce Goose couldn't fly. And in natural systems, too—a flea can jump to heights dozens of times its own size, but it couldn't even walk if it were scaled up to the size of a human.

After watching the man-computer thing from close up, for nearly thirty years, I am convinced that the matter of scale is a critical factor. Our earlier capabilities for judgment and intuition about the nature and effects of projected change simply aren't going to be applicable.

On the one hand, things that will start to change about our ways of thinking and working will catch us by surprise—in the framework within which we grew up, they just weren't candidates for being changed. Also, shifts in phenomena-scaling (number and degree of changes) are moving us into a qualitatively different, whole-environment domain. For our intuition and judgment to continue serving us, they will have to be reconditioned—a process only accomplished by experience.

A PERSONAL FOCUS

I am turning my focus toward developing specially equipped and specially trained "high-performance augmented teams." To produce examples and gain experience is the only way that I can see, today, to take on effective pursuit of the augmentation potential. A team, of from five to ten people, will serve as a prototype organizational model. Here, we can experiment with much higher levels of specialty skills and knowledge, and can work out effective modes of high-performance collaboration and new organizational roles. Conscious evolution in the whole-system character of a team can be carried out far more quickly and economically than with larger organizational units.

I also aim to awaken interest in some larger organizations that want to begin developing internal mechanisms and experiences for establishing an effective mode of organizational evolution—gearing up for the "hill climbing." Let's say that they are willing to start investing now toward evolving into a "high-performance organization." As our laboratory begins to turn out a succession of working-prototype, high-performance augmented teams, we will want them to be used in support of real-life organizational needs. The participating organizations will serve an important role in helping establish the application targets, and in providing field-test environments and constructive feedback. There seems to be good likelihood that the applications for such teams can be selected to provide very effective facilitation of the organization's hill-climbing process—a sort of "bootstrapping" strategy.

Much of the development and experience represented in the following pages will be used as a base. With the "integrative and evolutionary" character of AUGMENT, we can, for instance, attach the highest-quality terminal equipment, very easily extend the computer horsepower per worker, and, in a straightforward manner, bring almost any existing software into "reach-through" access. And for any-sized extension of functional capability, our User Interface System enables us, very flexibly, to extend the command language and evolve a powerful and coherent grammar and vocabulary.

REFERENCES

(Note: Reference 1 is the following reprint.)

1.   Engelbart, D. C., "Toward Integrated, Evolutionary Office Automation Systems," Proceedings of the Joint Engineering Management Conference, Denver, Colo., 16-18 Oct. 78, pp. 63-68.

2.   Drucker, Peter F., "Age of Discontinuity: Guidelines to Our Changing Society," Harper & Row, New York. 1969.

3.   Engelbart, D. C., "Augmenting Human Intellect: A Conceptual Framework," Stanford Research Institute, Research report, sponsored by the Air Force Office of Scientific Research—AFOSR-3223, AD-289 565, October 1962.

4.   Engelbart, D. C., "A Conceptual Framework for the Augmentation of Man's Intellect," in Vistas in Information Handling, Howerton and Weeks (Editors), Spartan Books, Washington, D.C., 1963, pp. 1-29.

PART B

INTEGRATED, EVOLUTIONARY
OFFICE AUTOMATION SYSTEMS

Douglas C. Engelbart
Tymshare, Inc.
Cupertino, Ca.

INTRODUCTION

Office Automation involves the planned application of integrated information handling tools and methods to improve the productivity of people in office operations. Although the handling of information by office people is the focus of this new technology, other aspects of the office will be affected. These include factors such as the organization of functions and lines of reporting, training for new methods, work space design, travel patterns, branch office location, home vs. office work, hours of work, employee morale, and job classifications. Organizations that harness office automation products will need to deal with many more than just technological issues.

About 22% of the U.S. work force is now in the office, with that percentage rising. Labor costs account for about 70% of the total office costs in our economy and salary costs are increasing about 6% each year. During the past 15 years there has been relatively little increase in productivity of the office work force, contrasting with the manufacturing sector where the average productivity has more than doubled.[1] The cost of new technology aimed at increasing the productivity of office workers is going down, while the capabilities of office automation systems have been rapidly increasing.

The U.S. "white collar" salary costs totaled $354 billion in 1974. This was divided into the following categories:[2]

	in $ billions	
Managers and Administrators	99	28.0%
Professional and Technical	150	42.4%
Other Clerical	83	23.4%
Secretaries and Typists	22	6.2%

Office automation will impact industry and government organizations in very significant ways with both *cost displacement* and *value-added* results. These two terms are now being used by people who are considering the potential payoffs of office automation to their organizations.

Cost displacement applications have the objective of achieving overall reductions in support staff costs or of increasing work volumes without adding support staff.

Such applications typically center around *word processing* and provide the base for the more advanced value-added applications.

Value-added applications are viewed as being directed toward improving managerial and professional staff productivity (and effectiveness) through use of more integrated office automation systems that can directly affect their work.

The value-added approach deals with far more fundamental issues than the replacement of some support staff positions with word processing pools. Its focus upon individuals and groups of managers and professionals as targets for productivity improvement brings with it opportunities for significant increases in organizational effectiveness and major cost benefits in the largest segment of the office cost spectrum.

For any organization, management choices at many levels will affect the balance between reducing total office costs (cost displacement) or increasing the total office effectiveness (value-added effects).

Word processing applications have, until recently, been equated with the term office automation. It is interesting to note that, on the average, typing tasks comprise only 30% of the secretaries' and typists' work—and thus account for only about 2% of the total office salaries.[2] The next few years will see a very rapid growth in the introduction of advanced technology into offices and in applications with more impact on managers and other non-clerical people, bringing with it broadened perceptions of what office automation really includes.

Office Automation is likely to become one of the fastest-growing and most significant new industries of the century. It will apply electronic technology to a broad new set of applications and bring significant change to many of the ways in which people and organizations work—*augmenting* their capabilities and increasing both the quantity and quality of their contributions.

EVOLUTION OF AN AUGMENTATION SYSTEM

At SRI International (formerly Stanford Research Institute), I began explicit planning in 1959 for an R&D program toward augmenting the human intellect by use of computer aids. The Air Force Office of Scientific Research supported my study for several years, resulting in a publication that provided a conceptual framework and a basic strategy for a long-term program.[3] In 1963, the Advanced Research Projects Agency began twelve years of continuous funding, during which there was also significant support from the Air Force Electronic Systems Division, NASA, Langley Research Center, Air Force Rome Air Development Center, and the Office of Naval Research.

By 1968, we had a core system, called NLS, that was quite powerful for editing mixed text and graphics, for managing project-sized knowledge bases for design, documentation and financial activities, and for supporting group collaboration. This was described in a paper in that year's Proceedings of the Fall Joint Computer Conference, held in San Francisco.[4] We also put on a real-time description and demonstration in a special session at the Conference, controlling the system from a workstation on the podium, piping video to San Francisco from Menlo Park via two specially leased TV links, and projecting video images of mixed camera views and computer displays on an 18-foot screen. In the course of the session, we made considerable use of direct, shared-screen collaboration between me (on the podium at the conference) and members of my staff in our laboratory at Menlo Park.

In the following years, we added some basic features to further facilitate collaboration. We also concentrated heavily upon system architecture to facilitate the subsequent evolution of a coherent "knowledge workshop," with a command-language interface providing consistency and easy expansion, and a general facility for inclusion of "foreign" application systems as workshop tools even if they are programmed in other languages, or run in other computers under other operating systems.

By 1974, after eleven years of evolution, a considerably matured NLS was running under TENEX on a DEC PDP-10, and we initiated a subscription service to make this system available to user organizations. Computer service was supplied by a dedicated PDP-10, owned, maintained and operated by a commercial facilities-management company, on their premises, under contract to us at SRI. We had mostly government clients who used the ARPANET for access communication. We conceived of this as our "Knowledge Workshop Utility service," providing a coordinated set of tools to support knowledge workers. We also emphasized personal support through field trainers and application consultants.

It may seem strange for a not-for-profit research institute to have fielded a commercial-grade service, but from a larger-system research viewpoint it was the only option: if we wanted to pursue significant augmentation results, it was absolutely necessary to have a community of real-world users. Within the whole augmentation-system domain, there are, to be sure, many significant technical problems remaining, but to my mind, by far the more numerous and challenging augmentation system problems lie in the human and organization domain—to learn how to harness the services that technology offers, toward human ends. For this purpose it is necessary to have a significant number of people who are stably and skillfully doing their everyday work with such tools, which requires in turn a solid, reliable set of computer-tool and people-support services.

In 1977, it was judged better to move the Utility-service and NLS-evolution activities out from the research-institute envrionment and into a suitable commercial environment. SRI advertised, entertained prospective bidders, made a selection, and negotiated a transfer of the business to TYMSHARE, Inc., of Cupertino, California. The system has been renamed AUGMENT, and is being marketed as part of TYMSHARE's integrated Office Automation services. Following is a brief outline of the features and services as brought over into that marketplace, organized under application areas of most relevance to the engineering-management theme of this conference.

DOCUMENT PRODUCTION

Almost all phases of any simple to complex document production process may be accomplished using AUGMENT. These include initial text entry by authors or by typists, editing, draft reviews (optionally printed-out), spelling correction, generation of tables of contents and indices, word counts, draft and final formatting (with provisions for graphics), routing for approvals, final proofing, printing or processing for photocomposition, and online filing (with electronic mail delivery optional).

AUGMENT features for document production include:

Powerful text editing, for example:
Display and hardcopy terminals

Mouse and keyset (optional) for added efficiency

Very large set of integrated commands (tools)

Commands in logically grouped subsets

Paragraphs (statements) as structural entities

Hierarchically-structured files

Flexible file view presentations: level and line clipping

Easy cross-file editing

Multi-display window viewing

Powerful reference-linking

Plus many general features, such as:
File privacy and integrity

Optional off-line text entry (also interfaces to other WP systems)

Geographically distributed user-access to AUGMENT system capabilities and working information through computer networks such as TYMNET and ARPANET

Spelling checking and correction

Tables of contents

Indexing and word counts

Pre-set and user-entered formatting

Electronic photocomposition

Remote collaboration during document development and production

Document filing, control, and retrieval

Calculating

Table manipulation

Sorting

Mixed text and graphics

Proofing

Forms design and presentation for data entry

INTER-OFFICE COMMUNICATIONS

To complement AUGMENT's powerful document production capabilities, online messages or long documents may be transmitted through "electronic mail" facilities to other users of the system. There is also a unique "shared screen" feature where two remotely separated (e.g., across the country) users both can share in viewing and controlling the same screen image on their respective display stations while talking together on the telephone. These two capabilities, described in Reference 5, provide users with a very useful, new kind of "dialogue support system" that has the following features:

Immediate or delayed delivery of messages or references

Individual or group distribution lists selected by the user

Action or information-copy specification

Indentification system for selecting distribution list data

Title, special comment, author, clerk, descriptors, and other document-related information capture, transmission, and filing

Permanent filing of all messages and documents for later retrieval

Forwarding of items to additional recipients

Indices of public items by number, author, and title keywords, for online access or hardcopy printout

Automatic indexing of individual recipients' mail by date

Entry of references to hardcopy documents for information and control purposes

PERSONAL INFORMATION MANAGEMENT

The foregoing features introduce many facilities and methods which are very effective for other applications as well, such as the management of an individual's day-to-day personal, working information. This value is particularly dependent upon the level of usage. When access to the AUGMENT system occurs regularly, preferably daily, a user can keep items such as reminders, agendas, calendars, notes, telephone numbers, and to-do lists structured as he or she prefers within AUGMENT files. When these are coordinated with documents being written, electronic mail transactions, and access to other database information, most of an individual's daily business can be aided by use of the AUGMENT system.

ORGANIZATIONAL INFORMATION MANAGEMENT

The document production and electronic mail features outlined above bring useful new capabilities into the office. The emphasis in those applications is on free textual information where the structural nodes are paragraphs, headings, citations, names and addresses, etc. These may be retrieved by scanning text "pages" while viewing different levels in the hierarchy, or by searching for strings of text.

There is also support for more structured approaches to information management. Flexible data structures can be defined using the basic features of AUGMENT where retrieval may be accomplished in a number of ways. Retrievals are aided by designating text strings as the "names" of nodes during the creation of such data bases. Special file searching is provided on these names, and their use for labeling data elements provides a simple means for organizing linked and structured data files with relatively rapid retrieval.

A special form of organizational entity where AUGMENT can be of significant value is an "engineering community."[6] Instead of being a coherent element in a monolithic, hierarchical organization, a community (in this sense of the word) is composed of elements from a number of such organizations, where community membership is established by being in a common discipline or a common mission. Examples: a community of groups each of whom is involved in some aspect of solar-power R&D; or a community of groups all of whom have inter-related responsibilities within a large project (members all may belong to scattered elements within one organization, or there may be many members from different organizations).

SOFTWARE ENGINEERING

AUGMENT provides an exceptional environment for the development and maintenance of large software systems.[7] The basic features discussed above are directly applicable to generating and managing the texts of specifications, source code, program libraries, and all levels of system documentation.

It should be noted that the hierarchical organization of AUGMENT's text files, the flexible level-clipping view control, and the built-in labelling features for paragraphs (statements) naturally support structured programming practices in a uniquely effective manner. (Under Air Force sponsorship, IBM conducted an evaluative study of NLS [AUGMENT] as a support system for their structured-program methodology.[8] From the report's Abstract: "This unique combination of capabilities can contribute positively to improved productivity and product reliability in programming development.")

There has also been continual evolution of debugging aids coordinated with the rest of the software engineer's "workshop."[9] With his workshop on Machine A, he has means for applying his full range of debugging tools in a uniform manner to debug processes on distant machines—including distributed processes that pass control from one machine to another. These processes can be running in mixed types of machines, under mixed types of operating systems, and can be programmed in mixed types of programming languages.

EVOLUTION AND OTHER-SYSTEM INTEGRATION

Perhaps the most important aspects of the system's design are (a) flexible provision for evolution, and (b) the ability to interface "through" AUGMENT to other systems while retaining a consistent user interface style. The underlying system of AUGMENT is designed to allow for all of a user's different data bases and application-program services to be integrated into one, coherent "knowledge workshop."[10] A Command Language Interpreter, operating upon the compiled "grammars" from descriptions written in a Command Meta Language, provides unique uniformity and flexibility in the user interface over a wide variety of application systems (new or old).[11],[12]

There are internal provisions for a user's commands to evoke "reach-through" operations to other systems that may run on another machine, and/or run under a different operating system, and/or be programmed in a different language.[13] Using the internal services of AUGMENT as his "home workplace" for preparing data or queries and for integrating remotely retrieved or processed data, a user may do a large share of the work related to other-system use within a familiar environment where fast, flexible study and manipulation are constantly used skills, and where special design attention has been given to the process of integrating information of varied form and source into working plans, reports, etc.

HIGH PAYOFF FOR LARGE ENGINEERING PROJECTS

In a "joint, engineering, and management" domain, the potential payoff of comprehensive, integrated office automation systems would seem extraordinarily large when applied in a whole-system fashion to the support of large projects. Here, a strong element of *value added* consideration is introduced—in this kind of application, there are significant *new ways for professionals to do their work.*

As individuals, the planners, designers, documenters, managers, or expediters will find considerable support for their particular types of work—as will the secretaries and clerks in the individual-work part of their support roles. But it is the impact at the organizational level, particularly for the distributed "community" form, where the special payoff will seem most dramatic.

Besides the basic capabilities outlined above, there have been developed special AUGMENT subsystems directly relevant to support of an engineering community: for financial and technical management of multi-project programs; for developing, maintaining, and querying directories of people and resources within a large community; for producing highly formatted and indexed, quality-publication "handbooks" from the directory information; and for cataloging, indexing, and controlling an extensive collection of hardcopy items (documents, letters, catalogs, clippings, etc.).

And new subsystems are under development to add special support for: calendar management; large-program budget development and review; large-program requisition generation and control; and reach-through services to other-machine data-base management systems.

The capability is directly available to connect AUGMENT to existing special systems for supporting design, analysis, testing and manufacturing, integrating these tools smoothly into the engineer's "coherent workshop."

For instance, selected diagrams, curves, and tables generated from these systems can be integrated automatically into an engineer's AUGMENT files as "illustrations" in his "engineering notebooks"—instead of his pasting photographs or plotter sheets into a binder. Besides providing for flexible studying and evolution of the individual's "notebook," the system enables flexible remote collaboration in developing plans, analyzing results, etc. And it is subsequently an easy matter to assemble selected components from this record for outputting through graphic printers to produce mixed, text-graphic documents (drafts, or high-quality productions).

A similar situation exists for managers within the large project: a valuable set of tools within AUGMENT providing a powerful "home workplace" with many special services to support the manager role; a capability for reaching through to other systems (e.g., PERT, IMS) and for integrating their products into the home workplace; and the multi-form means for communicating within the coherent, community working domain.

CONCLUSION

It is extremely important to note the multiple levels of synergism at work here:

(a) The synergistic effect of integrating many tools into one coherent workshop makes each tool considerably more valuable than if it were used alone—for instance, the value of teleconferencing is very much greater when the participants are already doing a large proportion of their everyday work on line, so that any of the working material is available for selective citing and accessing, and when the users are already at home with the basic techniques of preparing and studying on-line material and of organizing and finding related passages.

(b) And at another level, the synergistic effect of integrating many augmented individuals into one coherent community makes each element of augmentation considerably more valuable than if it were applied just to support its one individual—this is derived from the collaborative communication capabilities as applied through extended organizational methods to integrate the augmented capabilities of individuals into augmented teams and communities.

And finally, for any application of significant power—of which augmentation of an engineering project would be a good example—the adaptability and evolutionary flexibility of the computer-communication system is extremely important. The working methods of individuals will shift markedly as they settle into use of a comprehensive workshop, and with these new methods and skills will come payoff potential for changes and additions to their workshops—a cycle that will be significantly active for many years to come. A similar cycle will be even more dramatically evident at the organizational level.

An evolutionary approach seems the only viable alternative when the effects of a prospective change are not well known; and for many years to come this will be the case relative to the impacts of significant, prospective steps in office automation upon the operations of our organizations. We have an immense amount to learn about how people can better harness their basic capabilities toward individual and organizational ends.

It will be a long time before there is developed a stable framework within which to (a) design large next-step augmentation increments, or (b) plan an orderly transition for an organization that would adopt a large increment in one, discrete step.

Evolution of the service system, evolution of the individual's working life, and evolution of the organization's working mode—all must be provided for if an organization wants to capitalize significantly upon the potential of the technology that is arriving.

REFERENCES

1. Purchase, Alan, "Office of the Future," SRI Business Intelligence Program, Guidelines, April 1978.

2. Harkness, R. C., "Office Information Systems: an overview and agenda for public policy research," Telecommunications Policy, V. 2, No. 2, June 1978, pp. 91-105.

3. Engelbart, D. C., "A Conceptual Framework for the Augmentation of Man's Intellect," in Vistas in Information Handling, Howerton and Weeks (Editors), Spartan Books, Washington, D.C., 1963, pp. 1-29.

4. Engelbart, D. C., English William K., "A Research Center for Augmenting Human Intellect," AFIPS Conference Proceedings, Vol. 33, Fall Joint Computer Conference, San Francisco, December 1968, pp. 395-410.

5. Engelbart, D. C., "NLS Teleconferencing Features: The Journal, and Shared-Screen Telephoning," Proceedings of 1975 COMPCON, Washington, D.C., September 1975.

6. Engelbart, D. C., "Coordinated Information Services for a Discipline- or Mission-Oriented Community," Proceedings of the Second Annual Computer Communications Conference in San Jose, California, Jan 24, 1973—also, Proceedings of the NATO Conference on Computer Networks, University of Sussex, England, September 1974.

7. Victor, K. E., "A Software Engineering Environment," Proceedings of AIAA/NASA/IEEE/ACM Computers In Aerospace Conference, Los Angeles, Ca., October 31-November 2, 1977, pp. 399-403.

8. Hall, C., Kessler, M., Kinnie, G., Kopp, R., "NLS Support of Modern Programming Practices," Final Report, IBM Federal Systems Division, for AF Contract F30602-76-C-0115, September 1976, 72 pp.

9. Victor, K. E., "The Design and Implementation of DAD, a Multiprocess, Multimachine, Multilanguage Interactive Debugger," Proceedings of the Tenth Hawaii International Conference on System Sciences, University of Hawaii, 1977, pp. 196-199.

10. Engelbart, D. C., Watson, R. W., and Norton, J. C. "The Augmented Knowledge Workshop," AFIPS Conference Proceedings, Volume 42, pp. 9-21, National Computer Conference, June 4-8, 1973.

11. Watson, R. W., "User Interface Design Issues for a Large Interactive System," AFIPS Conference Proceedings, NCC Vol. 45, 1976, pp. 357-364.

12. Irby, C. H., "The Command Meta Language System," AFIPS Conference Proceedings, NCC Vol. 45, 1976.

13. White, J. E., "A High-Level Framework for Network-based Resource Sharing," AFIPS Conference Proceedings, 1976, NCC, Vol. 45.

CHAPTER 19

SOME NEW APPROACHES TO THE EMERGING OFFICE INFORMATION SYSTEMS

Robert M. Landau, Editor
President, Science Information Association
Kensington, MD

INTRODUCTION

The preceding chapters represent the best collection of papers to date that concentrate on the human and organizational aspects of our emerging office systems. Most are retrospective and anecdotal. This chapter focuses on the broader systems approaches that have been taken and then provides some prescriptive discussions from several newly emerging human factors oriented approaches to design methodologies being applied to the emerging office information systems. These approaches include: transaction; administrative/decision support; multi-media; integration; activity (work) stations; productivity enhancement; and Information Resources Management.

TRADITIONAL INFORMATION SYSTEM DESIGN APPROACHES

1. One of the more popular approaches is the *Hardware/Software* approach. The appropriate individuals in the organization are contacted by hardware/software vendors who, in effect, say: "We have a 'solution' for your information handling problems. Just place our equipment in your organization and your information activities will reorganize themselves around our 'solution' and you will be doing your information work faster, cheaper, etc." That may or may not be true (usually not true), but it invariably creates irrational system relationships, uneven and unnecessary expensive system development, and undesirable over-dependence on hardware and outside vendor personnel.

2. *Information/Process Flow* concentrates on the organization structure and the process relationships between the various components of the organization. The needs of the actual users and the information organization and content are quite often neglected. In its own way, this approach is as mechanistic as is the hardware/software approach.

3. *Major Operation Replacement* takes the approach that the ongoing operation cannot be improved without undue interference with existing operations. A completely new information operation is set up separately from the existing one and is run in parallel until debugged. At that time, the old operation is terminated and the new one put on stream. This approach is costly and takes a long time with no assurance of meaningful improvement in cost effectiveness, productivity or individual work enrichment.

4. The *Personnel Oriented* approach makes the presumption that the easiest way to control the activities/growth of an organization is by controlling the size (in terms of numbers of people and/or salaries) of the organization. No significant attention is given to: the information organization, content or flow; the possibility of more effective or efficient information tools; or the possibility of better decision making. The x% cut-across-the-board action is a good example of this approach.

5. Another approach is to have a *Budget Driven* operation. Here, the appropriation amount is considered to be the controlling factor. This approach has the same attributes and disadvantages as #4 above.

6. The *Modular (or incremental) Growth* approach tackles the possibility of information systems improvement one-step-at-a-time. Areas of most likely possible improvement are identified and appropriate system upgrading is accomplished. Examples are the installation of word processors or the 'computerization' of an existing process with little (or no) system analysis. Although usually better than any of the above, this approach may lead to: hard-to-cost-justify situations and uneven and incompatible subsystem development, even though, in some cases, there is subsystem optimization.

7. The *Requirement Specification* is probably the most effective of the traditional approaches in that it requires some systematic consideration of the organizational requirements. This approach focuses on the determination of explicit needs (or goals) of the organization, thus avoiding many of the disadvantages described in the preceding approaches. The disadvantages of this approach usually are: little attention is paid to the possible integration of the processes, flows and new technologies; potential productive gains are not considered; and the human factors aspects of more job fulfillment, satisfaction and effectiveness are not taken into account.

Large organizations seldom consciously pursue any one or combination of the above approaches. There is usually an undirected (or separately directed, as a matter of policy) blending of many, if not all, of the various approaches throughout the organization. The computer or MIS people will often favor approaches #1, 2, 3, 6 or 7; the personnel people, #4; the financial people, #5; and the records managers, #2. Regardless of the nature of the pattern, what is usually missing is an overall, evolutionary strategy of information system change within the context of careful concern for each individual's needs for improved physical, psychological, emotional and operational activities.

NEWLY EMERGING INFORMATION SYSTEM DESIGN APPROACHES

1. The large computer oriented *Transaction/Direct Access/Real Time* approach developed and expanded in the decade of the '70s. Millions of searches per year are being made on terminals over telephone lines by thousands of

people in hundreds of data bases in dozens of computers in various parts of the United States. The average interactive search lasts about five to 10 minutes and costs about $1.00 per minute for all but the terminal costs. A variety of CRT or printer terminals are available for under $1,000. Using these same type terminals, tens of thousands of people are sending and receiving millions of computer messages over telephone lines per year in dozens of systems. These messages average a few lines in length and a few minutes in duration for a cost of a few pennies per minute.

The above-described activities have been made possible by the rapidly declining costs of: fast developing online, interactive, transaction-based computer hardware and software systems; electronically switched digital transmission voice systems; and large data bases and/or indexes in digital form.

Equivalent (in terms of cost and performance) data processing (DP) facilities are fast becoming available in mini- and micro-based systems, which can easily be placed in office environments for use by millions of people. This same technology has caused a rapid installation of thousands of word processing (WP) machines which is greatly influencing how text is being processed in offices. These two facilities (DP and WP) are rapidly blending; DP machines are being provided WP software packages and WP machines are being provided DP software packages. Such combined DP/WP/ terminal equipment can now be purchased for under $2,000, the price of a simple terminal only a few years ago. These developments are just beginning to make an impact on the perceptions of how this will impact office information system evolution.

2. The *Administrative/Decision Support* approach has, in part, evolved from the MIS approach of the '70s. It extends the computer oriented techniques and systems philosophy from the computer room to the domain of the administrator and decision maker. The situation is somewhat reminiscent of the computer hardware and software business/scientific dichotomy of the '60s. The dichotomy has escalated (collapsed?) into the mini and micro worlds and right into the office! Unfortunately, the office is not just a digital/compu- tational world. Well over 80% of all information in most large organizations is still on paper. The alphanumeric information has been, on the average, rekeyboarded twice and there is an

average of seven identical copies of all documents, thanks to the ubiquity of convenience copiers.

3. The *Multi-Media* approach addresses the dilemma described above. It recognizes that there must be a blending of the text, data, voice and image information processes, systems and technologies to use the paper, microform and digital (alphanumeric and image) media in the proper proportion, as appropriate. The tests for usefulness include such factors as cost, convenience, response time, flexibility, readability, etc. The thrust of this approach is that the usefulness tests should be applied even-handedly without any preconceived notion that everything should be on paper or in digital form or on microform. It is often difficult to be so neutral when the major thrust for change comes from uni-media vendors.

4. The evolution to the *Integration* approach is a natural one from acceptance of the premise and limitations of the multi-media approach. It is similar to (but at a broader level than) the need and desire to systematize the processes involved in the use of a computer (e.g., MIS).

Integration can be approached at several levels: process; procedural; logical; intellectual; psychological; and technical. There are encouraging promises and pitfalls at each level. All levels should be considered to assure the most successful evolution of office information systems.

A number of writers, consulting companies and equipment manufacturers are describing, recommending and producing numerous systems that integrate a few functions (e.g., WP + DP; OCR + WP; DP + COM; microform storage + computer index; composite video graphics + overlaid alphanumerics; digital voice systems; video image display of microforms; etc. Few, however, have tried to look at complete integration of all processes, functions, media and technologies. One company, Micronet, Inc., which operates the Paperless Office in Washington, DC, has produced the most 'integrated' office in existence today.

The Paperless Office is modeled after the configuration of processes, functions and equipment shown in Figure 1, the Integrated Office System. Figure 1 attempts to show possible information system processes, functions and equipment and the relationships between them.

There are a number of vendor oriented approaches to how office information system integration will evolve in the

Figure 1

THE INTEGRATED OFFICE SYSTEM

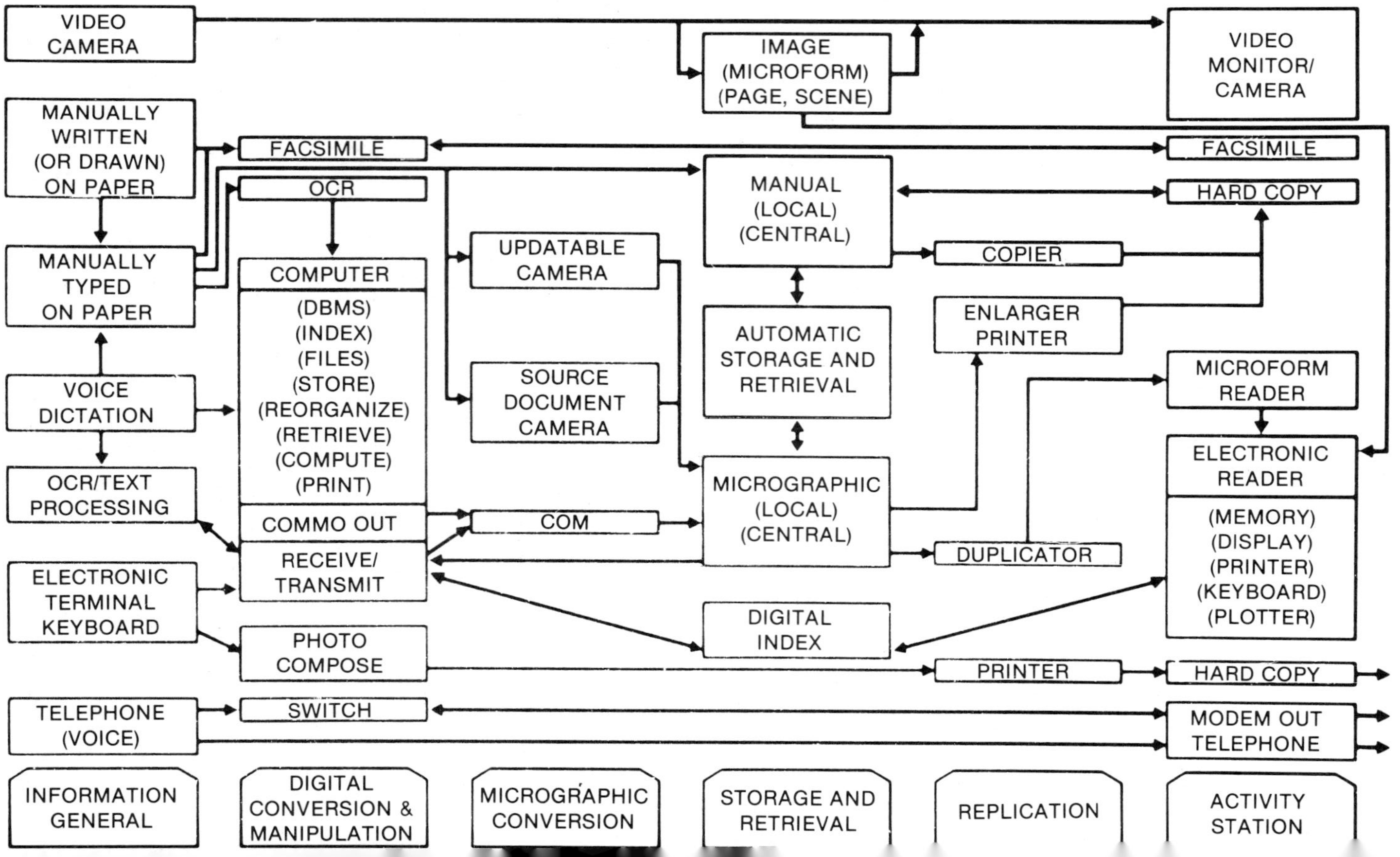

| ACTIVITY STATION | REPLICATION | STORAGE AND RETRIEVAL | MICROGRAPHIC CONVERSION | DIGITAL CONVERSION & MANIPULATION | INFORMATION GENERAL |

'80s. The *Intelligent Public Network* (see Figure 2) approach taken by AT&T presumes that computers, terminals, copiers, printers, facsimile units, etc. will be integrated into the public telephone system. The *Central Data-Processing Computer* approach (see Figure 2) taken by IBM presumes that data bases, terminals, slave minis, etc. will be integrated through a large computer serving hundreds to thousands of people. The *Intelligent PBX* approach (see Figure 2) taken by Rolm, Intecom and Mitel presume that telephones, facsimile, terminals, DP computers, WP units, intelligent copiers, etc. will be integrated through a digital PABX in the form of a computer control switching system. The *Coaxial Cable* (e.g., broadband bus) (see Figure 2) approach taken by Xerox, DEC and Intel visualizes DP computers, facsimile units, terminals, WP units and intelligent copiers/printers connected to and integrated by broadband coaxial cables. This approach, as well as the three others, implies very sophisticated software architecture, with each significantly different from and incompatible with the others.

The above approaches to office information system integration presume that essentially the information is in digital form, a far cry from the present reality. None of the above approaches consider: the integration of all media, as appropriate; the possibility of each user having an intelligent microprocessor within the terminal to do a large amount of local WP and DP work, thus down-loading a significant proportion of processing which would otherwise require communication facilities; and the human factors aspects of integration at all six levels listed at the beginning of this section (#4) on integration.

5. Because of the above described limitations, a fifth approach, the *Activity (Work) Station* is being considered by those office information systems designers who are particularly concerned about how we can improve the physical, intellectual and psychological environment of each individual office worker. That is the real key to improved office information systems productivity! The word 'activity' is used rather than 'work' to distinguish the intellectual activity of the office worker from the factory or production worker at a station.

Figure 2 shows the general activity station components; Figure 3 describes the details of the various elements of the activity station. Not all stations will have all elements; different

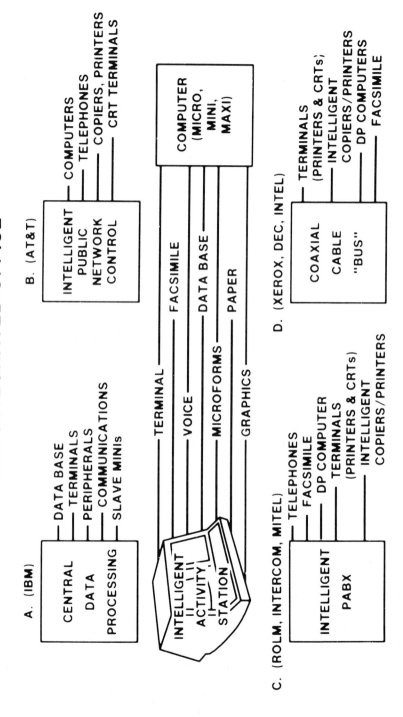

Figure 2

ALTERNATIVE APPROACHES TO THE INTEGRATED OFFICE

A. (IBM)

CENTRAL DATA PROCESSING
- DATA BASE
- TERMINALS
- PERIPHERALS
- COMMUNICATIONS
- SLAVE MINIs

INTELLIGENT ACTIVITY STATION
- TERMINAL
- FACSIMILE
- VOICE
- DATA BASE
- MICROFORMS
- PAPER
- GRAPHICS

B. (AT&T)

INTELLIGENT PUBLIC NETWORK CONTROL
- COMPUTERS
- TELEPHONES
- COPIERS, PRINTERS
- CRT TERMINALS

COMPUTER (MICRO, MINI, MAXI)

C. (ROLM, INTERCOM, MITEL)

INTELLIGENT PABX
- TELEPHONES
- FACSIMILE
- DP COMPUTER
- TERMINALS (PRINTERS & CRTs)
- INTELLIGENT COPIERS/PRINTERS

D. (XEROX, DEC, INTEL)

COAXIAL CABLE "BUS"
- TERMINALS (PRINTERS & CRTs)
- INTELLIGENT COPIERS/PRINTERS
- DP COMPUTERS
- FACSIMILE

Figure 3

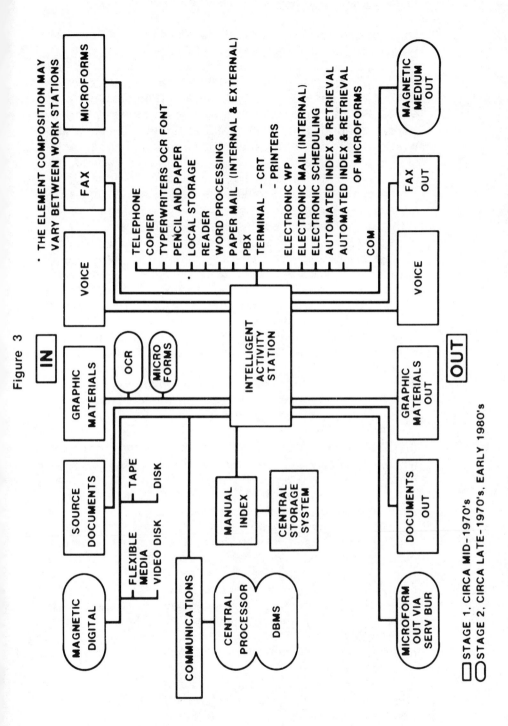

* THE ELEMENT COMPOSITION MAY VARY BETWEEN WORK STATIONS

IN

OUT

MICROFORMS
FAX
VOICE

GRAPHIC MATERIALS
OCR
MICRO FORMS

SOURCE DOCUMENTS
TAPE
DISK

MAGNETIC DIGITAL
FLEXIBLE MEDIA
VIDEO DISK

COMMUNICATIONS

CENTRAL PROCESSOR
DBMS

MANUAL INDEX
CENTRAL STORAGE SYSTEM

INTELLIGENT ACTIVITY STATION

TELEPHONE
COPIER
TYPEWRITERS OCR FONT
PENCIL AND PAPER
LOCAL STORAGE
READER
WORD PROCESSING
PAPER MAIL (INTERNAL & EXTERNAL)
PBX
TERMINAL - CRT
        - PRINTERS
ELECTRONIC WP
ELECTRONIC MAIL (INTERNAL)
ELECTRONIC SCHEDULING
AUTOMATED INDEX & RETRIEVAL
AUTOMATED INDEX & RETRIEVAL
        OF MICROFORMS
COM

MAGNETIC MEDIUM OUT
FAX OUT
VOICE

GRAPHIC MATERIALS OUT
DOCUMENTS OUT
MICROFORM OUT VIA SERV BUR

☐ STAGE 1, CIRCA MID-1970's
◯ STAGE 2, CIRCA LATE-1970's, EARLY 1980's

317

kinds of users will be provided those elements as appropriate to accomplish the particular required tasks.

Figure 4 provides a comprehensive list of activity station task support facilities under the five major categories: WP; CMS (Computer Message System); PIM (Personal Information Management); Correspondence Management and OIM (Organizational Information Management). These facilities would be provided to each user through his/her activity station to accomplish the various types, categories and nature of individual activities listed in Figure 5. Various types of operational and professional users are listed in Figure 6. By appropriate analysis techniques, it can be determined which activities are performed by each type of user.

6. There is still another approach beyond the system integration and the human factors oriented activity station approaches called *Productivity Enhancement*. A number of recently completed and ongoing studies and pilot operations indicate that we can expect significant productivy improvement in many areas and in many ways as these new approaches are applied to the emerging office information systems. Figure 7 lists a number of ideas that apply to improved office information system productivity. They include items relating to: the quality of the information; the needs of people; the adequacy of the tools; the rationality of the process; and the organization.

Productivity improvement can be considered in terms of the functions of process, decision and control. The various actions that may be taken on behalf of (or by) the several types of users relative to those three functions are listed in Figure 8. The matrix approach allows for easy analysis and identification of critical intersections.

It is now generally recognized that overall organizational effectiveness is a function of the quality of human productivity. That quality depends upon information content, form, precision, and timeliness. Productivity depends upon information cost, convenience and availablity. Information resources can be planned and evaluated on the basis of their impact of quality and productivity. Thus the organization's effectiveness can be directly affected by the quality of the management program that manages those information resources.

7. The question can be raised: Is it possible to somehow rationalize and combine the various apparently unrelated approaches described above?

Figure 4
Activity Station Task Support Facilities

1.0 Word Processing
    1.1 Prepare Correspondence, Reports and Other Textual Material
    1.2 Prepare Forms (e.g., travel, training, etc.)
    1.3 Perform Editing and Formatting
    1.4 Use Spelling Dictionary
    1.5 Build Index
    1.6 Store and Retrieve
    1.7 Prepare Hardcopy
    1.8 Reorganize and Delete Files and Records

2.0 Computer Message System (Electronic Mail)
    2.1 Compose and Edit Message
    2.2 Send Message and Select Receiver Group
    2.3 Scan and Read Incoming Messages
    2.4 Prepare and Use Canned Messages
    2.5 Build and Reorganize Files by Functional Categories
    2.6 Prepare and Maintain Distribution List
    2.7 Print Individual Messages as Desired
    2.8 Print or Send to Tape or COM All Messages Periodically for Back-Up
    2.9 Delete Messages

2.0 Personal Information Management
    3.1 Maintain Calendars (personal, public, event)
    3.2 Maintain Telephone Log, Diary & Correspondence Log
    3.3 Maintain Telephone and Other Directories
    3.4 Maintain Tickler File for Assignments, Action Items, etc.
    3.5 Use (or Create) Calculation, Math, Modeling, and Other Special Packages
    3.6 Create, Maintain and Use Personal Microform Index Lookup System

4.0 Correspondence Management
    4.1 Create, Store and Retrieve Correspondence Files as Required
    4.2 Assign Classification Codes, Index Terms, Names, Source and Item Identifiers, etc.

Figure 4 (continued)
Activity Station Task Support Facilities

4.3   Create Search Files
4.4   Create a Tracking Mechanism
4.5   Perform Queries
4.6   Prepare Statistical Reports

5.0   Organizational Information Management
    5.1   Use Local Organizational Data Bases (i.e., personnel, financial, etc.)
    5.2   Search External Data Bases
    5.3   Use Program Monitoring System for Status, Tracking, etc.
    5.4   Use Organizational Electronic Bulletin Board (i.e., Notices, Car Pool Information, etc.)
    5.5   Use Organizational Correspondence System
    5.6   Use Organizational Microform Index Lookup System

Figure 5
Analysis of Activities to Increase Productivity

1.0   Types of Personal Information Activities
    1.1.1   Write
    1.1.2   Read
    1.1.3   Proofread
    1.1.4   File
    1.1.5   Search
    1.1.6   Think
    1.1.7   Organize
    1.1.8   Calculate
    1.1.9   Schedule
    1.1.10   Memorize
    1.1.11   Index
    1.1.12   Correlate
    1.1.13   Compare
    1.1.14   Replicate
    1.1.15   Classify
    1.1.16   Record
    1.1.17   Learn
    1.1.18   Type

Figure 5 (continued)
Analysis of Activities to Increase Productivity

    1.1.19 Sort
    1.1.20 Travel
    1.1.21 Decide
    1.1.22 Wait
    1.1.23 Review

1.2.0 Interpersonal
    1.2.1 Meet
        1.2.1.1 Talk (1 : 1)
        1.2.1.2 Speak (1 : many)
        1.2.1.3 Listen
        1.2.1.4 Watch
    1.2.2 Telephone
    1.2.3 Teach
    1.2.4 Learn
    1.2.5 Dictate
    1.2.6 Supervise

2.0 Categories of Activity
    2.1 Transaction
    2.2 Personal Activity
    2.3 Organizational Activity
    2.4 Personal Decision Making
    2.5 Interpersonal (Organizational)
    2.6 Organizational Process

3.0 Nature of Activity
    3.1 Personal Processing
    3.2 Transaction Processing
    3.3 Information Retrieval
    3.4 Information Transfer
    3.5 Activities Management
    3.6 Structured Decision Making
    3.7 Unstructured Decision Making

4.0 Methods
    4.1 Process Substitution
    4.2 Process Elimination
    4.3 Personal Decision Making
    4.4 Interpersonal Decision Making

Figure 6
Exemplary Types of Information Users

1.0 Operational
    1.1   Executive
    1.2   Manager
    1.3   Supervisor
    1.4   Typist
    1.5   Secretary
    1.6   Clerk
    1.7   Administrative Assistant
    1.8   Equipment Operator
    1.9   Others

2.0 Professional
    2.1   Engineer
    2.2   Doctor
    2.3   Lawyer
    2.4   Accountant
    2.5   Economist
    2.6   Computer Programmer
    2.7   Budget Analyst
    2.8   Planner
    2.9   Salesman
    2.10 Others

Many would suggest that the answer might be found in the significant body of knowledge and operational techniques, known as *Management Information Systems* (MIS), which has developed over the past 20 years. The purpose behind MIS is to rationalize the methods and techniques used in providing better information to managers through the support of computers. In the late 1960s and early 1970s, we were talking about concepts such as the fully integrated system and integrated systems support packages. The implication was that these computer-driven systems could meet all the information processing needs of an organization.

We have since come to understand that these promises could not be kept. What we have discovered is that the computer has made significant and cost-effective contributions to the more routine operations of an organization. These are shown as level 1 in Figure 9, which lists the three levels of management activities requiring information resources analysis.

Figure 7
Factors Contributing to Improved Office Productivity

A. The Quality of the *Information*

   1. Accuracy
   2. Timeliness
   3. From a Reliable Source
   4. Relevant
   5. Properly Organized, Structured and Indexed
   6. Accessible (physically, logically, and at the proper time)

B. The Needs of the *People*

   1. Properly Trained
   2. Motivated (financially & emotionally)
   3. Properly Placed in Task Assignment
   4. Organizational/Social Requirements Met
   5. Proper Working Environment
   6. Provided Proper Working Tools

C. The Adequacy of the *Tools*

   1. Are they matched to the tasks?
   2. Are they being properly used?
   3. Are they the most effective for the tasks?
   4. Are they at the right level of integration?
   5. Are they designed for maximum ease of use?
   6. Are they the most cost effective?

D. The Rationality of the *Processes*

   1. Are they media independent as possible?
   2. Are they optimized logically?
   3. Are they being performed by the right people in terms of sequence and complexity?
   4. Are the right tools being used?
   5. Do they provide the right people the right information at the right time?
   6. Are they the most cost effective, individually and collectively?

E. The *Organization*

   1. Properly structured to operate effectively
   2. Appropriately positioned in its environment
   3. Designed to meet stated goals
   4. Properly responsive to individual needs.

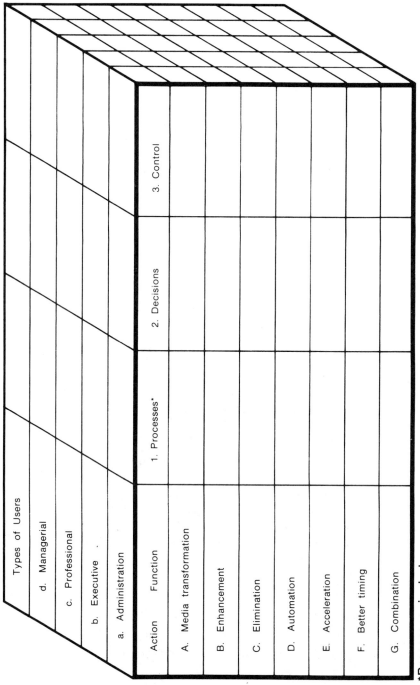

Figure 8
The Action/Function/User Matrix

Types of Users

d. Managerial
c. Professional
b. Executive
a. Administration

Action Function	1. Processes*	2. Decisions	3. Control
A. Media transformation			
B. Enhancement			
C. Elimination			
D. Automation			
E. Acceleration			
F. Better timing			
G. Combination			

*Processes include:

1.1 Creation	1.3 Storage	1.5 Transmission	1.7 Maintenance
1.2 Organization	1.4 Retrieval	1.6 Display	1.8 Disposition

Figure 9
Levels of Organizational Activities

LEVEL 1: Routine Operations and Reflex Actions

1.1 Recording of Customer Orders
1.2 Breakdown into Parts
1.3 Determining Net Requirements of Parts & Material
1.4 Shop Floor Data Collection
1.5 Preparation of Work Tickets
1.6 Maintaining Inventory Records
1.7 Reordering Parts and Materials
1.8 Production of Purchase Orders
1.9 Goods Receiving
1.10 Payment of Suppliers
1.11 Accounts Payable
1.12 Goods Shipping
1.13 Invoicing
1.14 Accounts Receivable
1.15 General Ledger
1.16 Budget Accounting
1.17 Costing
1.18 Payroll
1.19 Quality Control

LEVEL 2: Well-Defined Management Operations

2.1 Setting Working Budgets
2.2 Planning Working Capital
2.3 Determining Prices
2.4 Choosing Suppliers
2.5 Sales Management
2.6 Short-Term Forecasts
2.7 Production Scheduling
2.8 Shop Floor Expediting
2.9 Maintenance Management
2.10 Routine Personnel Administration
2.11 Formulating Rules for Routine Operations
2.12 Systems Analysis
2.13 Correspondence Management Program
2.14 Correspondence Guidelines
2.15 Reports Management Program
2.16 Forms Management Program
2.17 Forms Control System

Figure 9 (continued)
Levels of Organizational Activities

2.18 Directives Management Program
2.19 Directives System
2.20 Mail Management
2.21 Microform Programs
2.22 Files Classification System
2.23 Records Disposition
2.24 Quick Copy Controls
2.25 ADP Records Management
2.26 Vital Records
2.27 Word Processing Programs
2.28 Computers, Data Banks & Information Systems
2.29 Records Programs and Depositories
2.30 Reports Control and Inventories
2.31 Statistical Programs and Data
2.32 Libraries and Information Centers
2.33 Printing and Reprographic Programs

LEVEL 3: Strategic Planning and Creative Decision Making

3.1 Determination of Markets
3.2 Long-Range Forecasting
3.3 Directing Research
3.4 Choosing New Product Lines
3.5 Setting Financial Policies
3.6 Setting Personnel Policies

As we moved into the online interactive system of the late 1970s, computers began to provide significant support for the more well-defined management operations shown at level 2. MIS-based systems have as yet provided little help for the level 3 management activities of strategic planning and creative decision making.

The MIS systems have failed to accomplish the truly integrated systems for a second reason. The computer-driven systems have not been able to encompass all the activities listed in Figure 9. Proponents of MIS insist that it is only a matter of time before all these activities will be included.

There is an alternative scenario: *Information Resources Management* (IRM). Most organizational activities are supported by paper, voice, word and micrographic systems, as well as data processing systems. The principles behind IRM encompass the idea that all media and technologies can be combined in a way that will optimize the productivity of the individuals in the organization, thereby optimizing the total information handling activities. In essence, the principles of IRM look beyond MIS, which is primarily computer-based, but still employ the system approach to the larger information problems of an organization.

There are a number of quality and productivity benefits that accrue from the implementation of an IRM program. These include the following:

A. Improved decision making.
B. Accountability checkpoints.
C. Improved external relations.
D. Increased managerial and professional productivity.
E. More effective organizational structure.
F. Clerical job enrichment.
G. More responsive service activities.
H. The reduction or displacement of operating costs.
I. Better operational control.

THE IRM APPROACH

In order for an information resource management program to be successful, there must be top management comprehension and commitment. Until they are obtained, there is little hope for success. Two general approaches may be considered, depending upon the initial commitment of top management. If such commitment is only tentative, the best approach is to prepare a short paper outlining some of the procedures, the functional activities, the organization and activities that are concerned with information handling, and the major organizational activities that could benefit from such a program.

The paper should also contain a section itemizing some of the potential benefits and a section on the possible evolution from the present MIS organization, for example, to the new approaches made possible by IRM. The advantages of looking at all the functional activities and the explanation of the interrelationships between the various voice, word processing, data processing and micrographic systems can be explained.

A planning staff member who understands the organization, its processes and the IRM principles described in this chapter should be able to complete such a short study and paper in a matter of days or weeks. If this document has been properly prepared, and if management is generally made aware of the improvements that can be made in organizational productivity, top management should then be favorably disposed toward the more extensive plan required for full implementation of the changes. The IRM action plan can be started immediately if there is initial top level endorsement.

Before the action plan can be initiated, it is necessary to ascertain that the appropriate individuals, selected either within the organization or through a consulting arrangement, have a thorough understanding of:

A. The perceptions described above and displayed in Figures 1 through 9.
B. The major organizational components listed in Figure 10.
C. The Information Handling Organizations listed in Figure 11.
D. The Office Information Tools listed in Figure 12.

It should be expected that in order to obtain appropriate competence in all areas, a team of individuals will have to be selected. One person may have sufficient knowledge in two or more of the listed areas, but not in all of them. If an outside consulting group is brought in, there still should be significant representation by appropriate personnel within the organization. The director of the project should have sufficient training and experience to understand the complex relationships between the various areas. The team could be set up an an entirely separate entity in the planning area at a high level in the corporation, or it could be made up of individuals drawn from the various parts of the organization on a temporary basis.

There are a number of management and technical actions that should be initiated (or ratified and continued) in conjunction with the IRM planning and implementation programs. Exemplary actions are listed in Figure 13.

Many organizations already have data-base administrators, MIS directors, planning directors, and planning staff who may already be involved in a number of tasks related closely to those that would become part of the IRM program. Suitable arrangements would have to be made to accommodate these other ongoing operations.

Figure 10
Major Organizational Components (OC)

1.0 Management
    1.1 Executive Control
    1.2 Administrative Support

2.0 Planning
    2.1 Budgeting
    2.2 Forecasting

3.0 Accounting
    3.1 Accounts Payable
    3.2 Accounts Receivable
    3.3 Cost Accounting
    3.4 General Ledger & Budget Accounting
    3.5 Labor Costing
    3.6 Payroll

4.0 Personnel
    4.1 Hiring & Terminating
    4.2 Retirement Programs
    4.3 Standards & Procedures

5.0 Logistics
    5.1 Adjust Controls
    5.2 Gross Material Requirements
    5.3 Inventory
    5.4 Net Material Requirements
    5.5 Purchasing
    5.7 Receiving

6.0 Production
    6.1 Job Dispatching
    6.2 Production Scheduling
    6.3 Shipping
    6.4 Shop Floor Control

7.0 Engineering
    7.1 Development of New Product Specifications
    7.2 Quality Control
    7.3 Costing/Estimating
    7.4 Production Planning

Figure 10 (continued)
Major Organizational Components (OC)

8.0 Sales
    8.1 Billing
    8.2 Order Entry
    8.3 Special Order Costing
    8.4 Special Order Processing

9.0 Research and Development

Figure 11
Information Handling Organizations

1.0 Organizations Which are "Data Handling" in Character

    1.1 Computer Centers
    1.2 Printing & Reproduction Services
    1.3 Mailrooms & Message Centers
    1.4 Libraries & Information Analysis Centers
    1.5 Reports Control Offices
    1.6 Communication & Telecommunication Centers
    1.7 Statistical Services
    1.8 Record Centers & Repositories
    1.9 Clearinghouses & Information Referral Centers
    1.10 Data Centers & Documentation Centers
    1.11 Paperwork Management Offices
    1.12 MIS Services
    1.13 Legal Services
    1.14 Research & Development Centers
    1.15 Operating Divisions
    1.16 Information Resources Management

Figure 12
Office Information Tools

1.0 Hardware

    1.1.0 Text Systems
        1.1.1 Manual Typewriters
        1.1.2 Electric Typewriters
        1.1.3 Electronic Typewriters
        1.1.4 Word Processors (printer and/or CRT)
        1.1.5 Terminal Keyboards (printer and/or CRT)

Figure 12 (continued)
Office Information Tools

1.2.0 Image Systems
    1.2.1.0 Microform
        1.2.1.1 Computer Output Microform (COM)
        1.2.1.2 Computer Input Microform (CIM)
        1.2.1.3 Cameras (fiche and film)
        1.2.1.4 Updatable Microfiche Camera
        1.2.1.5 Microform Storage and Retrieval
        1.2.1.6 Readers/Viewers
        1.2.1.7 Microform Duplicators
        1.2.1.8 Microform to Hardcopy Printers
    1.2.2.0 Paper Systems
        1.2.2.1.0 Duplicators
            1.2.2.1.1 Copiers
            1.2.2.1.2 Offset
            1.2.2.1.3 Mimeographics
        1.2.2.2 Facsimile
        1.2.2.4 Optical Character Recognition (OCR)
        1.2.2.4 Photocomposition
    1.2.3.0 Digital
        1.2.3.1 Color Graphic Systems
        1.2.3.2 Graphic Tablets
        1.2.3.3 Plazma Display Systems
    1.2.4.0 Video
        1.2.4.1 Disk Systems
        1.2.4.2 Closed Circuit TV Systems
        1.2.4.3 Broadcast TV Systems
    1.2.5.0 Photographic
    1.2.6.0 Graphic Image Systems

1.3.0 Data
    1.3.1 Mainframe Computer Systems
    1.3.2 Mini/Micro Computer Systems
    1.3.3 Terminals
    1.3.4 Storage
    1.3.5 Communications
    1.3.6 Calculation

1.4.0 Voice
    1.4.1 Local PBX Systems
    1.4.2 Digital PBX Systems
    1.4.3 Voice Recording Systems
    1.4.4 Voice Transcription Systems
    1.4.5 Voice Recognition Systems

Figure 12 (continued)
Office Information Tools

1.4.6   Voice Generation Systems
1.4.7   Telephone

1.5.0   Activity (Work) Stations
   1.5.1   Work Surfaces
   1.5.2   Equipment Modules
   1.5.3   Light Source Equipment
   1.5.4   Power Source Equipment and Distribution
   1.5.5   Containers
   1.5.6   Area Dividers
   1.5.7   Ambient Conditioners (heat, ventilation)

2.0   Software

2.1.0   Digital System Support Packages (DP)
   2.1.1.0   Personal File Support
   2.1.1.2   Directories
   2.1.1.3   Calendar
   2.1.1.4   Tickler
   2.1.1.5   Calculation
   2.1.1.6   Microform Index
   2.1.2.0   Computer Message Systems (Electronic Mail,
           Teleconferencing)
      2.1.2.1   Compose
      2.1.2.2   Edit
      2.1.2.3   Send
      2.1.2.4   Retrieve
      2.1.2.5   File
      2.1.2.6   Delete
   2.1.3.0   Word Procesing Systems
      2.1.3.1   Letters
      2.1.3.2   Forms
      2.1.3.3   General
      2.1.3.4   Text Editing
      2.1.3.5   Storage and Retrieval
      2.1.3.6   Spelling Dictionary
   2.1.4.0   Correspondence Management
      2.1.4.1   Indexing
      2.1.4.2   Filing
      2.1.4.3   Queries
      2.1.4.4   Tracking
      2.1.4.5   Statistics

Figure 12 (continued)
Office Information Tools

2.1.5.0 Organizational Information Management
    2.1.5.1 DBMS
    2.1.5.2 Program Monitoring
    2.1.5.3 Bulletin Boards
    2.1.5.4 Decision Analysis
    2.1.5.5 Statistical Modeling
    2.1.5.6 Graphic Packages
    2.1.5.7 Natural Language Query Systems
    2.1.5.8 Business Applications

2.2.0 Integrated System Support Packages
  2.2.1.0 Word Processing (WP)
    2.2.1.1 WP to and from DP
    2.2.1.2 WP Combined with DP
    2.2.1.3 WP to Printer
    2.2.1.4 WP plus Communications
    2.2.1.5 WP to Photocomposition
  2.2.2.0 Micrographics
    2.2.2.1 Computer Output Microform (COM)
    2.2.2.2 Computer Input Microform (CIM)
    2.2.2.3 Microform to Hardcopy
    2.2.2.4 Microform Duplication
    2.2.2.5 Microform to Offset
    2.2.2.6 Automated Microform Retrieval
  2.2.3.0 Optical Character Recognition (OCR)
    2.2.3.1 OCR to WP
    2.2.3.2 OCR to DP
    2.2.3.3 OCR to Photocomposition
  2.2.4.0 Video
    2.2.4.1 Combined Video and Digital Display
    2.2.4.2 Video Storage with Digital Index
    2.2.4.3 Digitally Controlled Video Transmission
    2.2.4.4 Video to Hardcopy
    2.2.4.5 Video to Microform
  2.2.5.0 Data Processing (DP)
    2.2.5.1 DP to Phototypesetting
    2.2.5.2 DP to Voice
  2.2.6.0 Voice
    2.2.6.1 Digitally Controlled PBX
    2.2.6.2 Voice to WP
    2.2.6.3 Voice to DP

Figure 12 (con't.)

2.2.6.4 Digitally Controlled Voice Switching
               Communication
2.2.6.5 Voice and Video Systems
2.2.7.0 Media to Media Conversion
2.2.8.0 Automated Hardcopy File/Retrieval
2.2.9.0 Photographic (Audio/Visual)

AN IRM ACTION PLAN

The purpose of the action plan is to present top management with a scenario of reorganization, utilizing the principles of IRM, to increase the productivity of the organization's information handling activities. There are, of course, a number of additional purposes that could be the aim of a particular organization. Examples of these were listed above. The emphasis of the plan will be on documentation; as a rule, most organizations have relatively little documentation, much of it uncoordinated, in the various information handling areas.

An individual or a group should be assigned to the following tasks:

PHASE 1

STEP 1   Identify, select and code appropriate task support facilities to be catalogued (Figure 4).

STEP 2   Identify, select and code appropriate activities to be catalogued (Figure 5).

STEP 3   Select and code individual users to be affected by planned change (Figure 6).

STEP 4   Determine the critical interaction of the Action/
(Macro)   Function/User Matrix (Figure 8).

STEP 5   Determine the critical intersections of the
(Detailed)   elements of the above three arrays by matrix analysis (e.g., a manager 6-1.2) organizes 5-1.1.7) his calendar (4-3.1) or a WP operator (6-1.8) writes (5-1.1.1) to edit (4-1.3).

PHASE 2

STEP 1   Identify, select and code appropriate organizational activities (Figure 9).

STEP 2   Identify and code appropriate organizational components (Figure 10).

STEP 3   Identify and code appropriate information handling organizations (Figure 11.)

STEP 4   Determine the critical intersections of the elements in the above three arrays by matrix analysis (e.g., the record center (11-1.8) stores the retired payroll department's (10-3.6) payroll records (9-1.18) or engineering production planning (10-7.4) supports the R&D center (11-1.14) to develop the production scheduling plan (9-2.7).

Figure 13
Actions Required to Augment an IRM Program

Management Actions

Appoint an organization-wide information resources manager.

Appoint a data-base administrator.

Identify suitable subject data bases.

Set-up a planned sequence of projects for data-base evolution.

Provide planned education and experience dissemination from any pilot projects conducted.

Establish a conversion strategy and program specifications to allow existing manual systems to evolve smoothly.

Establish a policy and program to set-up multi-function work stations (permanent and portable) to utilize a multi-media, integrated information system.

Technical Actions

Develop online data entry and word processing systems.

Capture data at source wherever possible.

Develop online operations systems.

Have user groups adopt easy-to-use interrogation systems.

Plan the interrelation of geographically separate microform data bases.

Extend data communications network.

Plan use of distributed microform data bases.

Improve data searching capabilities.

Implement distributed data base network.

Adopt an organizationwide data description language.

Select data-base management software with good data independence.

Establish a data dictionary.

Establish accuracy controls.

Establish security and privacy controls.

Establish information quality controls.

Establish aids for data base monitoring and performance improvement.

PHASE 3

STEP 1   Determine which office information tools (one or more) (Figure 12) are required at the critical intersections in Step 5, Phase 1. In the first example, a terminal (12-1.3.3) computer message system (12-2.1.2), telephone (12-1.4.7) and a computer (12-1.3.1) are needed. In the second example, a word processing system (12-1.14) is needed.

STEP 2   Determine which office information tools (one or more) are required at the crucial intersections in Step 4, Phase 2. In the first example, a microform storage and retrieval system (12-1.2.1.5) is needed. In the second example, a color graphics system (12-1.2.3.1) with a statistical modeling software package (12-2.1.5.5) is needed.

Phases 1 and 2 can be performed simultaneously, but both 1 and 2 must precede Phase 3. To execute this plan, all the above described newly emerging information system design approaches will have to be used.

The data developed in executing the IRM action plan will provide the basis for comparing the cost of doing the present activities (at both the organization and individual levels) vs. performing the newly defined tasks with the appropriate technology by the proper individuals (system users) in the right organizational component and/or by the appropriate information handling organization.

The plan just described is by no means complete. Detailed methods of calculating the life cycle of information, relating costs to value, determining the best information budgeting mode (incremental, adjusted incremental, comprehensive, value/use), assessing information use, determining information-related expenses, constructing an information object classification system, applying appropriate accounting methods, and the rest are beyond the scope of this paper. These must be developed by experts in the various appropriate professional fields to fit the individual needs of each particular organization.

The preparation of the plan will absorb the attention of many people over many months. It will never be complete, but should be designed to contain numerous checkpoints, subgoals, and modifications, as appropriate. If the right pilots are chosen, short-term benefits (one to two years) should accrue. Many ongoing efforts will have to be carefully redirected to accomplish, in an evolutionary fashion, the proper selection, direction and timing of the integration of appropriate processes and technologies.

The problem is complex; the opportunities are great; the IRM tool is powerful; the technology is unstoppable. For those who take action, the rewards will be satisfying.

INDEX